VOICES
OF
SCOTLAND

Association for Scottish Literary Studies
Scottish Literature, 7 University Gardens
University of Glasgow, Glasgow G12 8QH
www.asls.org.uk

ASLS is a registered charity no. SC006535

First published 2019

Design and illustrations by Mark Mechan, Red Axe Design

The editors would like to thank Duncan Jones and Margaret Renton (ASLS) and
Lindsey Duncan (Education Scotland) for their assistance in producing this book.

British Library Cataloguing in Publication Data

A CIP record for this book is available
from the British Library

ISBN 978-1-906841-34-8

The Association for Scottish Literary Studies
acknowledges the support of the Scottish Government
towards the publication of this book

Contents

Contributors

James Alison
Morna Fleming
John Hodgart
Robert Hume
Ann MacKinnon
Christopher Nichol
Ronald W. Renton
Lorna Smith

Edited by

Morna Fleming
and Lorna Smith

Voices of Scotland is an anthology of Scottish poetry with related activities which has been designed for teachers working with students at Second and Third Levels of Curriculum for Excellence. It is the product of the Education Committee of the Association for Scottish Literary Studies. From their wide experience of teaching in Scottish schools, the members of the committee selected poems which are accessible and enjoyable and give students a flavour of the richness and breadth of Scotland's literary and linguistic heritage from the earliest ballads to very recent writing. The selection covers a broad range of themes and aims to reflect the linguistic variety of Scottish poetry and, in particular, the diverse voices of Scotland today.

The anthology features poems in English, Scots and Gaelic. The Scots poems employ a variety of dictions and tones, some in rich Scots, some in lightly accented English. There are poems in the distinctive language of the ballads, the urban Scots of Glasgow, the Doric of the North-east and Shetland dialect. It would be helpful to have a copy of the *Concise Scots Dictionary* in the classroom.

In each case, the text of the poem is presented in full. The anthology is indexed by title and by key words, allowing teachers to find poems relating to specific themes and intercurricular areas. Brief biographies of each poet and a glossary of Older Scots words are included.

A wide range of reading, writing, listening and talking activities will cover many of the outcomes for English. These activities are in no way prescriptive or exhaustive, but are designed to give an idea of how best the poems could be taught and explored. Suggestions are given for students to create their own imaginative responses in writing and drama and to further develop their work into other areas of the curriculum.

We hope that this anthology will provide teachers with a wide-ranging and practical resource which will enhance students' understanding, appreciation and enjoyment of poetry.

Voices of Scotland

Marion Angus

Alas! Poor Queen

She was skilled in music and the dance
And the old arts of love
At the court of the poisoned rose
And the perfumed glove,
And gave her beautiful hand
To the pale Dauphin
A triple crown to win –
And she loved little dogs
And parrots
And red-legged partridges
And the golden fishes of the Duc de Guise
And a pigeon with a blue ruff
She had from Monsieur d'Elboeuf.

Master John Knox was no friend to her;
She spoke him soft and kind,
Her honeyed words were Satan's lure
The unwary soul to bind.
'Good sir, doth a lissome shape
And a comely face
Offend your God His Grace
Whose Wisdom maketh these
Golden fishes of the Duc de Guise?'

She rode through Liddesdale with a song;
'Ye streams sae wondrous strang,
Oh, mak' me a wrack as I come back
But spare me as I gang.'
While a hill-bird cried and cried
Like a spirit lost
By the grey storm-wind tost.

Consider the way she had to go,
Think of the hungry snare,
The net she herself had woven,
Aware or unaware,
Of the dancing feet grown still,
The blinded eyes –
Queens should be cold and wise,
And she loved little things,
Parrots
And red-legged partridges
And the golden fishes of the Duc de Guise
And the pigeon with the blue ruff
She had from Monsieur d'Elboeuf.

Marion Angus

Alas! Poor Queen

Introduction

Although the poet does not name the queen, the references to 'the pale Dauphin' and 'Master John Knox' make it clear that she is referring to Mary Queen of Scots. Pupils' knowledge of the facts of Mary Queen of Scots' life may be patchy, but the poem can speak for itself. Verses one and two describe the queen's accomplishments which were well suited to the culture of the French court. Amidst the beauty, however, is the threat of treachery. Verses three to five explore the tragic course she followed after the death of her first husband, the King of France's son. Returning to Scotland at the age of eighteen to be queen, she faced bitter political and religious divisions. The poet suggests she had both spirit and wit in her responses to John Knox but the ballad lines which follow and the reference to the hill-bird's ghostly cries are full of foreboding. The poet urges her readers not to judge Mary while acknowledging that Mary herself may have been implicated in the murder of her second husband, Darnley, and the Catholic plot against her cousin, Queen Elizabeth I of England. The final verse contrasts Mary, by implication, with Elizabeth. Mary was emotional and artistically accomplished but lacked the statecraft and political cunning of the English queen. The repetition of the lines from verse two intensify the pathos and tragedy of Mary Stuart's life.

THIRD LEVEL
Related Texts:
Anon., 'The Four Maries'
Robert Burns, 'Lament of Mary Queen of Scots'

KEY WORDS:

Death

History

Lament

Royalty

Some key questions for class/group discussion

- What does the title suggest about the poet's attitude to her subject?

- What does verse one tell us about Mary Queen of Scots' life at the French court?

- What does the line 'At the court of the poisoned rose' suggest?

- In verse two, what do Mary's words suggest about her response to John Knox's criticisms of her?

- Why does the poet introduce the cries of the hill-bird in verse three?

- In the lines 'Consider the way she had to go/ Think of the hungry snare' what is the poet urging us not to do?

- What is the poet suggesting about Mary's own behaviour in lines two and three of verse four?

- In the final verse who is the poet contrasting Mary with?

- The final six lines of the poem are a repetition of the last six lines in verse one. Why do you think the poet chose to end the poem in this way?

Imaginative/creative writing

At the age of six in 1548, Mary was sent to France to marry the King's son, the Dauphin. Write a short story, entitled *A New Life*, in which a young person tells of his or her experiences beginning a new life in a new community and shares the feelings which this change aroused.

Further Development

Research the historical facts of Mary Queen of Scots' life, then prepare a short talk to explain why you think she remains one of the most famous figures in Scottish history.

Anon.

Arran

Arran of the many stags,
The sea strikes against her shoulder;
Isle in which companies are fed,
Ridges on which blue spears are reddened.

Skittish deer are on her peaks,
Mellow blaeberries on her heaths,
Cool water in her streams,
Mast upon her brown oaks.

Greyhounds are there and beagles,
Brambles and sloes of the dark blackthorn,
Her dwellings close against the woods,
Deer scattered about her oak-woods.

Gleaning of purple lichen on her rocks,
Flawless grass upon her slopes;
Over her fair shapely crags
Noise of dappled fawns a-skipping.

Smooth is her level land, fat are her swine,
Bright are her fields,
Her nuts on the boughs of her hazel-wood,
Long galleys sailing past her.

Delightful it is when the fair season comes,
Trout under the brinks of her rivers,
Seagulls answer each other round her white cliff;
Delightful at all times is Arran!

(Translated from Gaelic by Kuno Meyer)

Anon.

Arran

Introduction

'Arran' has been translated from an anonymous Gaelic poem which occurs within a medieval Irish collection of tales of the legendary bard Ossian. It belongs to the Celtic tradition of praise poetry in which a place or a person is enthusiastically celebrated and idealised, sometimes at the behest of a patron. Historically the isle of Arran in the Clyde estuary lay well within the zone of Celtic culture. The poem celebrates the natural flora and fauna of the island in an idealised manner, employing the format of a list, an accumulation of images, and deals with a cherished location. Students should be reminded that the text is a translation from Gaelic, with no attempt to create a formal stanzaic structure.

SECOND LEVEL
Related texts:
Janet Hamilton, 'Oor Location'

KEY WORDS:

Arran

Deer

Islands

Landscape

Weather

Some key questions for class/group discussion

- What animal seems to be of most interest to the poet?

- What signs are there of human beings on Arran?

- What kinds of food are available for them?

- What impressions do you get of the landscape and climate of the island?

- Are there any hints of flaws or disadvantages that Arran may have?

Imaginative/creative writing

- Build up a word picture of your own favourite place. It could be where you have gone on holiday or only visited briefly; it could be where you live.

- Write a brief advertisement addressed to tourists encouraging them to visit your chosen area. (How will you handle any disadvantages such as narrow roads or rainy climate?)

- Try to convey in prose or verse an impression of a location that you thoroughly dislike. Read, for example, Janet Hamilton's 'Oor Location'.

Further development

Here is an extract from a recent tourist advertisement for Arran: 'Welcome to Arran: Arran is alive with wildlife, countryside, beaches, pubs and restaurants, golf courses and much more ... how will you spend your island time?'

- Search out some current promotional literature for Arran and write your own brief report on what the island may, or may not, have to attract young visitors.

- What traces of the Gaelic language remain in Arran today?

Anon.

The Bewteis of the Fute-ball

Brissit brawnis and brokin banis,
Stryf, discord and waistie wanis.
Crukit in eild syne halt withal,
Thir are the bewties of the fute-ball.

In modern Scots:
Birsed brawns an breuken banes,
Strife, discord an wastie hames.
Creukit in eild syne haut withaw,
Thir are the beauties o the fitbaw.

The poem might be translated into modern English as:
Torn muscles and broken bones,
Strife, discord and impoverished homes.
Stooping in old age then lameness too,
Those are the beauties of football.

Anon.

The Bewteis of the Fute-ball

Introduction

The earliest reference to football in Scotland is from 1424 when King James I passed a law making the playing of football illegal; in 1457 James II decreed that the 'futeba an gowf be utterly cryt doon an nocht yaisit.' Various burgh councils issued similar laws, suggesting that the bans were unsuccessful. Some of these laws were aimed at ensuring young men spent more time practising their weaponry, but some were also concerned with the violence and trouble caused by football. These early versions of the sport had few if any rules and were more like a mob free-for-all, something that survives in customs like the New Year 'ba game' between the 'uppies' and 'doonies' in Kirkwall, Orkney. This poem, found in the Maitland Folio Manuscript dating from the later sixteenth century, is very short (only four lines) but very dense in its Scots. It is given in the original Middle Scots, along with modern Scots and English versions.

SECOND/THIRD LEVEL
Related Texts:
Iain Crichton Smith,
'Rhythm' (p. 62)
Matt McGinn, 'The Footba'
Referee'

KEY WORDS:

Competition

Football

History

Middle Ages

Sport

Violence

Some key questions for class/group discussion

- According to the poet, what are the physical dangers of the game and the long term consequences for your health? How does it affect families and communities?

- What is the poet's opinion of the game? Why does he or she say these are the 'bewteis'? How do we know this is meant to be sarcastic or ironic?

- Which word or expression do you think best describes the hazards of the game?

- Look at the use of sound effects (alliteration, assonance, stress and rhyme) and pick one example to show how they are used effectively in the poem.

- Do you think the problems of football today are worse, better or the same? Why?

Imaginative/creative writing

- Pupils could try their hand at writing their own poem or song about the 'beauties' of football or another game.

- Script an interview with an injured or aggrieved player or with an angry spectator who has seen some foul play which was not picked up by the referee.

Further development

- Research could be undertaken on the history of the game in Scotland and elsewhere, and also about how we helped spread the game to the rest of the world. A visit to the National Football Museum at Hampden Park is highly recommended.

- Find out about the New Year 'ba game' in Kirkwall, how it originated, and how it is currently played.

Anon.

The Bonnie Earl o' Moray

Ye Hielands and ye Lowlands,
O, whaur hae ye been?
They hae slain the Earl o' Moray,
And laid him on the green.
He was a braw gallant,
And he rade at the ring,
And the bonny Earl o' Moray,
He might hae been a king.
O lang will his lady
Lok frae the Castle Doune
Ere she see the Earl o' Moray
Come soundin' through the toun.

Now wae be to ye, Huntly,
And wherefore did ye sae?
I bade ye bring him wi' ye,
And forbade ye him to slay.
He was a braw gallant,
And he played at the glove;
And the bonny Earl o' Moray,
He was the Queen's true love.
O lang will his lady
Lok frae the Castle Doune
Ere she see the Earl o' Moray
Come soundin' through the toun.

Anon.

The Bonnie Earl o' Moray

Introduction

Like 'Bonnie George Campbell', this ballad is based on an actual historical event: the murder of the Earl of Moray by the Earl of Huntly in 1592, something that involved the most powerful people in the land, including King James VI. It focuses on the loss of a young man rather than the events themselves, though we are provided with some detail about his murder and some possible motives. This ballad is direct about stating admiration for the dead man, enumerating his attributes and accomplishments, which clearly made him a popular hero in the eyes of many, but also possibly made him some powerful enemies.

**SECOND/THIRD LEVEL
Related Texts:**
Anon., **'Bonnie George Campbell'** (p. 10)
Anon., **'The Twa Corbies'** (p. 28)
Anon., **'The Wife of Usher's Well'** (p. 30)

KEY WORDS:

Ballads

Death

History

Music

Murder

Royalty

Tragedy

Some key questions for class/group discussion

- How do we know right at the start that this was an event of national importance?

- Whose voice is quoted in verse two and why do you think this is included?

- Can we take his words at face value? Can we believe him?

- What motive might this person have had for wanting him dead?

- Which word choice in the chorus suggests he perhaps liked to make an entrance and exit?

- What else might he have done to make others jealous?

- Who would miss him most? (The lady in the chorus was his mother, not his wife).

Imaginative/creative writing

- Following research into historical events, write character profiles of victim and suspects, or compose a series of secret letters among the conspirators planning the deed.

- Write a newspaper report on the murder, in the form of a contemporary tabloid.

- Write a modern ballad about an important event today.

Further development

Find out what 'rade (or run) at the ring' and 'played at the glove' mean in this context. What was their purpose? Are there modern equivalents?

Anon.

Bonnie George Campbell

Hie upone Highlands,
and lay upon Tay.
Bonnie George Campbell
rode out on a day.

He saddled, and bridled,
so gallant rode he.
And hame cam his guid horse,
but never cam he.

Out cam his mother dear,
greeting fu sair.
Out cam his bonnie bryde,
riving her hair.

'The meadow lies green,
and the corn is unshorn.
The barn, it is empty,
the baby unborn!'

Saddled and bridled
and booted rode he,
A plume in his helmet,
a sword at his knee.

But toom cam his saddle
all bloody to see.
Oh, hame cam his guid horse,
but never cam he.

Anon.

Bonnie George Campbell

Introduction

Many ballads are about a real person who suffered a violent death. This ballad is possibly about Archibald or James Campbell who was killed in the Battle of Glenlivet in 1594, or Sir John Campbell of Calder who was murdered by another Campbell around the same time. This ballad gives no historical background to the event, giving only the bare bones of the story. Of the various recorded versions available online, probably the best is the one sung by Lesley Hale of Bitter Withy, as she respects the original language of the song.

The use of repetition and contrasts throughout the ballad builds the emotional intensity to a dramatic climax in the final verse. The first verse portrays young George Campbell as a braw gallant, cutting a fine figure on his horse as he rides away, but there is no reason given for his departure. The fourth line, however, abruptly suggests the tragic outcome without directly stating it. The spoken words of his mother and his bride heighten the dramatic intensity of the situation, culminating in his bride's statement that her child will be born fatherless. The final verse repeats the picture of the braw gallant riding away but confirms what was hinted at in the first verse, that he is riding out to fight in battle. The ballad reaches its dramatic climax in the third line of this verse which reveals that the empty saddle was covered in blood. The final line of the ballad repeats the last line of the first verse, reinforcing the tragedy of a young man cut down in his prime.

SECOND/THIRD LEVEL
Related Texts:
   Anon., 'The Bonnie Earl o' Moray' (p. 8)
   Anon., 'The Twa Corbies' (p. 28)
   Anon., 'The Wife of Usher's Well' (p. 30)
   Ewart Alan Mackintosh, 'In Memoriam' (p. 150)

KEY WORDS:

Ballads

Death

Drama

History

Music

Tragedy

War

Some key questions for class/group discussion

- Does the first verse give any hint of his reason for riding out?

- What does the word 'gallant' suggest about George Campbell?

- What do you think has happened to him?

- Which line of the ballad suggests this?

- How are his mother and bride affected?

- How do we know that, had he returned, he would have had much to look forward to?

- This is a short ballad with many gaps in the story. What do you feel makes it so dramatic?

Imaginative/creative writing

The ballad tells the universal story of a young man who does not return from battle. Write a story of your own, set in a historical or contemporary period of your own choosing, which tells the story either in the third person or from the point of view of the person closest to him.

Further Development

The Scottish poet Ewart Alan Mackintosh did not return from the battlefields of France. Prepare a short presentation which gives the key facts of his life and death, using one or two of his poems to illustrate his experiences in the First World War.

Anon.

The Bonnie Lass o' Fyvie

There was a troop o' Irish Dragoons
Cam' a-marchin' doon through Fyvie o,
An' their captain's fa'n in love wi' a very
 bonnie lass,
An' her name it was ca'd pretty Peggy o.

Chorus
There's mony a bonny lass in the Howe o'
 Auchterless,
There's mony a bonny lass in the Garioch o,
There's mony a bonny Jean in the toon o'
 Aiberdeen,
But the flooer o' them a' is in Fyvie o.

Oh it's 'Come doon the stair, pretty Peggy my
 dear,
Oh come doon the stair, pretty Peggy o,
Oh come doon the stair, kame back your
 yellow hair,
Tak' a last farewell o' yer daddy o.

'For it's I'll gie ye ribbons for your bonnie
 gowden hair,
I'll gie ye a necklace o' amber o,
I'll gie ye silken petticoats wi' flounces tae the
 knee,
If ye'll convoy me doon tae my chaumer o.'

'Oh I hae got ribbons for my bonnie gowden
 hair,
An' I hae got a necklace o' amber o,
An' I hae got petticoats befitting my degree,
An' I'd scorn tae be seen in your chaumer o.'

'What would your mammy think if she heard
 the guineas clink,
An' the hautboys playing afore ye o?
What would your mammy think when she
 heard the guineas clink,
An' kent ye had married a sodger o?

'Oh a sodger's wife I never shall be,
A sodger shall never enjoy me o.
For I never do intend to go to a foreign land,
So I never shall marry a soldier o.'

'A sodger's wife ye never shall be,
For ye'll be the captain's lady o,
An' the regiments shall stand wi' their hats
 intae their hands,
And they'll bow in the presence o'my Peggy o.

'It's braw, aye, it's braw a captain's lady tae be,
It's braw tae be a captain's lady o.
It's braw tae rant an' rove an' tae follow at his
 word,
An' tae march when your captain he is ready o.'

But the Colonel he cries 'Now mount, boys,
 mount!'
The Captain he cries 'Oh tarry o.
Oh gang nae awa for anither day or twa,
Till we see if this bonnie lass will marry o.'

It was early next morning that we rode awa,
An' oh but oor captain was sorry o.
The drums they did beat owre the bonnie
 braes o' Gight
An' the band played 'The Lowlands o' Fyvie' o.

Lang ere we wan intae auld Meldrum toon
It's we had oor captain to carry o.
An' lang ere we wan intae bonnie Aiberdeen
It's we had oor captain tae bury o.

Green grow the birk upon bonnie Ythanside
An' law lie the lawlands o' Fyvie o.
The captain's name was Ned an' he died for a
 maid;
He died for the bonnie lass o' Fyvie o.

Anon.

The Bonnie Lass o' Fyvie

Introduction

The ballad 'The Bonnie Lass o' Fyvie' appears to have its origins in a short English song called 'Pretty Peggy of Derby, O' in which the heroine, who had been obliged by her father to turn down her penniless sweetheart, rejected the offer of marriage from a handsome soldier called Captain Wade, a recruiting officer in a company of the Irish Dragoons. It found its way to Aberdeenshire at the beginning of the nineteenth century, was expanded in length and became 'naturalised' using many local place-names and with much of its language in Scots. Versions of it have been sung by Bob Dylan, Joan Baez and Simon and Garfunkel.

The Scottish version given here tells the story of a beautiful girl, Pretty Peggy, who lives in the Aberdeenshire village of Fyvie. She is courted by an officer of the Irish Dragoons who are temporarily quartered there. He offers her prosperity and the chance to see the world if she marries him but she steadfastly refuses. When his regiment departs she refuses to go with him and, heartbroken, his health rapidly deteriorates as they march south until he dies when they reach Aberdeen. The chorus emphasises the beauty of Peggy whilst the melancholy tone of the last verse evokes pity for the death of the captain. To prepare for the study of this ballad students might enjoy listening to the stimulating singing of it by The Corries.

> **SECOND LEVEL**
> **Related Texts:**
> Anon., 'Barbara Allan'
> Walter Scott, **'Jock o' Hazeldean'** (p. 198)
> Walter Scott, **'Lochinvar'** (p. 200)
> Walter Scott, **'Proud Maisie'** (p. 202)
>
> **KEY WORDS:**
>
> **Ballads**
>
> **Death**
>
> **Love**
>
> **North-east Scotland**
>
> **Soldiers**

Some key questions for class/group discussion

- Using a map of Aberdeenshire try to locate Aberdeen, Fyvie, the Garioch and Old Meldrum.

- It is likely that the captain was a recruiting officer. What would be the purpose of his regiment's visit to Fyvie?

- With what inducements does the captain try to persuade Peggy to marry him?

- Why do you think Peggy does not wish to marry him? There could be several reasons.

- The chorus is usually sung after every stanza. What is emphasised by doing this?

- The ballad grows very sad in the last four stanzas. How does the writer achieve this?

Imaginative/creative writing

Write a short story set in modern times in which the marriage plans of a young woman and a young man are upset because the young man has joined the army.

Further development

Create a storyboard which tells the story of the captain in eight scenes: (1) As the regiment marches into Fyvie, the captain sees Pretty Peggy. (2) The captain begs her to marry him. (3) She refuses him. (4) The colonel orders the regiment to leave Fyvie. (5) The captain begs the colonel to delay their departure. (6) They leave the next morning to the beating of the drums. (7) The captain is so heartbroken he has to be carried into Old Meldrum, a dying man. (8) The captain is buried in Aberdeen.

Anon.

The Bonnie Ship 'The Diamond'

The Diamond is a ship, my lads, for the Davis Strait she's bound,
And the quay it is all garnished with bonnie lasses 'round;
When Captain Thompson gives the order to sail the ocean wide,
Where the sun it never sets, my lads, no darkness dims the sky.

Chorus
So it's cheer up my lads,
let your hearts never fail,
While the bonnie ship the Diamond,
goes a-searching for the whale.

Along the quay at Peterhead, the lasses stand aroon,
Wi' their shawls all pulled about them and the saut tears runnin' doon;
Don't you weep, my bonny lass, though you be left behind,
For the rose will grow on Greenland's ice before we change our mind.

Here's a health to the Resolution, likewise the Eliza Swan,
Here's a health to the Battler of Montrose and the Diamond, ship of fame;
We wear the trousers o' the white and the jacket o' the blue,
When we return to Peterhead, they'll hae sweethearts anoo.

It will be bricht both day and nicht when the Greenland lads come hame,
Wi' a ship that's fu' of oil, my lads, and money to our name;
We'll make the cradles for to rock and the blankets for to tear,
And every lass in Peterhead sing 'Hushabye, my dear'.

Anon.

The Bonnie Ship 'The Diamond'

Introduction

The *Diamond* was a ship added to the Aberdeen whaling fleet in 1812. It went on yearly voyages until 1819, when it was lost in the ice. It is thought this song was first written in 1812. This is a work song from the whaling communities of north-east Scotland. It is important that the piece be enjoyed first and foremost as a song.

The theme is the impending departure of the whaler and the mood is one of celebration, camaraderie and macho swagger. The sailors are full of optimism as they prepare to sail into Arctic waters in pursuit of whales. The second verse describes the girls on the quayside weeping as they bid farewell to their loved ones, but the bravado of the men quickly dispels the sombre mood. The third verse celebrates the crews of various whaling ships, evoking the pride of the men and anticipating their successful return. The final verse promises their future prosperity when the ship returns full of whale oil.

There are several versions of the song available online.

SECOND LEVEL

Related Texts:

Andy Barnes, 'The Last of the Great Whales'
Helen B. Cruickshank, 'Overdue'
William McGonagall, 'The Famous Tay Whale'
George Scroggie, 'Fareweel Tae Tarwathie'

KEY WORDS:

| Environment |
| History |
| Music |
| North-east Scotland |
| Peterhead |
| The sea |
| Ships |
| Work |

Some key questions for class/group discussion

- Who are the singers?

- What is their purpose and destination?

- What are the dominant feelings of the men?

- Who are they leaving behind and what are these folk feeling?

- In verse one, what does 'garnished' mean in this context?

- What promises are made in the last verse?

Imaginative/creative writing

Write a dialogue between a whaler and his wife, either on the point of the ship's departure or its return, bringing out the contrast between the man and woman's feelings and attitudes to the expedition.

Further Development

Research the history of the whaling industry in Scotland, particularly the fate of the *Diamond* and the hazards of the Davis Straits.

Anon. (also attributed to James Hogg)

The Dowie Houms o Yarrow

Late at e'en, drinkin' the wine,
And ere they paid the lawin',
They set a combat them between,
To fight it in the dawin'.

'O stay at hame, my noble lord!
Oh, stay at hame, my marrow!
My cruel brother will you betray
On the dowie houms o Yarrow.'

'Oh, fare ye weel, my lady gay!
Oh, fare ye weel, my Sarah!
For I maun gae, tho' I ne'er return,
Frae the dowie banks o Yarrow.'

She kiss'd his cheek, she kamed his hair,
As she had done before, O;
She belted him with his noble brand,
And he's awa to Yarrow.

O he's gane up yon high, high hill –
I wat he gaed wi' sorrow –
An' in a den spied nine armed men,
I' the dowie houms o Yarrow.

'O are ye come to drink the wine,
As ye hae doon before, O;
Or are ye come to wield the brand,
On the bonnie banks o Yarrow?'

'I am no come to drink the wine,
As I hae done before, O,
But I am come to wield the brand,
On the dowie houms o Yarrow.'

Four he hurt, an' five he slew,
On the dowie houms of Yarrow,
Till that stubborn knight came him behind,
And ran his body thorrow.

'Gae hame, gae hame, good-brother John,
An' tell your sister Sarah,
To come an' lift her noble lord,
Who's sleepin' sound on Yarrow.'

'Yestreen I dream'd a dolefu' dream;
I ken'd there wad be sorrow;
I dream'd I pu'd the heather green,
On the dowie houms o Yarrow.'

She gaed up yon high, high hill –
I wat she gaed wi' sorrow –
An' in a den spy'd nine armed men,
On the dowie houms o Yarrow.

She kiss'd his cheek, she kamed his hair,
As oft she did before, O;
She drank the red blood frae him ran,
On the dowie houms o Yarrow.

'O haud your tongue, my douchter dear!
For what needs a' this sorrow?
I'll wed ye on a better lord
Than him you lost on Yarrow.'

'Oh, haud your tongue, my father dear,
An' dinna grieve your Sarah;
A better lord was never born
Than him I lost on Yarrow.

'Tak hame your ousen, tak hame your kye,
For they hae bred our sorrow;
I wiss that they had a' gane mad
When they cam first to Yarrow.'

Anon. (also attributed to James Hogg)

The Dowie Houms o Yarrow

Introduction

The secluded valley of the Yarrow Water lies in Ettrick Forest south-west of Selkirk in the Scottish Borders. For centuries the area suffered from vicious feuding and cattle-reiving among rival families. The first verses introduce the grim tale with chilling brevity. Language is mostly monosyllabic; pronouns help to hide the nature and identity of the characters and the causes of the quarrel; the location in an inn is merely implied, and the passage of time is tersely suggested. Students might start by listening to a related form of the ballad sung by Willie Scott who was himself a shepherd in Ettrick, or by his friend Alison McMorland. Thereafter they can tease out questions of meaning and issues.

> **THIRD LEVEL**
> **Related texts:**
>   Anon., 'Rare Willie's
>   Drowned in Yarrow'
>   Anon., **'Son David'** (p. 24)
>
> **KEY WORDS:**
>
> **Ballads**
>
> **Borders**
>
> **Family**
>
> **Grief**
>
> **Honour**
>
> **Love**
>
> **Music**
>
> **Treachery**

Some key questions for class/group discussion

- Can you suggest what is happening in the first verse and the possible identity of 'they'?

- Surveying the whole ballad, identify the four main participants in the action. Who, for example, is speaking in the verse beginning 'Yestreen I dream'd a dolefu' dream'?

- Consider why the lord feels that he 'maun gae' even though he may not return from Yarrow.

- What do you make of Sarah's behaviour?

- What does the final verse suggest about the possible causes of the tragedy?

Imaginative/creative writing

- This ballad has marked cinematic qualities: the tavern brawl cuts quickly to the home of the lord and his lady Sarah, then as quickly over the hills to the fatal rendezvous in the den by the river with both dialogue and bloody action. Produce a simple storyboard and script for part of the ballad.

- Nothing is said of the feelings of Sarah's mother. How do you think she felt? Compose in Scots or English some of her thoughts on the affair.

- Write in one ballad stanza a brief gravestone epitaph for the dead lord.

Further development

- The countryside of Yarrow has become famed for its associations with the Border ballad traditions. Research and write a brief report on what the locality is like today.

- The most famous poet of the area is James Hogg, known as 'The Ettrick Shepherd'. Find out about his works.

Anon.

Drumdelgie

There's a fairm toon up in Cairnie,
That's kent baith far an wide,
Tae be the Hash o Drumdelgie,
Upon sweet Deveronside.
The fairmer o yon muckle toon,
He is baith hard an sair,
An the cauldest day that iver blaws
His servants get their share.

At five o'clock we quickly rise
An hurry doon the stair;
It's there tae corn oor horses,
Likewise tae straicht their hair.
Syne, aifter workin half an oor,
Each tae the kitchie goes,
It's there we get oor breakfast,
Which generally is brose.

We haena got oor brose weel suppit,
An gien oor pints a tie,
Fin the foreman he cries 'Oot,
My lads, the oor is drawing nigh!'
At sax o' clock the mill's put on,
Tae gie us aa straucht wark;
It taks fower o us tae mak tae her,
Till ye could wring oor sark.

An fin the watter is put aff,
We hurry doon the stair,
Tae get some quarters through the fan
Till daylicht dis appear.
Fin daylicht dis begin tae peep,
An the sky begins tae clear,
The grieve he cries 'Come on my lads,
Ye'll bide nae langer here!

'There's sax o you'll ging tae the ploo,
An twa tae ca the neeps,
An the baillies they'll be be aifter you
Wi strae raips roon their queets.'
But fin that we were gyaun furth,
An turnin oot tae yoke,
The sna dank on sae thick an fast
That we were like to choke.

The frost it wis sae very hard,
The ploo she widna go;
An sae oor cairtin days commenced
Amang the frost and sna.
Oor horses being but young an sma,
The cairts they didna fill;
They aft required the saiddler
Chains tae drive them up the hill.

The termin time has come at last,
An we will get wir brass,
An we'll awa tae Huntly Fair
Tae hae a pairtin glass.
An we'll gyang in tae Huntly toon
An there gyang on the spree;
An then the fun it will commence
The quinies for tae see.

Sae fare ye weel Drumdelgie,
For I maun gyang awa;
Sae fare ye weel Drumdelgie,
Yer weety weather and aa!
Sae fare ye weel Drumdelgie,
I bid ye aa adieu;
An I'll leave ye as I got ye,
A maist unceevil crew!

Anon.

Drumdelgie

Introduction

This is a nineteenth-century song, written in Doric, dating from a time when farmers employed gangs of male agricultural workers who lived together in primitive outbuildings called bothies. Bothy ballads such as 'Drumdelgie' were part of the farm-workers' home-grown entertainment. Sometimes they would provide their own music with fiddles, concertinas, pipes and whistles.

The theme of this song is a complaint about the harsh working conditions prevailing on a large farm near Huntly in Aberdeenshire. Its mood satirically mingles resentment, defiance and gleeful anticipation. The farmer is hard on his workers. Even on the coldest days their work starts at five a.m. with little time allowed for breakfast. Their tasks included feeding and combing the horses, milling the corn, ploughing and pulling turnips. When the ground is frozen and snow is falling thick and fast, they struggle to drive the horses and carts up the hill. The singer is so disenchanted by his treatment at Drumdelgie farm that he intends to quit when his contract ends and spend his hard-earned wages 'on the spree' in Huntly. The song ends with a defiant farewell to the farmer, the foreman, the grieve and his fellow workers.

SECOND/THIRD LEVEL
Related Texts:
Anon., 'The Barn Yards o Delgaty'
Anon., **'The Bonnie Ship "The Diamond"'** (p. 14)
G. S. Morris, 'A Pair o Nicky Tams'

KEY WORDS:

Bothy ballads

Drama

Farming

History

Music

North-east Scotland

Scots language

Weather

Work

Some key questions for class/group discussion

- Are there any clues as to the time of year?

- What are the main tasks that the workers are tackling?

- What exactly has the singer got to complain about?

- How does the singer intend to celebrate?

- Who are the 'crew' mentioned in the final line?

- In what ways does the singer consider them to be uncivil?

Imaginative/creative writing

- Create a short dialogue (in Scots or English) that takes place between the singer and the farmer when he reveals that he will not be seeking another term at Drumdelgie farm.

- Write a humorous poem which complains about a hard day's work at school.

Further Development

- Find out how the bothy system worked in nineteenth century Scotland.

- The language of the song is a lively, strong Doric. It could provide the stimulus for an exploration of Doric as a distinctive dialect of Scots. With the help of dictionaries students can clarify expressions which are unfamiliar to them, in particular the jargon of obsolete farming practices.

Anon.

Get Up and Bar the Door

It fell about the Martinmas time,
And a gay time it was then,
When our goodwife got puddings to make,
And she's boil'd them in the pan.

The wind sae cauld blew south and north,
And blew into the floor;
Quoth our goodman to our goodwife,
'Gae out and bar the door.'

'My hand is in my hussyfskap,
Goodman, as ye may see;
An it shou'd nae be barr'd this hundred year,
It's no be barr'd for me.'

They made a paction 'tween them twa,
They made it firm and sure,
That the first word whae'er shou'd speak,
Shou'd rise and bar the door.

Then by there came two gentlemen,
At twelve o' clock at night,
And they could neither see house nor hall,
Nor coal nor candle-light.

'Now whether is this a rich man's house,
Or whether is it a poor?'
But ne'er a word wad ane o' them speak,
For barring of the door.

And first they ate the white puddings,
And then they ate the black;
Tho' muckle thought the goodwife to hersel,
Yet ne'er a word she spake.

Then said the one unto the other,
'Here, man, tak ye my knife;
Do ye tak aff the auld man's beard,
And I'll kiss the goodwife.'

'But there's nae water in the house,
And what shall we do than?'
'What ails ye at the pudding-bree,
That boils into the pan?'

O up then started our goodman,
An angry man was he:
'Will ye kiss my wife before my een,
And scad me wi' pudding-bree?'

Then up and started our goodwife,
Gied three skips on the floor:
'Goodman, you've spoken the foremost word,
Get up and bar the door.'

Anon.

Get Up and Bar the Door

Introduction

There are very few light-hearted poems in the canon of Scotland's traditional ballads. However, one small group does offer comic treatments of domestic squabblings. The theme of 'Get Up and Bar the Door' is the struggle between wives and husbands as to who should have the upper hand, and the last word, in married life.

Historically Martinmas was the busy period in November when farm beasts were slaughtered and salted to provide food for winter. The by-products of the butchery were used to make offal dishes such as black puddings, mealie puddings and haggis which could be stored. 'Gay' probably does not here mean joyful; it has the Scots sense of 'gey', meaning considerable, demanding, difficult. The wife would have her hands gey full with her kitchen duties.

SECOND LEVEL
Related texts:

Anon., 'The Wee Cooper of Fife'
Anon., **'The Wife of Usher's Well'** (p. 30)
Robert Burns, 'Kellyburn Braes'

KEY WORDS:

Ballads

Drama

Family

Food

Home Economics

Marriage

Martinmas

Some key questions for class/group discussion:

- Why should the husband order his wife to shut the door?

- Why does she refuse?

- What is demanding her attention?

- What do you think a 'paction' is?

- Do the travellers knock before entering the house?

- Are they hungry?

- What do you suppose the wife was thinking to herself?

- What might have prompted the travellers to threaten as they do?

- Do they behave as 'gentlemen'?

- Why would the wife 'Gie three skips on the floor'?

- Finally, how do you think the husband felt?

Imaginative /creative writing

This is one of the most vigorously dramatic of all the ballads. It is tightly constructed with sharp dialogue, and offers a rich opportunity for groups and/or class to work up, script and enact a comic performance of the episode.

- Write the script complete with all necessary stage directions which will be acted out.

- Compose a brief monologue in which either the husband or the wife expresses his/her feelings after the event.

Further development

Research and report to the class how 'puddings' were traditionally made in Scotland.

Anon.

MacPherson's Rant

Fareweel ye dungeons dark and strong,
Fareweel, fareweel to thee.
MacPherson's rant will nae be long
On yonder gallows tree.

Chorus:
Sae rantinly, sae wantonly
Sae dantinly gaed he –
He played a tune and he danced it roun',
Below the gallows tree.

It was by a woman's treacherous hand
That I was condemned to dee.
Abune a ledge at a window she stood
And a blanket she threw ower me.

The Laird o' Grant that Highland saunt
That first laid hands on me,
He pled the cause o' Peter Broon,
To let MacPherson dee.

Untie these bands fra off my hands
And gie tae me my sword,
An' there's no' a man in a' Scotland
But I'll brave him at a word.

There's some cam here to see me hanged
And some to buy my fiddle –
But afore that I would part wi' her
I'd brak her through the middle.

He took the fiddle intae baith o' his hands
And he brak it ower a stane.
Says, there's nae ither hand sall play on thee
When I am deid and gane.

O little did my mother think
When first she cradled me,
That I would turn a rovin' boy
And die on the gallows tree.

The reprieve was comin' ower the brig o' Banff
To set MacPherson free;
Bit they pit the clock a quarter afore
An' they hanged him tae the tree.

Anon.

MacPherson's Rant

Introduction

This song belongs to a popular group of ballads reporting the last words of criminals at public executions. It dramatises the fact that James MacPherson, an 'Egyptian' or gypsy, was tried and hanged as a thief at Banff in Moray in 1700. The song's theme involves treachery, swaggering courage, injustice and the power of music. A 'rant' is a stirring Scottish dance melody played on fiddle or pipes. One of the legends associated with MacPherson was that he was a fine fiddler, and that at the gallows he composed the tune which still bears his name.

There are two distinct voices in this song. Although most of the story is told in the voice of MacPherson himself, the voice of an anonymous narrator reports the condemned man's last defiant words and actions, and in the last verse reveals the extent of the injustice done to him. MacPherson bitterly denounces the powerful authorities who had condemned him to the gallows and in a final act of desperate defiance, breaks his fiddle over a stone to ensure that it cannot be played ever again. His last words, however, in stark contrast to his angry accusatory rant, have a pathos which evokes sympathy. In the final verse the narrator reveals the act of treachery which seals his fate, reinforcing the sense that a great injustice had been cruelly carried out.

Students can listen to Jimmy Macbeath's singing and Hamish Henderson's account of the background to the episode on the website **www.tobarandualchais.co.uk**.

> ### SECOND/THIRD LEVEL
> **Related Texts:**
> Anon., 'The Gypsy Laddies'
> Anon., **'The Bonnie Earl o Moray'** (p. 8)
>
> ### KEY WORDS:
> **Ballads**
> **Banff**
> **Death**
> **Drama**
> **Execution**
> **History**
> **Justice**
> **Music**
> **Travellers**
> **Treachery**

Some key questions for class/group discussion

- What two distinct voices are heard in this song?

- How was MacPherson captured? What part do you think Peter Broon might have played?

- 'The Laird o' Grant that Highland saunt' … that phrase seems to be an insult; can you explain it?

- What does MacPherson seem most proud of?

- What are the motives of those who have gathered to see him hanged?

- Who are 'they' in the last verse?

- Would the song have been more effective if the last verse had been missed out?

Imaginative/creative writing

The song invites performance. Can someone in the class play the fiddle or other instrument? In groups, write a script in which there are roles for a narrator, a chorus of voices, the woman who betrayed him, the mother who mourns, and for MacPherson himself. Then prepare your script for performance.

Further Development

Part of the charge against MacPherson was that he was a gypsy vagabond, which was in itself a capital offence. For centuries Scottish travelling groups were treated as outcasts. Read and listen to the ballad 'The Gypsy Laddies'. What was the crime and punishment of these three laddies and how was a woman involved?

Anon.

Son David

'Oh, what's the blood 'it's on your sword?
My son David, ho, son David?
What's that blood 'it's on your sword?
Come, promise, tell me true.'

'Oh, that's the blood of my grey meer;
Hey, lady Mother, ho, lady Mother,
That's the blood of my grey meer
Because it wadnae rule by me.'

'Oh, that blood it is owre clear,
My son David, ho, son David,
That blood it is owre clear,
Come, promise, tell me true.'

'Oh, that's the blood of my greyhound
Hey, lady Mother, ho, lady Mother,
That's the blood of my greyhound
Because it wadnae rule by me.'

'Oh, that blood it is owre clear,
My son David, ho, son David,
That blood it is owre clear,
Come, promise, tell me true.'

'Oh, that's the blood of my huntin hawk,
Hey, lady Mother, ho, lady Mother,
That's the blood of my huntin hawk,
Because it wadnae rule by me.'

'Oh, that blood it is owre clear,
My son David, ho, son David,
That blood it is owre clear,
Come, promise, tell me true.'

'For that's the blood of my brother John,
Hey, lady Mother, ho, lady Mother,
That's the blood of my brother John
Because he wadnae rule by me.'

'Oh, I'm gaun awa in a bottomless boat,
In a bottomless boat, in a bottomless boat,
For I'm gaun awa in a bottomless boat,
An I'll never return again.'

'Oh, whan will you come back again,
My son David, ho, son David?
Whan will you come back again?
Come, promise, tell me true.'

'When the sun an the moon meet in yon glen,
Hey, lady Mother, ho, lady Mother,
When the sun an the moon meet in yon glen,
Fore I'll return again.'

Anon.

Son David

Introduction

Like 'The Wife of Usher's Well' this tragic ballad involves a mother and her sons. Its theme is murderous fraternal rivalry. The horror of the episode builds up entirely in dialogue, in a sequence of formulaic question-and-answer verses. The version printed here has been notably sung by the traditional singer Jeannie Robertson, but as 'Son Davie' it was collected much earlier from the recitation of Mrs King, an old woman in Kilbarchan, Renfrewshire. Listen to Jeannie Robertson's singing, to be found on the website **www.tobarandualchais.co.uk**.

**SECOND LEVEL
Related texts:**

Anon., 'Edward'
Anon., 'Lord Randal'
Anon., **'The Twa Corbies'** (p. 28)
Anon., **'The Wife of Usher's Well'** (p. 30)

KEY WORDS:

Ballads

Brothers

Death

Drama

Family

Murder

Music

Supernatural

Some key questions for class/group discussion

- What clues are there to the background of the family?

- What is the meaning of the expressions 'Come promise tell me true' and 'Because it wadnae rule by me'?

- Do you think the mother suspects from the first what has happened?

- What might she mean by, 'That blood it is owre clear'?

- In what ways do the last three verses differ from the rest of the poem?

- The expression 'in a bottomless boat' is repeated four times in verse nine. What effect do you think the repetition has? What is the son telling his mother?

- Does the final verse contain a promise that he will actually come back again?

Imaginative/creative writing

The ballad does not tell us why David killed John. Consider the possibilities. Was it an accident or a quarrel? Which was the older brother? If they had quarrelled, what might have been the cause? Jealousy? Money? A girl? Their mother?

- Write a short story in which you develop the relationship to the point of the killing.

- Write a short report of what you imagine might have happened between the two brothers, as if for a witness statement in a court case.

- Make a playscript out of the ballad text, setting the scene, providing stage directions and adding any extra characters and dialogue that you need.

Further development

Listen to what Jeannie Robertson thought was the explanation of the killing. Do you agree?

Robert Burns

The Battle of Sherra-moor

O cam ye here the fight to shun,
　　Or herd the sheep wi' me, man,
Or were ye at the Sherra-moor,
　　Or did the battle see, man.
I saw the battle sair and teugh,
And reekin-red ran mony a sheugh,
My heart for fear gae sough for sough,
To hear the thuds, and see the cluds
O' clans frae woods, in tartan duds,
Wha glaum'd at kingdoms three, man.

The red-coat lads wi' black cockauds
　　To meet them were na slaw, man,
They rush'd, and push'd, and blude
　　outgush'd,
　　And mony a bouk did fa', man:
The great Argyle led on his files,
I wat they glanc'd for twenty miles,
They hough'd the Clans like nine-pin kyles,
They hack'd and hash'd while braid swords
　　clash'd,
And thro' they dash'd, and hew'd and
　　smash'd,
Till fey men di'd awa, man.

But had ye seen the philibegs
　　And skyrin tartan trews, man,
When in the teeth they dar'd our Whigs,
　　And covenant Trueblues, man;
In lines extended lang and large,
When baiginets o'erpower'd the targe,
And thousands hasten'd to the charge;
We' Highland wrath they frae the sheath
Drew blades o' death, till out o' breath
They fled like frighted dows, man.

O, how deil Tam can that be true,
　　The chace gaed frae the north, man;
I saw mysel, they did pursue
　　The horse-men back to Forth, man;
And at Dunblane in my ain sight
They took the brig wi' a' their might,
And straught to Stirling wing'd their flight,
But, cursed lot! the gates were shut
And mony a huntit, poor Red-coat
For fear amaist did swarf, man.

My sister Kate cam up the gate
　　Wi' crowdie unto me, man;
She swoor she saw some rebels run
　　To Perth and to Dundee, man:
Their left-hand General had nae skill;
The Angus lads had nae gude will,
That day their neebour's blude to spill;
For fear by foes that they should lose
Their cogs o' brose, they scar'd at blows
And homeward fast did flee, man.

They've lost some gallant gentlemen
　　Amang the Highland clans, man;
I fear my Lord Panmuir is slain,
　　Or in his en'mies hands, man.
Now wad ye sing this double flight,
Some fell for wrang and some for right,
And mony bade the warld gudenight;
Say pell and mell, wi' muskets knell
How Tories fell, and Whigs to hell
Flew off in frighted bands, man.

Robert Burns

The Battle of Sherra-moor

Introduction

Burns's song commemorates the battle between the Jacobites (supporters of the exiled Stuart, James III, 'the Old Pretender') and the Hanoverians (supporters of George I, from Hanover) during the 1715 Jacobite rising. The outcome of the battle at Sheriffmuir, north of Dunblane, on November 13, was inconclusive, or in modern sporting parlance a 'score-draw', something that gave rise to the famous line: 'some say that we wan an some say that they wan an some say that nane wan at a' man'. Written when Burns toured the Highlands in 1787, the song, based on an earlier ballad, takes the form of a dialogue between two shepherds giving opposing views: the first one arguing that 'the red-coat lads wi' black cockauds' defeated the Jacobites who 'fled like frighted dows' (doves), but the second is convinced that the redcoats 'wing'd their flight' back to Stirling Castle pursued by the lads wearing the white cockades (rosettes or hat badges). Both give detailed accounts of the savagery of the fighting, with many dying on both sides, the descriptions in many instances mirroring each other. Repetition is used very effectively to heighten the effect of the fighting.

THIRD LEVEL
Related Texts:
   Robert Burns, 'Killiecrankie'
   Robert Burns, 'Ye Jacobites by Name'
   James Hogg, 'Will Ye Go to Sheriffmuir?'

KEY WORDS:

- Ballads
- Battles
- History
- Jacobites
- Music
- War

Some key questions for class/group discussion

- How sure is each speaker about the outcome of the battle, and how do they try to convince the other that he is right?

- How do you think they felt about what they witnessed? Do they show any admiration, hatred, anger, sympathy, amusement, etc.?

- What impression are we given of (a) the ordinary soldiers; (b) their leaders?

- What evidence is there about how the men fighting in the battle felt or behaved? e.g. brave, afraid, savage, foolish, sorry, sad.

- How does the song help us to understand the confusion and chaos of the battle?

- What techniques are used to suggest the violence and bloodshed of the battle? e.g. word choice, imagery, repetition, alliteration, rhythm.

Imaginative/creative writing

- The song provides a rich resource for creating first-hand accounts, interviews and news reports of a historical event or scripting an argument between the various witnesses.

- Group readings and recordings of the song, or extracts, could also be attempted, or dramatic and artistic work featuring soldiers, witnesses and leaders.

Further development

Further research, perhaps with the History department, could be done on the battle, the people and the politics surrounding it.

Robert Burns

The Braw Wooer

Last May a braw wooer cam down the lang glen,
    And sair wi' his love he did deave me;
I said, there was naething I hated like men,
    The deuce gae wi'm, to believe me, believe me
    The deuce gae wi'm, to believe me.

He spak o' the darts in my bonie black een,
    And vow'd for my love he was dying;
I said, he might die when he liked for JEAN –
    The lord forgie me for lying, for lying,
    The Lord forgie me for lying!

A weel-stocked mailen, himself for the laird,
    And marriage aff-hand, were his proffers:
I never loot on that I kend it, or car'd,
    But thought I might hae waur offers, waur offers,
    But thought I might hae waur offers.

But what wad ye think? In a fortnight or less,
    The deil tak his taste to gae near her!
He up the lang loan to my black cousin, Bess,
    Guess ye how, the jad! I could bear her, could bear her,
    Guess ye how, the jad! I could bear her.

But a' the niest week as I petted wi' care,
    I gaed to the tryste o' Dalgarnock;
And wha but my fine, fickle lover was there,
    I glowr'd as I'd seen a warlock, a warlock,
    I glowr'd as I'd seen a warlock.

But owre my left shouther I gae him a blink,
    Least neebors might say I was saucy:
My wooer he caper'd as he'd been in drink,
    And vow'd I was his dear lassie, dear lassie,
    And vow'd I was his dear lassie.

I spier'd for my cousin fu' couthy and sweet,
    Gin she had recover'd her hearin,
And how her new shoon fit her auld shachl't feet;
    But, heavens! how he fell a swearin, a swearin,
    But, heavens! how he fell a swearin.

He begged, for Gudesake! I wad be his wife,
    Or else I wad kill him wi' sorrow:
So e'en to preserve the poor body in life,
    I think I maun wed him tomorrow, tomorrow,
    I think I maun wed him tomorrow.

Robert Burns

The Braw Wooer

Introduction

Like many of Burns's love songs, this is written from the female point of view as the poet adopts the persona of a young woman confiding in someone about her difficulties in winning the man she desires. It is a fine example of a dramatic song monologue which cleverly reveals the character of the speaker, making us laugh with her and also perhaps at her. The girl plays very hard to get by pretending to reject her wooer's passionate declaration of love, but her coolness almost backfires on her as he then seeks solace from her 'black cousin Bess' and she has to resort to more cunning tactics to win him back. The use of the word 'black' does not refer to Bess's skin or even necessarily her hair colour but expresses the speaker's jealousy and anger with her cousin, implying that she thinks she is less than clean, i.e. it's a dirty trick to steal her lover.

> **THIRD LEVEL**
> **Related Texts:**
> Anon., **'The Bonnie Lass o' Fyvie'** (p. 12)
> Robert Burns, 'What Can a Young Lassie Do Wi an Auld Man'
> Duncan Gray, 'My Tocher's the Jewel'
> T. T. Kilbucho, 'The Cobbler'
> Robert Henryson, 'Robin and Makyne'
>
> **KEY WORDS:**
>
> **Character**
>
> **Love**
>
> **Marriage**

Some key questions for class/group discussion

- How do we know that she is only pretending not to care for him?

- What do you think she sees as his main attractions? Why?

- How are the tables turned on her? Does she deserve this in your opinion? What would you have done in this situation if you were (a) her, and (b) him?

- How does she win him back and what do you think of her tactics?

- What do you think his apparent changes of heart reveal about him?

- Which words or phrases show how she feels at different stages and what aspects of her character are revealed by them? Do you admire her or not? Why?

Imaginative/creative writing

- Scripts could be written about the whole story, perhaps with each group writing a different scene, maybe including Bess's viewpoint on the speaker, whose name is never given.

- Letters could be written to an advice page or as a Facebook post expressing opinions on what she or he has done.

- Discussion might focus on whether she really loved him or was just after his money and on the general issue of whether pupils think you should marry for wealth or love.

Further development

Research some traditional wedding customs and compare them with modern wedding ceremonies and celebrations.

Robert Burns

To a Louse, On Seeing One on a Lady's Bonnet at Church

Ha! whare ye gaun, ye crowlan ferlie!
Your impudence protects you sairly:
I canna say but ye strunt rarely,
    Owre gawze and lace;
Tho' faith, I fear ye dine but sparely,
    On sic a place.

Ye ugly, creepan, blastet wonner,
Detested, shunn'd, by saunt an' sinner,
How daur ye set your fit upon her,
    Sae fine a Lady!
Gae somewhere else and seek your dinner,
    On some poor body.

Swith, in some beggar's haffet squattle;
There ye may creep, and sprawl, and sprattle,
Wi' ither kindred, jumping cattle,
    In shoals and nations;
Whare horn nor bane ne'er daur unsettle,
    Your thick plantations.

Now haud you there, ye're out o' sight,
Below the fatt'rels, snug and tight,
Na faith ye yet! ye'll no be right,
    Till ye've got on it,
The verra tapmost, towrin height
    O' Miss's bonnet.

My sooth! right bauld ye set your nose out,
As plump an' gray as onie grozet:
O for some rank, mercurial rozet,
    Or fell, red smeddum,
I'd gie you sic a hearty dose o't,
    Wad dress your droddum!

I wad na been surpriz'd to spy
You on an auld wife's flainen toy;
Or aiblins some bit duddie boy,
    On 's wylecoat;
But Miss's fine Lunardi, fye!
    How daur ye do 't?

O Jenny dinna toss your head,
An' set your beauties a' abread!
Ye little ken what cursed speed
    The blastie's makin!
Thae winks and finger-ends, I dread,
    Are notice takin!

O wad some Pow'r the giftie gie us
To see oursels as others see us!
It wad frae monie a blunder free us
    An' foolish notion:
What airs in dress an' gait wad lea'e us,
    And ev'n Devotion!

Robert Burns

To a Louse, On Seeing One on a Lady's Bonnet at Church

Introduction

This is one of the most popular poems by Robert Burns. The poem deals with an encounter he had while at the Kirk one Sunday. He sees a louse crawl from beneath the bonnet of a rather well-to-do young lady which sets him off to muse on the nature of life. He gives a vivid description of the louse's movements, telling it off for being in such an inappropriate setting, and suggesting the places it would feel more at home. Ultimately, the louse is used as a symbol of pride, both as the insect is climbing to the very top of the lady's hat, and as the lady herself is unaware of the infestation, showing herself off to the church congregation.

In the poem, Burns uses the traditional stanza form known as the 'Standard Habbie' which is also seen in other texts such as 'To a Mouse'. This stanza form, and the use of Scots adds life and energy to the text.

THIRD LEVEL
Related Texts:
  Robert Burns, 'To a Mouse'

KEY WORDS:

  Animals

  History

  Humanity

  Humour

  Nature

  Pride

  Standard Habbie

Some key questions for class/group discussion

• What kinds of descriptive language are used to describe the louse? Pick out some of the more vivid terms and explain why you like them.

• From what is said in the poem, what impression do you get of the young lady wearing the bonnet?

• In what ways does the use of Scots rather than English add life and detail to the points that Burns makes?

• In the last stanza, what is the key point that Burns makes about life and society?

Imaginative/creative writing

• Think about your favourite animal. List as many interesting words and phrases as you can to describe what the animal looks like and how it behaves. Try to use similes and metaphors and sound techniques.

• Write your own poem about this animal using the words and phrases from your list. You could write this as a word picture, an acrostic poem, or in any way you choose.

Further development

Most people in Burns's day would have carried lice and other afflictions on their persons and clothes. Use internet resources to find out what the most common ones were.

J. M. Caie

The Puddock

A puddock sat by the lochan's brim,
An' he thocht there was never a puddock like him.
He sat on his hurdies, he waggled his legs,
An' cockit his heid as he glowered throu' the seggs
The bigsy wee cratur' was feelin' that prood,
He gapit his mou' an' he croakit oot lood
'Gin ye'd a' like tae see a richt puddock,' quo' he,
'Ye'll never, I'll sweer, get a better nor me.
I've fem'lies an' wives an' a weel-plenished hame,
Wi' drink for my thrapple an' meat for my wame.
The lasses aye thocht me a fine strappin' chiel,
An' I ken I'm a rale bonny singer as weel.
I'm nae gaun tae blaw, but the truth I maun tell –
I believe I'm the verra MacPuddock himsel'.'

A heron was hungry an' needin' tae sup,
Sae he nabbit th' puddock and gollup't him up;
Syne runkled his feathers: 'A peer thing,' quo' he,
'But – puddocks is nae fat they eesed tae be.'

J. M. Caie

The Puddock

Introduction

John Morrison Caie, a native of Kincardineshire, wrote about the rural life of north-east Scotland in the early decades of the twentieth century, and, like his more famous contemporary author, James Leslie Mitchell, (better known as Lewis Grassic Gibbon) he often wrote about it in the language of the place itself, the tongue or 'speak' of the Mearns. His best-known poem is undoubtedly 'The Puddock', a grimly comic moral fable in which we hear an anonymous wry narrator introducing the puffed-up puddock (a frog or toad) who has a very high opinion of himself and his ability to satisfy 'families and wives', who clearly should think themselves lucky to have him. His very sudden end in the beak of a heron, which gives us the contrary voice and description of the creature, comically brings him down to size, as it were.

> **SECOND LEVEL**
> **Related Texts:**
> Robert Burns, 'To a Mouse'
> Robert Burns, **'To a Louse'** (p. 42)
> Norman MacCaig, **'Toad'** (p. 136)
> Angela McSeveney, **'Changing a Downie Cover'** (p. 164)
>
> **KEY WORDS:**
>
> **Amphibians**
>
> **Animals**
>
> **Fables**
>
> **Humour**
>
> **Nature**

Some key questions for class/group discussion

After listening to the poem (several good readings are available online) the students could read the poem to each other in pairs or small groups. If no glossary is available, ask groups to identify the words they don't know, possibly starting with 'puddock' itself and then ask the class to look up other words, such as hurdies (backside), thrapple (throat), wame (womb or stomach), syne (then) or Doric words like 'chiel' for chap or 'fat' for what. Of course there may well be English words which need checking out too, which could be done by a different group.

- If you didn't know what a puddock is, could you have guessed it from what happens in the poem? Why?

- How do the narrator's comments or description show or suggest that the puddock is a 'bigsy wee cratur'? What other words could you use for someone like this?

- What does the puddock say to confirm the narrator's opinion of him?

- What do you think he means by 'the verra MacPuddock himsel'?

- What is funny or ironic about the line 'I'm nae gaun tae blaw …' and also the last line of the poem?

- Do you feel sorry for the puddock? Why?

- Do you think the poem is really about animals or is it really about humans or both? What do you think the moral of the poem is?

Imaginative/creative writing

Individual and group readings or dramatisations could be recorded or filmed. The story could be rewritten in the students' own dialect for younger children, either in prose or as a short drama script.

Further development

Research the life cycles and food chains of frogs or any other riverbank or pond creature. Design a poster with drawings which conveys key information about the creature you have chosen.

Iain Camshron/John Cameron

Chì Mi na Mòr-bheanna / The Mist-Covered Mountains of Home

Sèist
O chì, chì mi na mòr-bheanna,
O chì, chì mi na còrr-bheanna,
O chì, chì mi na coireachan,
chì mi na sgoran fo cheò.

Chì mi gun dàil an t-àite san d' rugadh mi;
cuirear orm fàilte sa chànain a thuigeas mi;
gheibh mi ann aoidh agus gràdh nuair ruigeam
nach reicinn air thunnachan òir.

Chì mi ann coilltean, chi mi ann doireachan;
chì mi ann maghan bàna as torraiche;
chì mi na fèidh air làr nan coireachan,
falaicht' an trusgan de cheò.

Beanntaichean àrda as àillidh leacainnean;
sluagh ann a' còmhnaidh as còire
    cleachdainnean;
's aotrom mo cheum a' leum gam faicinn
is fanaidh mi tacan le deòin.

Fàilt' air na gorm-mheallaibh tholmach,
    thulachnach;
fàilt' air na còrr-bheannaibh mòra, mulanach;
fàilt' air na coilltean, is fàilt' air na h-uile –
O! 's sona bhith fuireach 'nan còir.

Chorus
Hoo, O! Soon shall I see them O;
Hee, O! See them, O see them O;
Ho ro! Soon shall I see them,
the mist-covered mountains of home.

There shall I visit the place of my birth;
and they'll give me a welcome, the warmest on
    earth;
all so loving and kind, full of music and mirth,
in the sweet-sounding language of home.

There shall I gaze on the mountains again,
on the fields and the woods and the burns in the
    glen;
and away 'mong the corries, beyond human ken,
in the haunts of the deer shall I roam.

There I'll converse with the hard-headed father,
and there shall I jest with the kind-hearted
    mother;
O, light is my heart as I turn my steps thither,
the ever-dear precincts of home.

Hail! to the mountains with summits of blue;
to the glens with their meadows of sunshine
    and dew;
to the women and men ever constant true,
ever ready to welcome one home.

John Cameron

Chì Mi na Mòr-bheanna / The Mist-Covered Mountains of Home

Introduction

The original name of this song/poem was 'Anticipation of Seeing Ballachulish on the First Day of Autumn, 1856'. It was written by John Cameron who was born and brought up there. It was later given the shorter title 'The Mist-Covered Mountains of Home'. It is now sung to a haunting slow air. The singer/speaker describes his keen anticipation of seeing again the high mountains of his Argyllshire home which are so frequently covered in mist. There he expects to renew his contacts with his family and the country of his early life, and everything to be perfect.

> **SECOND /THIRD LEVEL**
> **Related texts:**
> Iain Crichton Smith, 'Home' (short story)
> Duncan Macintyre, **'Final Farewell to the Bens'** (p. 148)
> Neil Munro, **'John o' Lorn'** (p. 178)
>
> **KEY WORDS:**
>
> **Argyll**
>
> **Countryside**
>
> **Exile**
>
> **Family**
>
> **Gaelic**
>
> **Highlands**
>
> **Nostalgia**

Some key questions for class/group discussion

- Read the poem through once or twice. Mist-covered hills need not be attractive, as they often mean it is raining or about to rain, but they are mentioned repeatedly in the chorus. Why are they so important to the singer/speaker?

- In the first verse he imagines himself back in his native village. What sort of reception does he expect to get? What is the 'sweet-sounding language of home' and why is it important?

- In the second verse, what aspects of nature does he expect to enjoy?

- In the third and fourth verses his expectation is that life will be perfect now he is back home with his family and in his own beautiful countryside. Is it likely that things will turn out as well as he expects? Find out what the word 'sentimental' means. Is this poem realistic or sentimental?

Imaginative/creative writing

Imagine you have been abroad for many years and have finally come home. In a short story describe your homecoming. Was it as wonderful as you expected?

Further development

Using a map of the Highlands (e.g. Ordnance Survey Landranger No. 41), try to locate the village of Ballachulish near Glencoe where the writer of this song/poem was born. Try to identify some of the high hills near the village which would have been his 'mist-covered mountains of home'. (On some maps you will see 'beinn' rather than 'ben'. 'Beinn' is the Gaelic spelling of 'ben'.)

Thomas Campbell

Lord Ullin's Daughter

A chieftain to the Highlands bound
Cries 'Boatman do not tarry!
And I'll give thee a silver pound
To row us o'er the ferry!'

'Now who be ye would cross Loch Gyle,
This dark and stormy water?'
'O I'm the chief of Ulva's isle,
And this Lord Ullin's daughter.

'And fast before her father's men
Three days we've fled together,
For should he find us in the glen,
My blood would stain the heather.

'His horsemen hard behind us ride –
Should they our steps discover,
Then who will cheer my bonnie bride,
When they have slain her lover?'

Out spoke the hardy highland wight,
'I'll go, my chief, I'm ready:
It is not for your silver bright,
But for your winsome lady.

'And by my word! The bonny bird
In danger shall not tarry;
So though the waves are raging white
I'll row your o'er the ferry.'

By this the storm grew loud apace,
The water wraith was shrieking;
And in the scowl of Heaven each face
Grew dark as they were speaking.

But still as wilder blew the wind,
And as the night grew drearer,
Adown the glen rode arméd men,
Their trampling sounded nearer.

'O haste thee, haste!' the lady cries,
'Though tempests round us gather;
I'll meet the raging of the skies,
But not an angry father.'

The boat has left a stormy land,
A stormy sea before her –
When, oh! too strong for human hand
The tempest gathered o'er her.

And still they row'd amidst the roar
Of waters fast prevailing:
Lord Ullin reached that fatal shore –
His wrath was changed to wailing.

For, sore dismay'd, through storm and shade
His child he did discover –
One lovely hand she stretched for aid,
And one was round her lover.

'Come back! Come back!' he cried in grief,
'Across this stormy water:
And I'll forgive your Highland chief,
My daughter! Oh, my daughter!'

'Twas vain: the loud waves lashed the shore,
Return or aid preventing:
The waters wild went o'er his child,
And he was left lamenting.

Thomas Campbell

Lord Ullin's Daughter

Introduction

Thomas Campbell's fame rests on his long poem 'The Pleasures of Hope' (1799), and stirring pieces like 'Hohenlinden' and 'Ye Mariners of England'. As a young man, he spent time as a tutor on the island of Mull where he heard the sad tale depicted in this poem. A young Highland chief has eloped with the daughter of Lord Ullin. Pursued by her angry father and his men, they make for the narrow strait between Mull and the small island of Ulva, the young chief's clan territory. When they reach the ferry, he offers the boatman 'a silver pound' to row them across. The seas are wild and the going hazardous but fear drives them on. When Lord Ullin and his retinue reach the shore, he sees the plight of his daughter. Moved by this he begs her to return and forgives her Highland chief for taking her from him. But it is too late: the seas overcome the lovers and they drown. The poem is straightforward, fast-moving and exciting; the girl's fear of her father's wrath is palpable; the description of the fierce weather is powerful; and a real note of tragedy is struck in the ending.

SECOND/THIRD LEVEL Related Texts:

Anon., **'The Bonnie Lass o' Fyvie'** (p. 12)
Lady Nairne, **'The Laird o' Cockpen'** (p. 182)
Sir Walter Scott, **'Jock o' Hazeldean'** (p. 198)
Sir Walter Scott, **'Lochinvar'** (p. 200)

KEY WORDS:

Disaster

Family

Geography

Highlands

Love

The sea

Weather

Some key questions for class/group discussion

- Why are the Highland chief and Lord Ullin's daughter desperate to cross to the island of Ulva?

- The chieftain offers the boatman a silver pound to row them across. What is his response to this?

- What is the weather like as the lovers try to cross the strait? Do you think the poet's description of it is good? Why?

- What is Lord Ullin's attitude at the end of the poem when he sees his daughter and her lover in such a perilous situation?

- How does the poem end?

Imaginative/creative writing

- Write a story in which a group of young people are out sailing in a small boat when the weather turns very nasty. On this occasion, however, there will be a happy ending.

- Write a modern-day story in which there are difficulties for two young people who want to get married because their parents do not approve of the match.

Further development

Have students examine Ordnance Survey Landranger Map 47: Tobermory and North Mull (A smaller scale map would be adequate.) They should look for Loch na Keal, which is the Loch Gyle of the poem. They should then locate the island of Ulva and identify the site of the tragedy.

W. D. Cocker

The Sniper

Two hundred yards away he saw his head;
He raised his rifle, took quick aim and shot him.
Two hundred yards away the man dropped dead;
With bright exulting eye he turned and said,
'By Jove, I got him!'
And he was jubilant; had he not won
The meed of praise his comrades haste to pay?
He smiled; he could not see what he had done;
The dead man lay two hundred yards away.
He could not see the dead, reproachful eyes,
The youthful face which Death had not defiled
But had transfigured when he claimed his prize.
Had he seen this perhaps he had not smiled.
He could not see the woman as she wept
To hear the news two hundred miles away,
Or through his every dream she would have crept,
And into all his thoughts by night and day.
Two hundred yards away, and, bending o'er
A body in a trench, rough men proclaim
Sadly, that Fritz, the merry is no more.
(Or shall we call him Jack? *It's all the same*.)

W. D. Cocker

The Sniper

Introduction

William Dixon Cocker wrote a number of poems about his experience of war and captivity: 'Up the Line to Poelkapelle', 'The Phantom Platoon', 'The Sniper', and a five-part sonnet cycle entitled 'Sonnets in Captivity'. 'The Sniper' focuses not on the sniper himself but on the effect his bullet has on his anonymous victim and his loved ones. We do not learn about the nationality of either the killer or the dead soldier, as the dead boy could be of any nationality, showing that the tragedy and cruelty of his loss are felt equally on all sides. This poem reveals the true nature of modern warfare with cold-blooded killing from a long distance, something that makes the killing of fellow human beings somehow easier.

THIRD LEVEL
Related Texts:
Geoffrey A. S. Kennedy, 'The Sniper'
Ewart Alan Mackintosh, **'In Memoriam'** (p. 150)
Ewart Alan Mackintosh, **'On Vimy Ridge'** (p. 152)
Robert W. Service, 'The Sniper'

KEY WORDS:

| Death |
| History |
| Loss |
| War |

Some key questions for class/group discussion

- How does the sniper feel about the killing and how does the author reveal this?

- How do his comrades react and how does this contrast with the reaction of the dead man's comrades?

- How does the poet arouse our sympathy for the dead soldier?

- What impact does his death have on the woman at home and how might this have affected the sniper if he could have seen her? What point do you think is being made here by the poet?

- What does he mean that 'it's all the same'? Why does he put this last sentence in italics?

- How does he emphasise the speed of the killing through word choice and sentence structure?

- The poet deploys a number of changing viewpoints in the poem. Outline them and explain how effective this technique is.

- Contrasts and repetition are important in the poem. Identify a couple of these and explain their effect.

Imaginative/creative writing

- All British soldiers were required to write a letter which could be sent home on the occasion of their death. Compose the letter which the sniper wrote after this event.

- Devise a script between the sniper and his colleagues, or between the dead soldier's colleagues, about Fritz or Jack.

Further development

Research could be undertaken into family history and local history leading to talks or presentations about the First World War. Older students could explore further comparisons with other war poems.

Stewart Conn

Heirloom

Learning on moving house to Edinburgh
that my grandfather's licensed grocers
had been in the High Street
made me feel less an interloper
than one who has been long away.

Next door to the police station
he would leave out, on wintry nights,
a dram for the man on the beat.
And his special-constable's baton
bearing the city's coat of arms,

presented during World War One,
hung in our front porch for years
on its frayed leather strap, for decoration
but within easy reach in the event of intruders.
Only to end up lost, presumed stolen.

Stewart Conn

Heirloom

Introduction

'Heirloom' is published in the collection *Ghosts at Cockcrow*, in the section which is about the poet's childhood and youth in Edinburgh. The poet is pleased to discover that he had relatives in Edinburgh in the past, as this made him feel as if he was coming back home rather than moving in from outside, and the little anecdote about his grandfather's generosity serves to cement his place. The heirloom of the title, his grandfather's special-constable's baton, is described in detail, but only the memory of it now remains.

SECOND/THIRD LEVEL
Related texts:

Jackie Kay, **'Grandpa's Soup'** (p. 112)
Catriona Nic Ìomhair Parsons / Catriona MacIvor Parsons, **'Memory'** / **'Cuimhne'** (p. 190)

KEY WORDS:

Family

History

Home

Memory

Nostalgia

Some key questions for class/group discussion

- Why was it important for the poet to find out that his grandfather had had a shop in Edinburgh in the past?

- What is a 'licensed grocer'?

- What is 'a dram' and why do you think his grandfather left one out for 'the man on the beat'?

- Why do you think the poet takes so many lines to describe the 'special-constable's baton'?

- Show how the poet uses a comic tone in the second last line of the poem.

- In what way is the fate of the baton very ironic?

- There is a feeling of time passing in this poem. Trace all the references to time/the past (remember that the tense of verbs can be significant) to justify the description of the poem as concerning memory.

Imaginative/creative writing

- Imagine a brief conversation between the poet's grandfather and the beat policeman on a cold winter's night when the dram is enjoyed.

- Imagine (or recall) moving to a house in a new town. What did you miss about your old house and old town, and what did you look forward to in your new location?

Further development

Find out what a special constable is/was, and what duties they performed.

Stewart Conn

Springtime

In front of me a girl with bare feet,
in a beribboned dress, picks white
flowers in a field somewhere near Pompeii.

Each day I look at her, head straight,
right hand outstretched as she delicately
plucks the stem. Was she there that night

the lava flowed, birds shrivelled in the sky
and lovers turned to ash, where they lay?
If so, what had she done to deserve it?

I wonder, will it ever be
Springtime again, the blood flow freely;
or has man blighted all hope of recovery?

We are on borrowed time, you and I
and have been from the outset.
All that is left, is to live lovingly.

Stewart Conn

Springtime

Introduction

Conn says that 'Springtime' reflects the sense of precariousness which is found in all his poetry. The poem describes a scene in southern Italy, near the town of Pompeii, which was destroyed by the eruption of Vesuvius in 79 CE. The poet observes a girl picking flowers, an everyday scene, and one which must have been repeated many times in that place, and it takes him back to the moment of destruction, and the many similar girls who perished in the eruption. He is very conscious of the role of chance in such events – the people of Pompeii were not being punished; they were simply in the wrong place at the wrong time. His thought moves from the particular scene to a wider consideration of man's place in the world, and what damage he is causing by his actions.

THIRD LEVEL
Related texts:

Sheena Blackhall, 'The Eruption of Vesuvius Letter No. 1' (p. 34)

KEY WORDS:

Death

Disaster

Environment

History

Nature

Romans

Seasons

Youth

Some key questions for class/group discussion

- Read the first five and a half lines. Why do you think the poet gives such a detailed description of the girl? What details has he left out?

- How do you know that this is not a single observation?

- What event is the poet describing in lines six to eight? Why do you think he chooses these images?

- How could this girl be involved in the eruption? What does the poet wish you to understand here?

- The poem becomes much more philosophical in the last two stanzas, where the poet is looking at man's destruction of the world, rather than the natural destructive power of the volcano. Put into your own words what the 'message' of these lines is. Who do you think 'you and I' are?

- Although there is no obvious rhyme, the poet often uses line-end words which have similar sounds, such as 'feet', 'white', 'straight', 'night'. There is a similar internal half-rhyme, as in 'straight' and 'outstretched'. What do you think is the effect of this?

Imaginative/creative writing

Read Sheena Blackhall's 'The Eruption of Vesuvius Letter No. 1' which will give you details of the eruption, and then imagine that you are this girl picking flowers near the town of Pompeii, but far enough away not to be affected by the eruption. Imagine that you see what is happening, and in your own style, write an account of the event.

Further development

Find out all you can about the eruption of Vesuvius, and the destruction (and preservation under the ash) of Pompeii. You could compare this natural effect with the human actions which are changing the climate and parts of the world.

James Copeland

Black Friday

Oot behind a lorry,
Peyin nae heed,
Ablow a double-decker,
A poor wean deid.

Perra worn sannies,
Wee durty knees,
Heh, errapolis.
Stand back, please!

Lookit the conductriss,
Face as white as chalk.
Heh, see the driver but,
Canny even talk.

Anyone a witness?
Naw, we never saw,
Glad ah'm no the polis
Goin tae tell its maw.

Weemen windae-hingin,
Herts in their mooth,
It's no oor close, Lizzie,
Oh Gawdstreuth!

Screams on the landin,
Two closes doon,
It's no wee Hughie!
Poor Nellie Broon.

Phone up the shipyard,
Oh, what a shame,
Yes, we'll inform him,
Please repeat the name.

See Big Hughie,
Jokin wi' the squad.
Better knock aff, Hughie,
O dear God.

Whit – no his lauddie?
Aw bloody hell!
D'ye see Hughie's face but,
He's jist a boy himsel.

James Copeland

Black Friday

Introduction

In this poem James Copeland gives a simple description of a fatal accident involving a young child. We hear the voices of ordinary Glaswegians trying to come to terms with this experience. The various voices in the poem form a chorus. Most of the speakers use the local dialect but some use Standard English. The poet shows that he has an eye and ear for the sadness in the everyday life of ordinary people. The use of speech and rhyme gives a rhythm to the poem which paints a vivid picture of tenement life in Glasgow. People who lived in tenements often shared each other's lives and this poem is a good example of that community feeling. The poem starts with a description of the accident, and sympathy is created by the reference to the 'Perra worn sannies/Wee durty knees' of the victim. The poet describes various reactions to the incident, using direct speech. Perhaps the most poignant line in the poem is the last one when the boy's father is described as 'jist a boy himsel'.

**SECOND LEVEL
Related Texts:**

Margaret Green, '**The Ballad of Janitor MacKay**' (p. 92)
Jim McLean, '**Farewell to Glasgow**' (p. 156)
Nancy Nicolson, '**Listen tae the Teacher**' (p. 186)

KEY WORDS:

Childhood

Death

Family

Glasgow

History

Modern Studies

Some key questions for class/group discussion

• Read the poem aloud and work out who is speaking each line. Assign different members of your group to read the different voices and have a narrator for the other parts. Who uses Standard English and why?

• Explain how the simile, 'face as white as chalk' emphasises the conductress's reaction.

• What does the alliteration in 'Weemin windae-hingin' add to the picture?

• Apart from the Brown family, whom do you feel sorry for in the poem?

Imaginative/creative writing

• Write a newspaper report of the incident in the poem. Most of the report will be in Standard English but you should use Glaswegian dialect for the eyewitness accounts.

• Produce a road safety leaflet which gets across the dangers on the roads.

Further development

The poem gives glimpses of life in the tenements. Research the way of life of tenement communities in the twentieth century.

Joe Corrie

The Image o' God

Crawlin' aboot like a snail in the mud,
Covered wi' clammy blae,
ME, made after the image o' God –
Jings! But it's laughable, tae.

Howkin' awa' 'neath a mountain o' stane,
Gaspin' for want o' air,
The sweat makin' streams doon my bare back-banes,
And my knees a' hauckit and sair.

Strainin' and cursin' the hale shift through,
Half-starved, half-blin', half-mad,
And the gaffer he says, 'Less dirt in that coal
Or ye go up the pit, my lad.'

So I gie my life tae the Nimmo squad
For eicht and fower a day.
Me! Made after the image o' God –
Jings! But it's laughable, tae.

Joe Corrie

The Image o' God

Introduction

This bitterly ironic poem, written in the 1930s from the perspective of a coalminer toiling in the darkness of the pit, ridicules the Old Testament story of Creation where God made man in his own image. Joe Corrie was a coal miner and wrote from his own experience and the experiences of the mining community to which he belonged. Some explanation may be necessary, like the concept of Creation in the Book of Genesis and the reference to the Nimmo Squad, which was either the name of the pit owner or the name of a ganger or sub-contractor who hired a team of men. The warning from the gaffer might also need explanation as miners were often paid by the ton and the foreman thinks the miner is trying to cheat him, when ironically the miner can hardly see in the darkness to separate coal from dirt. His meagre wages of 'eicht an fower a day' means eight shillings and four pence in pre-decimal currency (about 42p in today's money) which would mean a weekly wage of about £2.

THIRD LEVEL
Related Texts:
Anon., 'The Donibristle Disaster'
Anon., 'The Blantyre Explosion'
Ewan MacColl, 'Schooldays End/Schooldays Over'
Matt McGinn, 'The Miner's Lullaby'

KEY WORDS:

Environment

History

Mining

Modern Studies

Poverty

Religion

Work

Some key questions for class/group discussion

- How does the miner feel about the idea of being made in God's image?

- What different emotions does he express in the poem?

- Why do you think he puts 'ME' in capital letters?

- Why would he think he gives his life to the Nimmo squad?

- What does he mean by 'Jings! But it's laughable tae' and what does this suggest about God?

Imaginative/creative writing

Think about the vivid descriptions of working underground in the pit used by Joe Corrie in the poem and write a first-person account of a teenager's first day working as a miner.

Further development

- If any pupils have grandparents who worked in the pits, they could interview them about what it was like to work as a miner and how they felt about it. Perhaps they could invite former miners to visit the school and talk to the pupils about their lives, especially in a former mining area.

- Research could be undertaken into the history of mining in Scotland, the importance of coal as a fuel in our history and the human and environmental problems associated with it.

Robert Crawford

Alba Einstein

When proof of Einstein's Glaswegian birth
First hit the media everything else was dropped:
Logie Baird, Dundee painters, David Hume – all
Got the big E. Physics documentaries
Became peak-viewing; Scots publishers hurled awa
MacDiarmid like an overbaked potato, and swooped
On the memorabilia: *Einstein Used My Fruitshop*,
Einstein in Old Postcards, Einstein's Bearsden Relatives.
Hot on their heels came the A.E. Fun Park,
Quantum Court, Glen Einstein Highland Malt.
Glasgow was booming. Scotland rose to its feet
At Albert Suppers where The Toast to the General Theory
Was given by footballers, panto-dames, or restaurateurs.
In the US an ageing lab-technician recorded
How the Great Man when excited showed a telltale glottal stop.
He'd loved fiddlers' rallies. His favourite sport was curling.
Thanks to this, Scottish business expanded
Endlessly. His head grew toby-jug-shaped,
Ideal for keyrings. He'd always worn brogues.
Ate bannocks in exile. As a wee boy he'd read *The Beano*.
His name brought new energy: our culture was solidly based
On pride in our hero, The Universal Scot.

Robert Crawford

Alba Einstein

Introduction

The poem imagines what would happen if Albert Einstein were found to be Scottish, and in so doing pokes fun at the Scottish tendency to go overboard in claiming anyone who could possibly have a drop of Scottish blood and finding reasons for celebrating. The poem is not difficult in terms of diction, but gives many possibilities for investigating areas of contemporary Scottish culture. Famous and celebrated Scots are ignored in favour of Albert Einstein, roads and buildings are named after him, the Burns Supper becomes the Albert Supper and all sorts of unlikely 'facts' are unearthed to round out the picture.

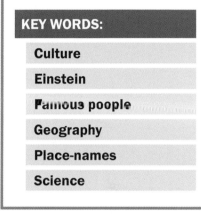

THIRD LEVEL
Related texts:
Robert Crawford, 'John Logie Baird'
Robert Crawford, 'A Scottish Assembly'

KEY WORDS:

Culture

Einstein

Famous people

Geography

Place-names

Science

Some key questions for class/group discussion

- What does the poet mean by 'the big E' in line four? Can you think of two entirely different meanings (hint – one related to Einstein's theory)?

- The only use of Scots is found in 'hurled awa' in line five. Why is it particularly appropriate here?

- What is the significance of the place-names in lines nine to ten?

- What evidence is cited in the last eight lines of the poem to 'prove' Einstein's Scottishness?

- Why is the poem called 'Alba Einstein'?

Imaginative/creative writing

In the vein of Robert Crawford's humorous and unlikely 'facts', write a newspaper report of an interview with the owner of the shop in *Einstein Used My Fruitshop*, or draft the Toast to the General Theory.

Further development

- The poem presents a rare opportunity for collaboration with the Science department.

- There are many possibilities for investigating the people named in the poem: Logie Baird, Dundee painters, David Hume, Hugh MacDiarmid.

- Investigate the features of the Burns Supper which are being transferred to the Albert Supper.

- In the context of Einstein's theory, investigate why the poet describes Scottish business as 'expanding endlessly' (lines seventeen to eighteen); says 'His name brought new energy' (line twenty-one), and calls him 'The Universal Scot' (line twenty-two).

Iain Crichton Smith

Rhythm

They dunno how it is. I smack a ball
right through the goals. But they dunno how the words
get muddled in my head, get tired somehow.
I look through the window, see. And there's a wall
I'd kick the ball against, just smack and smack.
Old Jerry he can't play, he don't know how,
not now at any rate. He's too flicking small.
See him in shorts, out in the crazy black.
Rythm, he says and ryme. See him at back.
He don't know nuthing about Law. He'd fall
flat on his face, just like a big sack,
when you're going down the wing, the wind behind you
And crossing into goalmouth, and they're roaring
the whole great crowd. They're up on their feet cheering.
The ball's at your feet and there it goes, just crack.

Iain Crichton Smith

Rhythm

Introduction

In 'Rhythm', Iain Crichton Smith makes use of sound to convey the boy's strong feelings about his inability to learn in the classroom whereas he can play football with ease. He knows the rhythm of the ball although he can't recognise words on the page. The poet uses 'dunno' to convey the way the boy might speak and he misspells 'rythm' and 'ryme' to show his problem with spelling. He makes use of both rhythm and rhyme to get the feeling of freedom and success the boy has when he is playing football. He shows his disdain for Old Jerry by saying he can't play football and he uses the vernacular in 'he's too flicking small'. This poem is a fine example of the poet getting into the head of a boy who is not good at schoolwork but really good at football. The uses of the word 'smack' convey both his frustration and his elation.

SECOND LEVEL

Related Texts:

Anon., 'The Bewteis of the Fute-ball' (p. 6)

Jim Douglas, 'The New Teacher' (p. 68)

Margaret Green, 'The Ballad of Janitor MacKay' (p. 92)

KEY WORDS:

Childhood

Football

Memory

Physical Education

School

Sport

Some key questions for class/group discussion

- In the first three lines, which word does the poet use to convey his frustration with words and which word does he use to convey his ability with a ball? How do these words differ in sound?

- Why does he repeat the word 'smack' in line five?

- What simile does he use to show that he is not impressed by 'him at back'?

- In the last four lines of the poem pick out all the words which show how happy he is when he is playing football.

- Why do you think he has used the word 'crack' in the last line and not 'smack' which he has used earlier for smashing the ball in?

Imaginative/creative writing

- Write about a skill you have and try to convey the pleasure you get out of it.

- Write a short story which finishes with 'They're up on their feet cheering'.

Further development

Football is sometimes referred to as 'poetry in motion'. See if you can find a football commentary on TV or radio or in a newspaper and pick out the similes and metaphors that are used to describe a goal or a good piece of playing.

Iain Mac a' Ghobhainn / Iain Crichton Smith

Nuair a Bha Sinn Òg / When We Were Young

Nuair a bha sinn òg bhiodh uisge ann,
is sinn a' bualadh chlachan air na pòlaichean
teileagraf gun stad.

Bhiodh aon neach na sheasamh ri balla
's am bùrn a' drùdhadh
's a chraiceann sleamhainn leis a' bhùrn ghlas.

Nuair a bha sinn òg bhiodh sinn a' cluich
cèiseball 's a' ghealach anns an adhar
mar chèiseball de dh' òr.

Nuair a bha sinn òg bhiodh cailleachan
ag ràdh rinn: 'Na dèan siud, dèan seo,'
air eagal na caillich-oidhche.

Nuair a bha sinn òg bha an t-adhar falamh
is dealbhan anns an leabhar, is talamh
uaine, fad' às.

Nuair a bha sinn òg, bha breugan ann,
nuair a tha sinn aost, 's e bhreug a th' ann
gun robh an òig' gun small.

When we were young it would be raining and we throwing stones
at the telegraph poles unceasingly.

One horse would be standing against a wall, drenched
by the rain, his skin slippery with the grey rain.

When we were young we would be playing football
with the moon in the sky like a football made of gold.

When we were young old women would be telling us,
'Don't do this, do that' for fear of the owl.

When we were young the sky would be empty, and
pictures in the book, and the green earth and distant.

When we were young, there would be lies, when we
are old the lie is that youth was without stain.

Iain Mac a' Ghobhainn / Iain Crichton Smith

Nuair a Bha Sinn Òg / When We Were Young

Introduction

Iain Crichton Smith had a rural upbringing in the village of Bayble on the island of Lewis. His poem reflects that upbringing. He uses contrasting images to describe his and other village children's experiences. He reflects nostalgically on some of the pastimes he enjoyed: the games of football in the long evenings under a golden moon and looking at pictures in the book which stirred his imagination. He remembers, perhaps with less nostalgia, the horse 'drenched by the rain' standing beside a wall under grey skies and the warnings of superstitious old women who scolded children for perceived misdemeanours. All are evocative of his Hebridean island upbringing which had left an indelible impression on him. The poem suggests the complexities inherent in nostalgia for a distant childhood. As adults, he states, we lie to ourselves that our youth was innocent and 'without stain'. The translation of this Gaelic poem is by the poet himself.

THIRD LEVEL
Related texts:
Catriona Parsons McIvor, **'Cuimhne/Memory'** (p. 190)
Robert Louis Stevenson, 'Sing me a song of a lad that is gone'
Robert Louis Stevenson, 'To R. S. Crockett'

KEY WORDS:

Childhood

Disillusionment

Memory

Youth

Some key questions for class/group discussion

- What does 'nostalgia' mean? Are the first five stanzas of this poem nostalgic?

- Why do you think the poet mentions the fact that it is raining and the horse is getting soaked?

- Why do you think he compares the moon to a 'football made of gold'?

- Is stanza six nostalgic or realistic? What is the 'lie' we tell about youth when we are old?

Imaginative/creative writing

It is often said that childhood is the happiest time in our lives. Imagine you could turn the clock back to your childhood and write a short story which explores the truth of this statement.

Further development

Research Scotland's traditional games. The classic book on this subject is Iona and Peter Opie's *The Lore and Language of Schoolchildren*, first published in 1960 and republished in 2001 by New York Review of Books. Develop your own class or group project on this subject using your own experiences, older relatives' experiences and research into the subject.

Christine De Luca

Russian Doll

You wid tink dey wir only ee dolly
aa sheeny an pentit an bricht,
triggit up i da flags o aa nations:
but some rippit – dat canna be richt?

Inside dat der a Wast European
wi a luik less uncan ta see.
You can tell fae da een der a blydeness
dat life's wirt livin an free.

Inside dat een you'll fin yet anidder
jost as boannie but peerier scale.
Dat's da British identity hoidin:
god ta delicht in as weel.

Inside dat een a Scot is hunkered
wi a baetin haert prood ta belang
tae a country still writin hits story,
transformin wi poems an sang.

Inside dat een, a ting o a dolly
wi a tongue tied ta love o a laand:
tae a ain place, a ain fock, a language
ta hadd i da lof o a haand.

Inside dat een, da mintiest dukkie:
but da key tae dem aa, jost da sam.
Hit waels aa da tochts, aa da feelins
sae da inner an ooter is wan.

Christine De Luca

Russian Doll

Introduction

Christine De Luca is a poet who writes in both English and Shetlandic. The Shetland dialect is a very distinctive dialect of Scots due to the many Norse words and idioms it contains. With the help of a glossary and by reading the poem out loud, pupils should not have difficulty in translating it.

The poet uses a Russian doll as the symbol for both the diversity of the human race, with its different nations and tribes, and the common humanity it shares. She develops her theme by making each successive, smaller doll represent a smaller entity, beginning with the nations of the world and continuing the metaphor in the following verses to include Western Europe, Britain, Scotland and her own Shetland Isles. In verse one she uses the image of the largest doll to express her concern that not all nations live in peace and the rhetorical question emphasises that concern. She celebrates Western European freedoms and British identity and expresses pride in a Scotland which is still creating its own identity in 'poems and sang'. In verse five she asserts the importance of the seemingly least important identity, that of being a Shetlander. 'A ting o a dolly' stands for the poet's love of her own Shetland language, the landscape and the people of the islands. In the final verse the poet uses the idea of the smallest, innermost doll, 'da mintiest dukkie', as a creator of harmony among the multifarious local, national and international identities to be found worldwide.

THIRD LEVEL
Related Texts:
Carol Ann Duffy, 'Originally'
Bashabi Fraser, 'Between My Two Worlds'
Hamish Henderson, 'The Freedom Come All Ye'
Adam McNaughtan, **'Yellow on the Broom'** (p. 162)
Nancy Nicolson, **'Listen tae the Teacher'** (p. 186)

KEY WORDS:

Geography

History

Identity

Shetlands

Some key questions for class/group discussion

- What does the largest, outermost doll represent?

- It is shiny and brightly painted but what is not right about its decoration?

- What do the eyes of the Western European doll tell about her?

- What feelings does the poet have about the British doll?

- What characteristics does the Scottish doll have?

- Why does the poet call the Shetland doll 'a ting o a dolly'?

- The poet attributes to the Shetland doll her own strongest feelings. What are they?

- What does the phrase 'ta hadd i da lof o a haand' add to the emotions expressed in this verse?

- In the final verse the poet makes 'da mintiest dukkie', sitting in the very heart of the collection of dolls, the most important doll? What does it do to merit this importance?

- What do think is the theme of the poem?

Imaginative/creative writing

Write a description of a place which means a great deal to you, including your reasons why it is so important to you.

Further development

Create the text and design of a tourist leaflet which is both informative and enthusiastic about the beauties and amenities of a place you know well.

Jim Douglas

The New Teacher

Is a dove a doo, Dad?
Is a doo a dove?
Is a cow a coo, Dad?
A sparrow just a speug?
Is a wall a waw, Dad?
Is a dog a dug?
She's gonny warm ma ear, Dad,
Insteid o skelp ma lug.
Ma teacher's awfy posh, Dad.
She changes aw oor names.
Wee Shuggie noo is Hugh, Dad,
And Jimmy's ayewis James.

Ah'm scunnered wi it aw, Dad,
The wey she shoogles words.
And I must be glaikit no tae ken
That feathered friends are birds.
Ye learnt me aw wrong, Dad,
Ye cawd a ball a baw.
Your wife is now my mother, Dad,
You said she wis ma maw.
Ah'm no shair hoo tae spell, Dad,
Ah'll niver pass ma test
What is this Ah'm wearin, Dad –
A simmit or a vest?

Chorus:
Is a dove a doo, Dad?
Is a doo a dove?
Is a cow a coo, Dad?
A sparrow just a speug?
Is a wall a waw, Dad?
Is a dog a dug?
She's gonny warm ma ear, Dad,
Insteid o skelp ma lug.

Ah gave ma nose a dicht, Dad,
When it began tae dreep.
She gave me sich a fricht, Dad,
Ah near fell aff ma seat.
'Haven't you a hankerchief?'
She roared as if in pain.
'Naw, ah jist use ma sleeve, miss,'
And wiped ma nose again.
Ah cawd a mouse a moose, Dad,
Ah shid hiv held ma tongue.
That's manure on yer bitts, Dad,
Nae longer is it dung.

It's turnips and potatoes,
No tatties noo and neeps.
She said I'd ripped my trousers
When Ah'd only torn ma breeks.
There's two words for awthin, Dad,
Aw jumbled in ma heid.
Hoo can Ah be well bred, Dad,
When Ah keep sayin breid?
Is a crow a craw, Dad?
Is a bull a bul?
Ah'll try tae get it richt, Dad,
I will, I will, Ah wull.

Jim Douglas

The New Teacher

Introduction

This humorous song describes a young boy's bewilderment and confusion after learning from his 'posh' new teacher that all his native and Scottish words or pronunciations are 'wrong'. It is a comic take on the very serious issues of linguistic snobbery and discrimination which have a damaging effect on children's sense of identity, self-worth and their ability to learn. The tune is an old 1950s rock and roll song, 'Putting on the Agony', by Lonnie Donegan. Although references in the song suggest that Jim Douglas was describing an earlier period in Scottish education when official attitudes discouraged children from speaking or writing Scots in the classroom, the message of the song is still relevant today.

**SECOND/THIRD LEVEL
Related Texts:**

Liz Lochhead, 'Kidspoem/
Bairnsang'
Nancy Nicolson, **'Listen tae
the Teacher'** (p. 186)

KEY WORDS:

Humour

Identity

Prejudice

School

Scots language

Some key questions for class/group discussion

- How long ago do you think this imagined conversation between a boy and his father took place?

- Why is the boy confused?

- What does the teacher make him feel?

- Which of the following phrases do you think are more descriptive: 'warm my ear' or 'skelp ma lug'; 'ripped my trousers' or 'torn ma breeks'; 'wiped ma nose again' or 'gave ma nose a dicht'? Can you give a reason or reasons for your choices?

Imaginative/creative writing

Write a short story in which a child who has moved to a new school in a different area, is made fun of because he or she has a different accent and uses local words. How is this situation resolved?

Further development

In groups a class could establish how many words in the song are known or used by group members. Parents and grandparents could also be consulted. The groups could then devise and illustrate their own Scots–English word book.

Carol Ann Duffy

The Loch Ness Monster's Husband

She's real. Ah married her and we bide
in the Loch. No weans. Ah'm a wee guy,
but she's as big as a legend, all monster, the one
who swims the dark wet miles to the surface
and sticks her neck oot. Ah thought love
was only true in fairy tales, but Ah went
for a dip one day and saw her face. Now,
Ah'm a believer.

Carol Ann Duffy

The Loch Ness Monster's Husband

Introduction

'The Loch Ness Monster's Husband' comes from a collection entitled *The Good Child's Guide to Rock and Roll*, which contains a number of humorous pieces like this one. The poet wrote a number of poems imagining the thoughts, feelings and attitudes of the wives of famous men, and this is a comic version of these. The poem depends on the tales and legends about the monster, but also on elements of popular culture, like the lines which will be recognised from the first *Shrek* film, but are actually from a Monkees song of the 1960s.

> **SECOND/THIRD LEVEL**
> **Related texts:**
> Carol Ann Duffy, '**Nippy Maclachlan**' (p. 72)
> Carol Ann Duffy, '**The Scottish Prince**' (p. 74)
> Edwin Morgan, '**The Loch Ness Monster's Song**' (p. 174)
>
> **KEYWORDS:**
>
> Character
>
> Humour
>
> Imagination
>
> Loch Ness
>
> Love
>
> Monsters

Some key questions for class/group discussion

- In saying 'She's real', what two points is the poet making about the monster?

- What does the speaker mean when he says 'No weans'?

- What is the effect of the simile 'as big as a legend'?

- What two meanings are there to 'sticks her neck oot'?

- The lines 'Ah thought love was only true in fairy tales … Now Ah'm a believer' are probably best known from the film *Shrek*. Why is this appropriate in this context?

- How do you picture the Loch Ness Monster's husband? What clues are you given in the poem?

Imaginative/creative writing

Imagine another legendary creature – yeti, centaur, minotaur, unicorn, harpie, etc. (you may have to look some of these up) and compose your own poem, writing as the creature's wife or husband as appropriate.

Further development

On the internet, see if you can find the full lyrics for the Monkees' 'I'm a Believer', as quoted in the poem, and make a comparison with this poem.

Carol Ann Duffy

Nippy Maclachlan

Nippy Maclachlan lives at the Border, the place
where language changes with water,
where flooers grow thistles and thustles grow flowers,
and eagles fly high clutching takeaway mice.
Nippy Maclachlan is nasty, not nice.

Nippy Maclachlan lives on the wire, the fence
between air, earth, water and fire, where milk in a coo
soors in the udder, if one acre's one man's, the other's
his brother's, where foxes' sly jaws are feathery, bloody.
Nippy Maclachlan's smelly and muddy.

Nippy Maclachlan lives at the crossing, the point
where everything has to reverse.
where rain turns to thunder and thunder to worse
and rats crawl on their bellies through sewer and ditch.
Nippy Maclachlan has warts and a twitch.

Nippy Maclachlan sharpens her stones, flings them
at folk who are far from their homes,
spits and hangs ribbons of phlegm on the wind,
snogs with a scarecrow out in the fields.
Do you think Nippy Maclachlan is real?

Carol Ann Duffy

Nippy Maclachlan

Introduction

Carol Ann Duffy has written meditations on home and displacement, such as 'Originally' and 'The Way My Mother speaks', and elements of this double-voiced utterance can be seen in 'Nippy Maclachlan' which is very much a poem about the borders, junctions between countries, atmospheres and languages. The first three stanzas delineate these kinds of border points, some of them natural, others very man-made, like wires and fences, examining the nastinesses which are part of the natural world, while the fourth concentrates on the title character as a thoroughly nasty piece of work. There are elements of something supernatural creeping even into discussions of the natural world, and a strong sense of identification with the land, and shutting out strangers.

THIRD LEVEL
Related texts:
   Christine De Luca, **'Russian Doll'** (p. 66)
   Jim Douglas, **'The New Teacher'** (p. 68)
   Margaret Green, **'The Ballad of Janitor MacKay'** (p. 92)

KEYWORDS:

Dullying

Character

Language

Outsiders

Some key questions for class/group discussion

- What point is the poet making in the third line of the first stanza?

- Read the second stanza out loud, and listen carefully to the sounds. Can you hear the internal rhyme ('on the wire … water and fire'; 'soors in the udder … his brother's')? How does the rhythm of this stanza help to stress this rhyme?

- What picture of the country do you get from this second stanza?

- The situation appears to be getting worse as the poem progresses. How does the poet want you to feel about the rats and the 'warts and a twitch' in the third stanza?

- In what way does the final stanza bring us to the 'truth' of what the poem is about? Do you think Nippy Maclachlan is real in any sense?

Imaginative/creative writing

- Imagine you have had to move away from your home to stay with relatives in a different part of the country where the accent is different, and you are obvious as a stranger. Using some of the ideas in the poem, write an account of an unpleasant meeting with one of the locals who does not want to make you feel welcome.

- Alternatively, imagine that you are Nippy Maclachlan, and write an account of how you showed an incomer who was boss.

Further development

Carry out your own research into a particular aspect of the history of emigration from Scotland, or immigration into Scotland. In both instances, individuals or families have left their native lands to become immigrants into a new country. Your research could be historical, or based on your own family's or relatives' experience.

Carol Ann Duffy

The Scottish Prince

Every summer, I visit the Scottish Prince
at his castle high on a hill outside Crieff.
We dine on haggis and tatties and neeps –
I drink water with mine and the Prince sips
at a peaty peppery dram. Then it's time for the dance.

O Scottish Prince, the heathery air sweetens the night.
Bats hang upside down in the pines like lamps waiting
for light. Ask me, ask me to dance to the skirl o' the pipes.

All the girls are in dresses. The boys are in kilts,
but no boy's so fine as the Prince in his tartan pleats.
I wait for a glance from the Prince, for the chance
to prance or flounce by his side, to bounce hand in hand
down the Gay Gordon line. Och, the pleasure's a' mine!

O Scottish Prince, the heathery air sweetens the night.
Bats hang upside down in the pines like lamps waiting
for light. Ask me, ask me to dance to the skirl o' the pipes.

At the end of summer, I say goodbye to the Scottish Prince
and catch a train to the South, over the border, the other side
of the purple hills, far from the blue and white flag, waving farewell
from the castle roof. The Prince will expect me back again
next year – here's a sprig of heather pressed in my hand as proof.

O Scottish Prince, the heathery air sweetens the night.
Bats hang upside down in the pines like lamps waiting
for light. Ask me, ask me to dance to the skirl o' the pipes.
Ask me, ask me, ask me to dance to the skirl o' the pipes.

Carol Ann Duffy

The Scottish Prince

Introduction

'The Scottish Prince' illustrates one of Duffy's preoccupations in poetry: the contrast between the English and Scottish views of life, often shown in use of Scottish diction. Readers will have to decide what is real and what is imagined, while working through the stereotypical picture of Scottish life. The visit described appears to be real, but the details are such as could be read about in a book or magazine article about the idea of Scotland. The stay in 'a castle high on a hill' is a convention of Scottish romantic writing, and the meal of 'haggis and tatties and neeps' is the stereotypical view of the Scots' meals. Does the Prince actually exist, or is he either a creation of the speaker or of the Scottish Tourist Board? There appear to be two voices in the poem, as the chorus has a much more poetic tone than the stanzas.

THIRD LEVEL
Related texts:

Marion Angus, '**Alas, Poor Queen**' (p. 2)
Carol Ann Duffy, '**Nippy Maclachlan**' (p. 72)
Jackie Kay, '**In My Country**' (p. 114)
Edwin Morgan, '**Canedolia**' (p. 170)

KEYWORDS:

Art & Design

Character

Scotland

Stereotypes

Some key questions for class/group discussion

- Why do you think the visit takes place 'at' rather than 'in' the castle in line two?

- What is the Prince's drink?

- The language used in the refrain is quite different from that of the verses. How would you describe it?

- In the second stanza, what is the effect of the internal rhyme (glance, chance, prance, flounce, bounce)? How does this introduce a rather comic note?

- What do you think the speaker is imagining in 'Och, the pleasure's a' mine!'?

- Do you think there really is a Scottish Prince? What evidence can you give for your answer?

- Why do you think the final refrain repeats the last line (with an additional 'ask me')?

Imaginative/creative writing

Imagine you are the person in the poem, and write the account of your journey to the summer holiday castle. Who is with you, how long is the train journey, what do you see from the carriage windows as you travel, how do you arrive at the castle, and who greets you there?

Further development

Collect some examples of brochures produced by VisitScotland and similar bodies promoting tourism in Scotland. What are the common features which are celebrated? Do you think the real Scotland is on view in this literature, or is it an idealised, unrealistic portrait? Create a tourist brochure for your home town, village or area which is truthful.

William Dunbar

I That in Heill Wes and Gladness

I that in heill wes and gladness
Am trublit now with greit seiknes
And feblit with infermite:
Timor mortis conturbat me.

Our pleasance heir is all vane glory;
This fals world is but transitory,
The flesch is brukle, the fend is sle:
Timor mortis conturbat me.

The stait of man dois change and vary;
Now sound, now seik, now blith, now sary,
Now dansand mery, now like to dee
Timor mortis conturbat me.

No stait in erd heir standis sicker.
As with the wynd wavis the wicker
So waueris this warldis vanite:
Timor mortis conturbat me.

On to the ded gois all estates:
Princis, prelotis and potestatis,
Baith rich and pur, of al degree:
Timor mortis conturbat me.

He takis the knythis in to feild,
Anarmyt under helme and scheild.
Victour he is at all melle:
Timor mortis conturbat me.

That strang unmercifull tyrant
Takis, on the moderis breast sowkand,
The bab, full of benignite:
Timor mortis conturbat me.

He takis the campion in the stour,
The capitane closit in the tour,
The lady in bour full of bewte:
Timor mortis conturbat me.

He sparis no lord for his piscence,
Na clerk for his intelligence;
His awful strak may no man fle:
Timor mortis conturbat me.

Sen for the ded remeid is none,
Best is that we for dede dispone,
Eftir our deid that lif may we:
Timor mortis conturbat me.

William Dunbar

I That in Heill Wes and Gladness

Introduction

The full version of this poem, often known as 'The Lament for the Makars', names a number of Scottish and English poets of Dunbar's own and earlier periods who have died, many of whom are known only from their mention in this poem. The court was both Dunbar's audience and his subject matter, and many of the poems take courtiers and their (often undignified) doings as their subjects for comic effect. Dunbar's poetry is very varied in style, subject matter and diction, showing brilliance and flexibility in expression. This poem, perhaps his most famous, derives from the tradition of moral lyrics concerned with death and mutability, in which he makes the point that however young, energetic, rich or powerful a person is, he will die, and sometimes sooner than he expects.

THIRD LEVEL
Related texts:
Anon., 'The Twa Corbies' (p. 28)
Anon., 'The Wife of Usher's Well' (p. 30)
Ewart Alan Mackintosh, 'In Memoriam' (p. 150)
Ewart Alan Mackintosh, 'Cha Till MacCruimein'

KEY WORDS:

Change

Death

Health

History

Poets

Some key questions for class/group discussion

- Each verse has a refrain '*Timor mortis conturbat me*' which means 'The fear of death distresses me'. Looking closely at the first four verses, what is it that makes the poet think about death at this time?

- In the seventh verse, Death comes for a tiny baby. Why do you think Dunbar puts this between the death of the knights on the battlefield in the sixth and eighth verses?

- Make a list of the descriptions Dunbar gives of Death, and the way he acts. Which strike you as most effective?

Imaginative/creative writing

Invent a refrain for yourself, on any topic you like, and then construct your own poem following Dunbar's model. It should be in four-line verses, rhyming aabb if possible, but it can have a much happier or even comic topic.

Further development

Find the full version of the poem, and try to find out who the various poets were, when they lived and the kind of poems they wrote. You will find the Scottish Poetry Library website particularly useful.

William Dunbar

The Magryme

My heid did yak yester nicht,
This day to mak that I na micht.
So sair the magryme dois me menyie
Perseing my brow as ony ganyie
That scant I luik may on the licht.

And now, schir, laitlie eftir mes
To dyt thocht I begowthe to dres,
The sentence lay full evill till find,
Vnsleipit in my heid behind,
Dullit in dulnes and distres.

Full oft at morrow I wpryse,
Quhen that my curage sleipeing lyis.
For mirth, for menstrallie and play,
For din nor dancing nor deray,
It will not walkin me no wise.

William Dunbar

The Magryme

Introduction

Although this short poem is six hundred years old and its language seems obsolete, it presents vividly an experience which is still very familiar today. It can be seen as a 'sick note' written by someone who is apologising and explaining why he has not been able to do his homework. Its author, the great makar, William Dunbar, was a member of the household of James IV, in which he served sometimes as a secretary, a priest and a semi-official royal poet. Among his duties would be the production of verses dealing with various moods, serious and comic, and with events in the court at Edinburgh and Stirling. In some of these he speaks very directly to the king ('Schir'). This example might well record the poet's feelings on a morning after the night before, involving the high jinks listed in the final stanza.

THIRD LEVEL
Related Texts:
Robert Burns, **'Address to the Toothache'** (p. 36)
Robert Garioch, 'Owre Weill'

KEY WORDS:

Disease

Health

History

Humour

Poets

Some key questions for class/group discussion

- Which Scots words have now dropped out of use completely (e.g. ganyie, a crossbow bolt)?

- Which are obviously related to words still current (e.g. magryme)?

- Which are contemporary English (e.g. dancing) ?

- Can you work out unfamiliar words from the context? (Scots dictionaries and the online *Dictionary of the Scots Language* can help if you get stuck.)

- What are the symptoms that trouble the poet?

- What effect do these have on his writing?

- In the mornings what is his mood when he awakens?

- What are the high jinks which are listed in the last verse?

- Do you think this is meant to be a humorous poem or is Dunbar really feeling very sorry for himself?

Imaginative/creative writing

James IV was also a poet. Write in Scots or English a short rhyming reply which he might have sent to Dunbar, or compose a conversation between the king and Dunbar concerning the latter's failure to meet his deadline for a poem.

Further development

Visit, if you can, the restored royal apartments at Stirling Castle which might well have been the setting for Dunbar's predicament. What do you think of them?

William Dunbar

Sir Jhon Sinclair Begowth to Dance

Sir Jhon Sinclair begowthe to dance
For he was new cum owt of France;
Ony thing that he do mycht
The ane futt yeid ay onrycht
And to the toher wald nocht gree.
Quod ane, 'Tak up the Quenis knycht!'
A mirrear dance mycht na man see.

Than cam in Maister Robert Schau;
He leuket as he culd lern tham a,
Bot ay his ane futt did waver.
He stackeret lyk ane strummall aver
That hobchackellt war aboin the kne.
To seik fra Sterling to Stranaver
A mirrear daunce mycht na man see.

Than cam in the maister almaser,
Ane hommiltye jommeltye juffler
Lyk a stirk stackarand in the ry.
His hippis gaff mony hoddous cry.
John Bute the fule said, 'Waes me,
He is bedirtin – fye, fy!'
A mirrear dance mycht na man se.

Than cam in Dunbar the mackar,
On all the flure thair was nane frackar,
And thair he dancet the dirrye dantoun.
He hoppet lyk a pillie wanton
For luff of Musgraeffe, men tellis me.
He trippet quhill he tint his panton;
A mirrear dance mycht na man see.

Than cam in Maesteres Musgraeffe;
Scho mycht heff lernit all the laeffe.
Quhen I schau hir sa trimlye dance,
Hir guid convoy and contenance,
Than for hir saek I wissit to be
The grytast erle or duk in France;
A mirrear dance mycht na man see.

Than cam in Dame Dounteboir;
God waett gif that schou louket sowr.
Schou maid sic morgeownis with hir hippis,
For lachtter nain mycht hald thair lippis.
Quhen schou was danceand bisselye
Ane blast of wind son fra hir slippis;
A mirrear dance mycht na man se.

Quhen thair was cum in five or sax,
The Quenis Dog begowthe to rax,
And of his band he maid a bred
And to the dancing soin he him med.
Quhou mastevlyk abowt yeid he;
He stinckett lyk a tyk, sum saed;
A mirrear dance mycht na man see.

William Dunbar

Sir Jhon Sinclair Begowth to Dance

Introduction

The court was both Dunbar's audience and his subject matter, and many of the poems, like this one, take courtiers and their (often undignified) doings as their subjects for comic effect. Part of Dunbar's role was to amuse the court with his writing, and it is easy to imagine the laughter at such well-observed characters. None of the characters appears to be able to put a foot right in the dance, and some of them suffer egregious social faux-pas. Dunbar puts himself in the poem, and shows that he is well prepared to laugh at himself. The court ladies were not excepted, either from the clumsiness or from the fart jokes, and the whole scene finally descends into the ridiculous when the queen's dog joins in.

THIRD LEVEL
Related texts:
Sir David Lyndsay, 'The Justing Betwix James Watsoun and Jhone Barbour' (p. 128)

KEY WORDS:

Character

Dance

History

Humour

Some key questions for class/group discussion

- In what way do Sir Jhon Sinclair and Maister Robert Schau suffer from the same disability in dancing? What words from the second verse would you pick out as being particularly descriptive?

- Dunbar makes particular fun of the master almoner. What unfortunate circumstance has happened to him? How does the language give you a clear picture of his appearance and activities?

- Note the contrasts between Mistress Musgrave and Dame Dounteboir in terms of the language used and the description of their activities in the dance.

- In what way is it appropriate that the Queen's dog should join the dance in terms of the language used to describe most of the other dancers? What do they all have in common?

- Look at the structure of the poem – how does the rhyme scheme that Dunbar has used, and the refrain echo the formalities of the court dance?

Imaginative/creative writing

Write your own account of perhaps a school disco where you describe the dancing actions of people with the same kind of comic effect as Dunbar has produced here. Ideally this should be a poem, but could equally be written in prose.

Further development

Try to find out about the court of James IV, specifically whether you can find out if these people are real. You will find plenty of information on the internet and in the library on historical sources, on James IV's building programme and the way he brought Renaissance ideas from Europe, specifically France (where Sir Jhon has come from in the poem).

Jean Elliot

The Flooers o' the Forest

I've heard the liltin at oor yowe-milkin,
Lassies a-liltin before break o day
Now there's a moanin on ilka green loanin –
The Flooers o' the Forest are a' wede awa.

At buchts, in the mornin, nae blythe lads are scornin,
Lassies are lanely and dowie and wae
Nae daffin, nae gabbin, but sighin and sabbin,
The Flooers o' the Forest are a' wede awa.

In hairst at the shearin, nae youths now are jeerin,
Bandsters are lyart and runkled and gray
At fair or at preachin, nae wooin, nae fleechin –
The Flooers o' the Forest are a' wede awa.

At e'en at the gloamin, nae swankies are roamin
'Bout stacks wi the lassies at bogle tae play
But ilk ane sits dreary, lamentin her deary –
The Flooers o' the Forest are a' wede awa.

Dule and wae for the order, sent oor lads to the Border
The English, for aince, by guile wan the day
The Flooers o' the Forest, that focht aye the foremost
The prime o' our land, lie cauld in the clay.

We hear nae mair liltin at oor yowe-milkin
Women and bairnies are heartless and wae
Sighin and moanin on ilka green loanin –
The Flooers o' the Forest are a' wede awa.

Jean Elliot

The Flooers o' the Forest

Introduction

The poem is a lament for the flower of Scottish manhood, slain with their king on Flodden field. On 9 September 1513 the Scots army, under King James IV, faced the English forces of King Henry VIII under the command of Thomas Howard, Earl of Surrey. The battle was ferocious and bloody, and a disastrous defeat for the Scots. Around 14,000 men died on both sides, including James IV, the last British king to die in battle.

The composition of the song began with a fragment of a very old ballad. Mrs Patrick Cockburn of Ormiston drew on this fragment to write a full song. Then in the mid-eighteenth century Jean Elliot drew on Mrs Cockburn's work to make this lyric a much finer piece of work.

In each stanza of the poem, the young men of the area are evoked by descriptions of what they are no longer doing, and by the effect of their absence on the girls and young women.

THIRD LEVEL
Related texts:
Janet Hamilton, 'Auld Mither Scotlan''
Tom Pow, 'Sorry'
Sir Walter Scott, 'Tale of Flodden Field' (in *Marmion*)
Dorcas Symms, 'Loss'

KEY WORDS:

Ballads

Battles

Death

Flodden

History

Lament

Music

Some key questions for class/group discussion

- The structure of the poem is deceptively simple, but what do you notice when you read it out loud? Listen to the way the words in the middle and at the end of lines one and three rhyme (internal rhyme). Why do you think the poet has done this?

- Who are 'the Flooers o' the Forest', and why are they so described?

- Why do you think the poet concentrates on the young women in the poem, when its actual subject is the dead of the battle?

- What are the important features of the description of the battle in stanza five?

- What is the effect of the near repetition in the final stanza?

Imaginative/creative writing

Write a series of diary entries in the persona of a young girl whose brothers have joined the army and marched south. This would start with the excitement of practising with weapons, joining the march, and then the tone would gradually change as the news filtered back from the battlefield.

Further development

- Find out about the background to the battle, and why it turned out to be such a disaster for the Scots. There are many possibilities for collaboration with the History department.

- Try to find a recording of the poem being sung. This could be a collaboration with the Music department.

Alec Finlay

New Model Glider

her nose a black bruise
of plasticine Dad launches

up she dips in cupped arcs
hiccupping over thistles and molehills

we watch her fly and wish
for a wee thermal

to scoop her magically
to the road or

even more wonderful
a disaster in the peaty burn

as the elastic band whirrs
unwound I run after

chasing the tail in my wellies
arms out to catch her

the moment before
she touches down on the turf

my ankles tumble over
smash goes the balsa

For Ailie

Alec Finlay

New Model Glider

Introduction

In this poem Alec Finlay recreates an incident from his childhood. His clever use of form and evocative word choice give his poem charm and humour. He conveys the pleasure and exhilaration he felt as a young boy flying his new model glider, perhaps for the first time. The poem's form helps to suggests the irregular flight of the glider and the boy's dash to catch her before she crashes on the turf. The use of 'she' rather than 'it' conveys a pride in the model glider which is as important to him as a ship is, for example, to her captain and crew. The image in the second stanza evokes the dipping and climbing of the craft as she tries to gain height, 'hiccupping over thistles and molehills'. The boy's hopes for 'a wee thermal', which would enable her to fly as far as the road, and his excited anticipation of the thrill of a crash in the burn convey his feelings most effectively. The final three stanzas describe his impetuous dash to catch the glider before she lands on the turf. In his eagerness, hampered perhaps by his wellies, he tumbles over and smashes the glider. The dramatic directness of the final line encapsulates the boy's rueful feelings with a self-deprecating humour.

SECOND LEVEL
Related Texts:
Charles Murray, **'The Whistle'** (p. 180)

KEY WORDS:

Art & Design

Childhood

Craft

Flight

Science

Technical Studies

Some key questions for class/group discussion

- The poem takes the form of a series of two-line stanzas and has no punctuation. What do you think Alec Finlay's purpose was in using this form of verse?

- What does the phrase 'her nose a black bruise/of plasticine' suggest about the making of the glider?

- Why does he refer to the glider as 'she' not 'it'?

- What does stanza two tell you about the flight of the glider?

- Look at stanzas four and five. The boy hopes that a thermal current will magically enable the glider to fly as far as the road. Why, therefore, do you think he says it would be 'even more wonderful' if the glider crashed in the burn?

- Look at the final three stanzas. The boy's dash to catch the glider ends in disaster but there is no self-pity in his account. Which parts of his account make you both sympathise and smile?

Imaginative/creative writing

- Write an account of your first attempt to fly a model plane or kite or control a model railway.

- Describe your experience of making an object or learning a skill or craft which both challenged you and gave you pleasure.

Further development

Carry out you own research into the history of a discovery or invention which has made people's lives better and organise your findings into a short classroom presentation.

Matthew Fitt

Captain Puggle

Captain Puggle flees his plane
Frae Tumshie Airport tae Bahrain
Gets the Smiths and their wee wean
Brings them aw back hame again.

Captain Puggle flees tae Barra
Skites aff like a shootin arra
But he'll soon be back the morra
Pechin like a puggled sparra.

Captain Puggle's oot o ile
Efter ainly twinty mile
Sae he had tae bide a while
In a field outside Carlisle.

Captain Puggle jets tae Crete
Wi his neebor, Bowfer Pete
In the cockpit, Bowfer's feet
Aye mak Captain Puggle greet.

Captain Puggle's sellt his plane
Says he'll never flee again
But next week he's aff tae Spain
In his brand-new Buhlitt Train.

Matthew Fitt

Captain Puggle

Introduction

This poem is in the established Scottish tradition of comic nonsense poems. When talking about the poem, Matthew Fitt tells us he used as his inspiration a 'mad pilot' called Mirek 'who has a plane and likes to fly it upside down and in bad weather just to scare everyone'. It is probably most like the familiar nonsense poems of Edward Lear – only with a Scottish twist. Its use of varied place names opens the way to considering the wide range of locations the bold Captain could have visited. But, if examined closely, it may be that it also suggests that Puggle has a rather ecology-friendly conscience, and has been thinking about his carbon footprint (although considering the poem as a critique of globalisation may be a step too far). The basic rhyme scheme, again, reminds us of limericks, and is easy to emulate.

SECOND LEVEL
Related texts:
Matthew Fitt, 'Fireworks aff the Castle'

KEY WORDS:

Flight

Geography

Humour

Place-names

Travel

Some key questions for class/group discussion

- How do the first two verses paint a detailed picture of Captain Puggle's high-speed lifestyle?

- List all the places in the poem that Captain Puggle visits. Where would you rather go (pick names which sound exotic/silly/Scottish/far-off and interesting)?

- Look closely at how Fitt uses some Scottish words effectively, e.g. 'skites', 'puggled' and 'neebor'. What are their more common English versions? And why are they more effective?

- List what you think are the reasons (given in the poem) why Captain Puggle turns from planes to trains.

Imaginative/creative writing

- Imagine you are one of the Smith family mentioned in the first stanza. Write the emails you would send back to your friends about the journey from 'Tumshie airport tae Bahrain' and back again.

- Script the conversation between Captain Puggle and Bowfer Pete (think about why he is called 'Bowfer').

Further development

Although this is a nonsense poem, transport links between the islands of Scotland and the mainland are vitally important. Using internet sources, research the various island airports and airfields (you will find that the Barra landing strip is on the beach, for instance), and report on how these flights help to maintain the island population.

Robert Garioch

I'm Neutral

Last nicht in Scotland Street I met a man
that gruppit my lapel – a kinna foreign
cratur he seemed; he tellt me, There's a war on
atween the Lang-nebs and the Big-heid Clan.

I wasna fasht, I took him for a moron,
naething byordnar, but he said, Ye're wan
of thae lang-nebbit folk, and if I can,
I'm gaunnae pash ye doun and rype your sporran.

Says he, I'll get a medal for this job;
we're watchan ye, we ken fine what ye're at,
ye're wi us or agin us, shut your gob.

He gied a clout that knockit aff my hat,
bawlan, A fecht! Come on, the Big-heid Mob!
Aweill, I caa'd him owre, and that was that.

Robert Garioch

I'm Neutral

Introduction

Robert Garioch loved writing in the Scots language and was greatly influenced by earlier Scottish poets such as Robert Fergusson and, interestingly, the eighteenth-century Italian poet Belli. Belli was famous for his sonnets, a type of poem of fourteen lines which Garioch uses here. You will see that it is divided into a section of eight lines followed by a section of six lines. Do you notice any difference in how the rhymes are arranged in the first eight lines and then in the following six lines? The poem concerns a 'war' between the Lang-nebs and the Big-heids, and although ridiculous, it rehearses the kinds of arguments which are often used in real fights and wars, and explores notions of allegiance.

THIRD LEVEL
Related texts:
Christine De Luca,
'**Russian Doll**' (p. 66)
Adam McNaughtan, '**Yellow on the Broom**' (p. 162)

KEY WORDS:

Belonging

History

Identity

Prejudice

War

Some key questions for class/group discussion

- The poet has gone to some trouble to make his poem seem like a casual street conversation between two fighting Scotsmen. But is it so casual? Look for the rhymes at the end of each line; do you see any pattern there?

- From what you learn in verse one, did these two men know each other? What evidence can you give for your answer?

- What reason did the man in Scotland Street give for attacking the speaker in verse two?

- What is your opinion of his reason for the attack on the speaker?

- 'Aweill, I caa'd him owre, and that was that.' Do you feel the victim is surprised, shocked or offended by the attack?

- The poet doesn't make any direct comment on these goings-on and says in the title 'I'm neutral'. Do you feel, however, he is? Or is he trying to steer us towards a particular view of this behaviour?

- What do you think that view might be? Is there a clue in the names of the 'tribes'?

Imaginative/creative writing

The poem is about two men from opposite sides or gangs in a 'war'. The fight here is between the Lang-nebs and the Big-heids, deliberately silly names to show up the silliness of their 'reasons' for fighting. Using what you have learned about the pointlessness of such taking of sides, write a story which shows up the daftness of fighting with people just because they are different in some way.

Further development

- There are some longstanding rivalries in the Scottish Borders towns which give rise to annual games. See if you can find out about the Selkirk ba' game, and, from the other end of the country, the Kirkwall ba' game.

- One of the kingdoms visited by Gulliver on his travels, in the novel by Jonathan Swift, sees perpetual conflict between the 'big-enders' and the 'little-enders' about the best way to open a boiled egg. Read this passage, and see what the satirist has to say about this kind of prejudice.

James Hogg

Lock the Door, Lariston

Lock, the door, Lariston, lion of Liddesdale,
Lock the door Lariston, Lowther comes on,
    The Armstrongs are flying,
    Their widows are crying,
The Castletown's burning, and Oliver's gone;
Lock the door, Lariston – high on the
    weather gleam
    See how the Saxon plumes bob on the sky,
    Yeoman and carbineer
    Billman and halberdier;
Fierce is the foray, and far is the cry.

Bewcastle brandishes high his broad
    scimitar,
Ridley is riding his fleet-footed grey,
    Hedley and Howard there,
    Wandale and Windermere, –
Lock the door, Lariston, hold them at bay.
Why dost thou smile, noble Elliot of
    Lariston?
Why do the joy-candles gleam in thine eye?
    Thou bold Border ranger,
    Beware of thy danger –
Thy foes are relentless, determined, and
    nigh.

Jock Elliot raised up his steel bonnet and
    lookit,
His hand grasp'd the sword with a nervous
    embrace;
    'Ah, welcome, brave foemen,
    On earth there are no men
More gallant to meet in the foray or chase!
Little know you of the hearts I have hidden
    here,
Little know you of our moss troopers' might,
    Lindhope and Sorby true,
    Sundhope and Milburn too,
Gentle in manner, but lions in fight!

'I've Mangerton, Gornberry, Raeburn and
    Netherby,
Old Sim of Whitram, and all his array;
    Come all Northumberland,
    Teesdale and Cumberland,
Here at the Breaken Tower end shall the fray.'
Scowl'd the broad sun o'er the links of green
    Liddesdale,
Red as the beacon-light tipp'd he the wold,
    Many a bold martial eye
    Mirror'd that morning sky,
Never more oped on his orbit of gold!

Shrill was the bugle's note, dreadful the
    warrior shout,
Lances and halberds in splinters were borne;
    Halberd and hauberk then
    Braved the claymore in vain,
Buckler and armlet in shivers were shorn.
See how they wane, the proud files of the
    Windermere,
Howard – Ah! Woe to thy hopes of the day!
    Hear the wide welkin rend,
    While the Scots' shouts ascend,
'Elliot of Lariston, Elliot for aye!'

James Hogg

Lock the Door, Lariston

Introduction

James Hogg, a friend of Sir Walter Scott, was expert in the history, ballads and songs of the Borders. 'Lock the Door, Lariston' captures the spirit of the battles of the Border reivers of Scotland and England who relentlessly and violently plundered each other's territories, especially during the sixteenth and seventeenth centuries. They were led by the chiefs of local important families and were virtually uncontrollable by their respective monarchs. The poem/song describes an attack by the English reivers on the Elliot stronghold of Lariston, in Liddesdale south of Hawick in what was called the Middle Marches. The Armstongs have already been slaughtered at Newcastleton ('The Castletown's burning', line five) and the English under Bewcastle, Ridley and others are approaching Lariston. The leader of the Elliots, Jock, prepares to defend his people and his property. He is supported by the local families – Lindhope, Sorby, Gornberry, Raeburn and others – and resolves that the matter will be resolved there and then at his fortified tower house, the Breaken Tower. At dawn a bitter battle commences. The English retreat and Elliot wins.

SECOND/THIRD LEVEL
Related Texts:
Ewart Alan MacIntosh, **'On Vimy Ridge'** (p. 152)
Sir Walter Scott, **'Lochinvar'** (p. 200)
Sir Walter Scott, 'Marmion'

KEY WORDS:

Battles

Borders

Geography

History

Reivers

War

Some key questions for class/group discussion

- Lariston is the name of the farm/village in Liddesdale from which Jock Elliot, the hero of the poem, takes his name. In line one he is called 'lion of Liddesdale'. What does this tell us about him?

- Who seems to have the upper hand in verse one and the first half of verse two?

- In verse three and the first half of verse four, why does Jock Elliot have such confidence?

- The Breaken Tower is the Elliots' fortified stronghold. What does Jock mean when he says: 'Here at the Breaken Tower end shall the fray'?

- Who wins? How do you know?

- Look up the words 'halberd', 'hauberk', 'claymore' and 'buckler'.

Imaginative/creative writing

Write a story in which you are one of the reivers on a raid into northern England, or in which you are a young Elliot in a tower house on the Scottish border helping your father to defend it from attack.

Further development

Pupils could listen to the stirring rendering of this song by The Corries. They could also examine Ordnance Survey Landranger Map 79 and look for Liddesdale and the farm of Larriston which is about six miles north of Newcastleton.

Jackie Kay

Darling

You might forget the exact sound of her voice
or how her face looked when sleeping.
You might forget the sound of her quiet weeping
curled into the shape of a half moon,

when smaller than her self, she seemed already to be leaving
before she left, when the blossom was on the trees
and the sun was out, and all seemed good in the world.
I held her hand and sang a song from when I was a girl –

Heel y'ho boys, let her go boys –
and when I stopped singing she had slipped away,
already a slip of a girl again, skipping off,
her heart light, her face almost smiling.

And what I didn't know or couldn't say then
was that she hadn't really gone.
The dead don't go till you do, loved ones.
The dead are still here holding our hands.

Jackie Kay
Darling

Introduction

This is a poem of great tenderness which expresses the poet's feelings about a loved one who has died. The poet does not reveal the person's identity or circumstances but there is the suggestion that the person knew she was dying as she wept 'curled into the shape of a half moon', and perhaps an allusion to the effects of ageing on the body's frame in the phrase 'smaller than herself'. By using the second person and repeating the phrase 'You might forget', in the first stanza, the poet includes the reader or listener immediately in her particular experience, voicing her regret that she might not remember the sound of her loved one's voice or her face when asleep. In the second stanza the contrast between the inevitability of death and the renewal of spring is poignant. The poet speaks now in the first person, stating simply and directly that she had held the loved one's hand and had sung to her as she passed away peacefully, the poet imagining the loved one as 'a slip of a girl again', free from care and suffering. The final stanza alludes to the complex feelings which the poet could not recognise or express in the immediate aftermath of death, then concludes with the strong, inclusive affirmation that the dead live on in our memories. They are still present, 'holding our hands', a continuing source of comfort and support.

THIRD LEVEL
Related texts:
> Marion Angus, **'Alas, Poor Queen'** (p. 2)
> Liz Lochhead, **'For My Grandmother Knitting'** (p. 124)
> Alastair Reid, **'My Father, Dying'** (p. 194)

KEY WORDS:

Death

Love

Memory

Some key questions for class/group discussion

- Why do you think the poet uses the second person, 'you' in the first stanza?

- What information about the person described in the first stanza is suggested by the phrase 'curled into the shape of a half moon'?

- Comment on the two apparent contradictions in the second stanza. What does the poet seem to be suggesting?

- Why does the poet use the images of blossom on the trees and the brightness of the sun in the second stanza?

- In the third stanza the poet tells us that she sang 'The Mingulay Boat Song', which she had learned as a girl, as her loved one passed away. The song, adapted from a Gaelic original, expresses the sailors' joyful looking forward to their return to Mingulay, the rhythm of the tune suggesting the boat's surge forward towards home. Why do you think the poet chose this song?

- Consider the final stanza. What realisation has the poet come to?

- Comment on the effectiveness of the final phrase 'holding our hands'.

Imaginative/creative writing

Describe some of your most treasured memories of a person who has meant a great deal to you.

Further development

Research the life and achievements of a historical person you admire then prepare a short talk, giving key information about that person's life and your reasons for your admiration.

Jackie Kay

Grandpa's Soup

No one makes soup like my Grandpa's,
with its diced carrots the perfect size
and its diced potatoes the perfect size
and its wee soft bits –
what are their names?
and its big bit of hough,
which rhymes with loch, floating
like a rich island in the middle of the soup sea.

I say, Grandpa, Grandpa your soup is the best soup in the whole world.
And Grandpa says, Och,
which rhymes with hough and loch,
Och, Don't be daft,
because he's shy about his soup, my Grandpa.
He knows I will grow up and pine for it.
I will fall ill and desperately need it.
I will long for it my whole life after he is gone.
Every soup will become sad and wrong after he is gone.
He knows when I'm older I will avoid soup altogether.
Oh Grandpa, Grandpa, why is your soup so glorious? I say
tucking into my fourth bowl in a day.

Barley! That's the name of the wee soft bits. Barley.

Jackie Kay

Grandpa's Soup

Introduction

This humorous and touching poem expresses a child's uninhibited delight in her grandpa's soup-making, her enjoyment of the finished product and her affection and admiration for him. By making the speaker a child, Jackie Kay recreates the spontaneity and directness of a child's response to her grandpa's soup-making, which reveals the strong bond between them. In contrast the grandpa's response to the child's enthusiasm is one of self-deprecation. The child's confident statement about the unmatched quality of her grandpa's soup is reinforced by the repetition of the phrase 'the perfect size' and the repeated idea in different words that his soup is 'the best soup/in the whole world'. The child's pleasure in playing with the sounds of words is emphasised in the connections she makes with soup, loch and sea. The lines from 'He knows I will grow up and pine for it' to the exclamatory question 'Oh Grandpa, Grandpa, why is your soup so glorious?' suggest that the child is taking us, the readers or listeners, into her confidence. They build up to a humorous climax which is also touching in the child's acceptance that her grandpa will not always be there. The final line brings the speaker back to earth when, as a sudden afterthought, she remembers the name of 'the wee soft bits'.

> **SECOND/THIRD LEVEL**
> **Related texts:**
> Robert Burns, 'To a Haggis'
> Liz Lochhead, **'For My Grandmother Knitting'** (p. 124)
>
> **KEY WORDS:**
> **Art & Design**
> **Childhood**
> **Family**
> **Food**
> **Geography**
> **Grandparents**
> **Home Economics**
> **Memory**

Some key questions for class/group discussion

- Look at line one. What does the speaker think of her grandpa's soup?

- Why do you think the child repeats the phrase 'the perfect size'?

- What is a 'bit of hough'?

- Why do you think the speaker adds the phrase 'rhymes with loch'?

- What figures of speech are used in the lines 'floating/like a rich island in the middle of a soup sea'? What do these lines tell us about the speaker?

- In the second section of the poem the speaker expresses the same idea that was expressed in the first line of the poem. What are her words in this instance? Why does she repeat the same idea?

- How does the grandpa react to these words?

- Comment on the lines beginning 'He knows I will grow up and pine for it' until the end of the second section of the poem. Why are they both humorous and touching?

- In what way does the last line of the poem reinforce the impression of a child speaking?

Imaginative/ creative writing

- Using 'Grandpa's Soup' as a model, write a poem of your own in praise of a person who means a lot to you.

- Write a descriptive account of how you learned a particular activity, skill or sport.

Further development

The poem refers to a soup often called Scotch Broth. Research traditional Scottish dishes or foods, perhaps investigating foods particular to your area (Orkney cheese, Arbroath smokies, cullen skink, Stornoway black pudding, Dundee cake, etc.). Then devise a menu for overseas visitors who are anxious to taste traditional Scottish food. You can add brief explanations of the dishes you are offering and make an attractive design for your menu.

Jackie Kay

In My Country

walking by the waters,
down where an honest river
shakes hands with the sea,
a woman passed round me
in a slow, watchful circle,
as if I were a superstition;

or the worst dregs of her imagination,
so when she finally spoke
her words spliced into bars
of an old wheel. A segment of air.
Where do you come from?
'Here,' I said, 'Here. These parts.'

From *Red Dust Road: an autobiographical journey*, by Jackie Kay
(Picador, 2010):

At the end of the summer of 1981, I return to Stirling for the beginning
of my third year at university. A friend and I decide to visit the castle,
thinking that it's weird that we've never yet been. A woman at the
castle says to me, 'Are you over from America, dear?' She can't hear my
obviously Scottish accent because she can only see my face. If you have
skin my colour, you must be a foreigner. She is not trying to be unkind,
and she has no idea that her question gets asked over and over again.
Where are you from, people have asked all my life. I used to say
Glasgow. Then they'd say and where are your parents from? And I used
to say Glasgow and Fife, which was the truth, but not the one they
were looking for. Sometimes I'd say, I'm adopted, my original father
was from Nigeria, and they'd nod, with a kind of a 'That explains it'
look on their face. (pp. 192–93)

Jackie Kay

In My Country

Introduction

'In My Country' is an intensely felt poem about Jackie Kay's own personal experience of racial prejudice. It expresses an unpalatable, universal truth about the darker aspects of human nature: the age-old fear of the stranger who is not of the tribe and the urge to attack or ostracise anyone who is of a different colour, culture or creed. The first three lines describe the speaker walking at the mouth of a river. The personification of the 'honest river' which 'shakes hands with the sea' suggests a natural harmony which the speaker identifies with. It is brutally shattered by the behaviour of a woman who walks round her like an animal circling its prey or witch-hunters choosing their victim.

The poet uses the paragraph break for dramatic effect, showing the speaker's intense hurt and anger at the woman's behaviour in the forceful line 'or the worst dregs of her imagination'. The colloquial directness of the following line 'so when she finally spoke' further intensifies the hurt and anger the speaker feels. By slowly emphasising each word of the question, '*Where do you come from?*', the woman reveals her deep-rooted prejudice and ignorance. By replying that she also comes from 'Here. These parts', the speaker proudly and defiantly asserts her identity and challenges the woman's prejudice. It is a fitting climax to the poem.

THIRD LEVEL
Related Texts:
  Christine De Luca,
  'Russian Doll' (p. 66)
  Carol Ann Duffy,
  'Originally'
  Bashabi Fraser, 'Between
  Two Worlds'
  Jackie Kay, 'English Cousin
  Comes to Scotland'

KEY WORDS:

Belonging

Identity

Prejudice

Racism

Some key questions for class/group discussion

- Describe the contrast between the speaker's description of her walk by the mouth of the river and her description of the woman's behaviour.

- Why does the poet have a stanza break before the line 'or the worst dregs of her imagination'?

- What do the lines 'her words spliced into bars/of an old wheel' reveal about the woman's attitude to the speaker?

- The poem builds to a climax in the last line. What does the speaker's reply reveal about her attitude towards the woman's prejudice?

Imaginative/creative writing

- Write a short story in which the main character challenges the prejudice of others.

- *In My Country*: using this title, write a poem which expresses some of your feelings, positive or negative or mixed, about where you live.

Further development

In her memoir *Red Dust Road*, Jackie Kay wrote in prose about an incident where she was perceived as different (the passage is printed below the text of the poem). In pairs, make a detailed comparison of the two incidents.

Jackie Kay

Maw Broon Visits a Therapist

Crivens! This is jist typical.
When it comes tae talking aboot me,
well, A' just clam up. Canny think whit
tae say.

Weel, weel. A'm here because
A' canny hawnle life, ken whit A' mean,
because everything is awfy
and A'm no masell.

A' dinny ken who Maw Broon is anymare.
A' canny remember ma Christian name.
A' remember when A' wis a wean,
folks cried me something.

The idea o' me ever being a bairn
is impossible. A' feel A've aye worn
This same pinnie and this heid scarf
A've got on the noo.

How come you've no got anything tae say?
You've no opened yir mooth.
Whit's wrang. Am A' no daeing it right?
A' dinny ken hoo yir supposed tae dae therapy.

Jings. Dae A' just talk on like this?
Michty. This is awfy awkward.
You've no said a dickie bird.
Tell you a dream? Crivens,

A've no had a dream since A' wis a wean.
An image? Whit kind of image?
What comes tae mind?
Whit represents whit?

Och. This therapy's making me crabbit.
A' thought this wuid mak me happy.
This is awfy. A' feel unweel.
How do A' see masell?

Weel. A'm fed up wey ma bun.
It is jist a big onion
at the back o'ma heid.
A' canny let ma hair doon.

A'm built like a bothy, hefty.
A'm constantly wabbit and crabbit.
Ma hale family taks me for grantit.
A'll aye be the wan tae dae it

whitever *it* is. Here – A'm quite guid
At this therapy lark eh?
Here, Maw Broon could be a therapist.
Sit there like you are, glaikit,

a box o tissues and a clock,
a few wee emmms and aaas.
Jings, it's money for auld rope.
There that's whit A' feel like –

A tatty auld rope
nibiddy wuid want tae climb
a' twistit and tangled
an, jings, this is exciting

A' could break. A' could jist give in.

Jackie Kay

Maw Broon Visits a Therapist

Introduction

'Maw Broon Visits a Therapist' is one of a series of poems Jackie Kay has written featuring the archetypal Scottish matriarch as depicted in D. C. Thomson's cartoon strip *The Broons*. Maw is a formidable mother of eight. She has to run every aspect of the household and keep her husband, Paw, in line. Kay puts her into totally alien situations, as here, where the comic effect comes from imagining the well-known comic strip character struggling with an aspect of the modern world. Maw Broon was 'born' fully formed as the unflappable mother who just copes with what life throws at her and the family, but now she has 'lost the place', which is completely unthinkable. She doesn't really understand how to deal with the 'therapy', but Kay creates a realistic character who is multi-dimensioned, and who epitomises the contemporary middle-aged mother who is trying to 'find herself'.

THIRD LEVEL
Related texts:
  Jackie Kay, 'The Broons'
  Bairn's Black'
  Jackie Kay, 'Maw Broon
  Goes for Colonic Irrigation'
  Jackie Kay, 'There's Trouble
  for Maw Broon'

KEY WORDS:

  Character

  Comics

  Family

  Humour

  Mothers

Some key questions for class/group discussion

- Pick out the aspects of Maw Broon's character which are depicted in the first four stanzas. (It would be helpful to have access to some of *The Broons* strips for this.)

- How does the poet create the impression of a conversation with only one speaker?

- In the ninth stanza, the poet uses the physical description of the bun to make a joke. What two meanings are contained in 'A' canny let ma hair doon', and what does that tell you about Maw Broon's personality?

- What does the comparison with 'a tatty auld rope' in the final stanza tell you about Maw Broon's feelings at the end of the poem?

Imaginative/creative writing

There are many opportunities for writing different versions of this kind of poem – either putting Maw Broon into other situations, such as 'at the school parents' night', where she could be discussing her son Horace (a bookish schoolboy forever trying to learn poetry by rote amidst the chaos of a do-it-yourself chimney-sweeping mishap or other domestic turmoil) – or writing a poem about one of the other characters, such as Daphne, forever trying to find a boyfriend.

Further development

Collect a number of *The Broons* strips (or indeed an annual volume) and look at the characters portrayed as Scottish stereotypes. How realistic do you find this family? Why do you think the strip has remained so popular for so long?

James Kennedy

The Highland Crofter

Frae Kenmore tae Ben More
The land is a' the Marquis's;
The mossy howes, the heathery knowes
An' ilka bonnie park is his;
The bearded goats, the towsie stots,
An' a' the braxie carcases;
Ilk crofter's rent, ilk tinkler's tent,
An ilka collie's bark is his;
The muir-cock's craw, the piper's blaw,
The ghillie's hard day's wark is his;
Frae Kenmore tae Ben More
The warld is a' the Marquis's.

The fish that swim, the birds that skim,
The fir, the ash, the birk is his;
The Castle ha' sae big an' braw,
Yon diamond-crusted dirk is his;
The roofless hame, a burning shame,
The factor's dirty wark is his;
The poor folk vexed, the lawyer's text,
Yon smirking legal shark is his;
Frae Kenmore tae Ben More
The warld is a' the Marquis's.

But near, mair near, God's voice we hear –
The dawn as weel's the dark is His;
The poet's dream, the patriot's theme,
The fire that lights the mirk is His.
They clearly show God's mills are slow
But sure the handiwork is His;
And in His grace our hope we place;
Fair Freedom's sheltering ark is His.
The men that toil should own the soil –
A note as clear's the lark is this –
Breadalbane's land – the fair, the grand –
Will no' be aye the Marquis's.

James Kennedy

The Highland Crofter

Introduction

This extraordinary poem about the Highland Clearances has a strange history. In 1988 the author was finally identified as James Kennedy, a crofter who had been expelled from his tenancy during the wholesale clearances inflicted on the lands around Loch Tay by the Marquis of Breadalbane in the 1830s. The poem begins in light-hearted tone, and even turns to the comic in allotting to the Marquis all the animal and man-made sounds heard on the land. In the second stanza, however, after enumerating the living things – fish, birds, trees – and the tangible assets – castle, jewelled dirk – that belong to the Marquis's estate, the tone turns darker with the introduction of 'the roofless hame' and 'the poor folk vexed' which tell of the clearances. Finally, the contrast between the Marquis's earthly dominion and God's eternal rule is the subject of the final stanza. Reinforced by the comic effects of triple and internal rhyming and punning, the theme of the poem develops as a powerful promise of retribution for aristocratic arrogance and rapacity.

**SECOND/THIRD LEVEL
Related texts:**
Donnchadh Bàn Mac an t-Saoir / Duncan Ban Macintyre, **Cead Deireannach nam Beann / Final Farewell to the Bens** (p. 148)
Derick Thomson, 'Strathnaver'

KEY WORDS:

Clearances

Farming

Highlands

History

Politics

Religion

Some key questions for class/group discussion

- The first stanza of this poem first appeared in a humorous magazine called *Punch*. Do you think it is funny? Why?

- Read the stanza aloud, exploring Scots expressions, the impact of stylistic devices, and mood. What is a Marquis? What is the distance between Kenmore and Ben More?

- Then look at the whole poem. Is the poem still amusing in any sense? How and where in the text does the mood start to change?

- What is the promise being made in the third stanza of the poem?

Imaginative/creative writing

- Using some of the language of the poem, and taking the role of a crofter on the estate, write a letter to relatives in the nearby town lamenting the harshness of life and the threats made by the factor (the man who comes to collect the rents) and the lawyer.

- Write the sermon preached by the minister in which he reassures his parishioners that their woes and worries are heard and understood.

Further development

'The men that toil should own the soil'. Do you agree? Debate this assertion in class or groups.

Tom Leonard

The Dropout

scrimpt nscraipt furryi
urryi grateful
no wan bit

speylt useless yi urr
twistid izza coarkscrew
cawz rows inan empty hooss

yir fathir nivirid yoor chance
pick n choozyir joab
a steady pey

well jiss take a lookit yirsell
naithur wurk nur wahnt
aw aye

yir clivir
damn clivir
but yi huvny a clue whutyir dayn

Tom Leonard

The Dropout

Introduction

This vernacular poem by one of Scotland's most radical poets has sometimes been seen as a comic sketch in language to be measured alongside entertainments such as Stanley Baxter's 'Parliamo Glasgow', but it is better understood as part of Leonard's concerns with the democracy of language and the authoritarian suppression of 'natural' language through an insistence on 'correctness'.

The class should be introduced to the poem through it being read aloud. Pupils could be asked to write down their reactions to the poem and how they feel it differs from their normal expectations of poetry. Some explanation of the poem might be needed. The poet's concern to prove the Glaswegian existence as the authentic stuff of poetry could be made clear. Pupils could be guided towards careful examination of the poem's language, where linguistic clichés and the portrayal of the Glaswegian dialect as comic in its spelling are carefully avoided. It might also be useful to use a recording of Leonard reading his poem as a means of introducing the class to sound poetry.

SECOND/THIRD LEVEL
Related Texts:
Tom Leonard, 'Feed Ma Lamz'
Tom Leonard, **'The Good Thief'** (p. 122)
Tom Leonard, 'Moral Philosophy'
Tom Leonard, 'Radical Renfrew'
Tom Leonard, 'A Summer's Day'

KEY WORDS:

Glasgow

Humour

Language

Politics

Some key questions for class/group discussion

- Try to say who the speaker is in the poem (male/female, older/younger), and who is the hapless listener (male/female, older/younger).

- What do you think is the relationship between them?

- What is it about the spelling of the words that is different from other spellings of Glasgow dialect you've seen?

- Why is the last verse also a joke?

Imaginative/creative writing

- Write a poem in a phonetic version of your own dialect.

- Write a prose piece based on this poem that shows the parent's attitude towards his/her feckless child, and why he/she thinks their child is 'clivir', but 'huvny a clue whutyir dayn'.

- Write the Dropout's response to his/her parent's complaint.

Further development

- The poem could be looked at alongside a range of vernacular poetry written in the 1960s by Leonard which supports his argument that the Glaswegian dialect is an authentic language for poetry.

- There are frequent discussions (often in the letters pages of newspapers) regarding local accents on BBC News, for instance. Make an online search to see what you can find. What are the arguments that people use in favour of and against regional accents as opposed to 'BBC English'? Write a report in which you balance the arguments for and against a variety of accents in factual radio and television programmes.

Tom Leonard

The Good Thief

heh jimmy
yawright ih
stull wayiz urryi
ih

heh jimmy
ma right insane yirra pape
ma right insane yirwanny us jimmy
see it nyir eyes
wanny uz

heh

heh jimmy
lookslik wirgonny miss thi gemm
gonny miss thi GEMM jimmy
nearly three a cloke thinoo

dork init
good jobe theyve gote thi lights

Tom Leonard

The Good Thief

Introduction

'The Good Thief' is the first of 'Six Glasgow Poems' published in 1969. As in many of Tom Leonard's poems he uses the Glasgow vernacular and speech patterns. In using this language he is questioning our linguistic prejudices and in the last of the six poems, 'Good Style', he is dismissive of people who will not take the trouble to read his work: 'if yi canny unnirston thim jiss clear aff then'. He encodes his work by writing in this style and some effort is needed to read it.

All six of the poems have some biblical connotations and Tom Leonard says 'The Good Thief' is about the crucifixion and Catholic/Protestant bigotry. Jimmy, the generic name for a Glaswegian, is being asked about his religion and is made to feel as if he is on the side of the questioner.

Ostensibly they are on their way to a football match and are late. The darkness at three o'clock hints at the crucifixion. 'The Good Thief' is the unknown character who was crucified alongside Christ. The thief, at first, verbally abused Christ, then repented and asked Jesus to remember him – just as the good thief of the poem starts off aggressively and then realises that he, 'Jimmy', is one of them.

THIRD LEVEL
Related Texts:
> Robert Garioch, **'I'm Neutral'** (p. 88)
> Alexander Gray, 'There Cam Thrie Kings'
> Josephine Neill, 'A Christmas Poem'
> Margaret Tollick, **'Mairi's Sang'** (p. 222)

KEY WORDS:

Easter

Football

Glasgow

Language

Prejudice

Religion

Some key questions for class/group discussion

- The poet uses repetition of a key phrase. What is it and why do you think he does this?

- Look at the second line of the second stanza. What two meanings might be taken from the word, 'insane'?

- Pick a point in the poem where you are aware of a biblical reference and discuss it.

- What two meanings can be taken from the last line?

Imaginative/creative Writing

- Write about a time when you 'missed the gemm'. It can be any kind of 'gemm'.

- Write a piece of dialogue between two strangers in the Glasgow dialect.

Further development

Find out more about the crucifixion and the significance of the title of the poem.

Liz Lochhead

For My Grandmother Knitting

There is no need they say
but the needles still move
their rhythms in the working of your hands
as easily
as if your hands
were once again those sure and skilful hands
of the fisher-girl.

You are old now
and your grasp of things is not so good
but master of your moments then
deft and swift
you slit the still-ticking quick silver fish.
Hard work it was too
of necessity.

But now they say there is no need
as the needles move
in the working of your hands
once the hands of the bride
with the hand-span waist
once the hands of the miner's wife
who scrubbed his back
in a tin bath by the coal fire
once the hands of the mother
of six who made do and mended
scraped and slaved slapped sometimes
when necessary.

But now they say there is no need
the kids they say grandma
have too much already
more than they can wear
too many scarves and cardigans –
gran you do too much
there's no necessity ...

At your window you wave
them goodbye Sunday.
With your painful hands
big on shrunken wrists.
Swollen-jointed. Red. Arthritic. Old.
But the needles still move
their rhythms in the working of your hands
easily
as if your hands remembered
of their own accord the pattern
as if your hands had forgotten
how to stop

Liz Lochhead

For My Grandmother Knitting

Introduction

Liz Lochhead wrote this poem in praise of her grandmother. She describes her grandmother in old age still knitting for her grandchildren, although there is not the same need of her skills. The poet emphasises the skills her grandmother still practises, 'their rhythms in the working' of her hands and refers back to her grandmother's job as a fisher girl. She describes the dexterity with which she 'slit the still-ticking quick silver fish' and comments on the hard work her grandmother experienced. In stanza three she uses repetition to describe the life that 'the hands' have led. The poignancy of the fact that her grandchildren no longer need her knitted offerings is well described in stanza four, using the words of the children's parents. The description of her hands in the last stanza shows how old she is but she still knits, as if her 'hands had forgotten/how to stop'. The poem is a heartfelt tribute to the poet's grandmother, to her endurance, hard work and self-sacrifice and evokes a way of life which has largely disappeared.

SECOND/THIRD LEVEL Related Texts:

Jackie Kay, 'Grandpa's Soup' (p. 112)
Norman MacCaig, 'Aunt Julia' (p. 132)
Alastair Reid, 'My Father, Dying' (p. 194)
Alan Riach, 'A Short Introduction to my Uncle Glen' (p. 196)
Christopher Rush, 'My Grandmother'
Derick Thomson, 'Clann Nighean An Sgadain/The Herring Girls' (p. 216)

KEY WORDS:

Childhood

Family

Grandparents

History

Memory

Old age

Some key questions for class/group discussion

- Look at the number of times 'need', 'necessity' and 'necessary' are used in the poem. Why are these words repeated?

- In stanza four, repetition is used to describe stages in the grandmother's life. What were her roles in life and how does the poet create a vivid picture of her way of life?

- Discuss the feelings the poet has for her grandmother and pick out two lines which you consider most effectively express her feelings.

- Which lines in the last stanza link up with those in the first stanza and in what way is this last stanza a fitting conclusion to the poem?

Imaginative/creative writing

- Choose a person who has made a strong impression on you. Write a descriptive account of some of your memories of this person.

- Imagine that the grandmother is interviewed about her life. Write the interview.

Further development

See what you can find out about the herring-fishing industry in the late nineteenth and early twentieth century and the role of the fisher girls.

Liz Lochhead

The Metal Raw

was what we used to call
what must've really been the *un*metalled
    road or row,
a no-cars scratch across two farmers' tracts
between ours, with its brand new scheme,
and the next
ex-mining village.

At four, or five or six or so, I thought
it meant the colour, though. *Metal raw*
was crude red (*rid*) gravel that you'd
better not brake your bike on and that
    surfaced
just the first hundred yards or so
then patched the worst of the ruts
on the dirt and mud and clinker of the rest
    of it. Rust
on corrugated iron, that was *metal* and *raw*,
    both.
A real remnant of *The Iron Curtain* for all I
    knew,
torn and gouged with nail holes along edges
that you'd to *watch they wouldnae rip the
    hand off you.*

Sheets of this stuff crumbled to red dust
    along the Metal Raw
among the black cold fires and rags and bits
    of brick
around the place the tinkers still camped
a week or two each Spring
with their piebald ponies.
Always some story
among us weans around the scheme or at
    the swings
about somebody's big cousin creeping close
    enough
to kick the boiling billycan over, about a
    shaken fist
cursing and swearing and how far, on the
    light nights,
that big man with the stick had hunted him.

I was wee enough then,
on a Sunday walk along the Metal Raw
with Mum and Dad in my good coat,
for the tinks' big black dog that *wouldnae do
    me any harm*
to knock me flying in the mulchy ditch
    among
flag iris and the reeds I called *bullrushes*
and that might have harboured Baby Moses
and not one bit surprised me.
See, I am talking of the time when I mixed
    up
Old Meg she was a gipsy
and that old woman up the Metal Raw
smoking a pipe outside a tilting lean-to of
    tarred and
patched tarpaulin stretched on hawthorn.

And this was the nineteen fifties.
We slept under a *mushroom cloud,*
feared *Kruschev and Bulgarin,* men in
    Cossack hats
in blizzards of interference on the tiny grey
    T.V. screens
of *the Cold War.*

This was the time when our mothers down
    the New Houses
Stood on *Red Cardinal* doorsteps
far too scared not to buy the tinkers' pegs
    and prophesies.

Liz Lochhead

The Metal Raw

Introduction

Much of Liz Lochhead's work is autobiographical and this poem is a good illustration of how a childhood incident can give a very sharp description of life in a certain era. The 'metal raw' of the title is shown to mean many different things to the child in the poem. It was a 'red gravel' road where you had to be careful 'not to brake your bike' but it also represented the 'iron curtain' between one culture and another. Although the adults have very definite boundaries the child mixes up the two cultures and sees the 'Old Meg' of the song as the old tinker lady she sees on the 'metal raw'. As an adult looking back she is aware of the 'Cold War' but, at the time, she was only aware of the fear of the tinkers as is illustrated by the parents being 'too scared not to buy the tinkers' pegs'.

THIRD LEVEL
Related Texts:
Liz Lochhead, **'For My Grandmother Knitting'** (p. 124)
Norman MacCaig, **'Aunt Julia'** (p. 132)
Adam McNaughtan, **'Yellow on the Broom'** (p. 162)
Stephen Mulrine, 'The Coming of The Wee Malkies'

KEY WORDS:

Childhood

History

Memory

Prejudice

Travellers

Some key questions for class/group discussion

- How does the poet explain what the 'metal raw' was in the first stanza?

- In the second stanza show how words like 'Rust' and 'clinker' add to the description of the 'raw'.

- Why is '*watch they wouldnae rip the hand off you*' in italics?

- What stories are told against the tinkers?

- What is the difference between the poet's parents and the tinkers and how is it shown in stanza four?

- Comment on the use of the word '*bullrushes*' in that stanza.

- Why are '*mushroom cloud*' and '*Kruschev and Bulgarin*' in italics?

Imaginative/creative Writing

- Write about a place that you remember from your childhood and explain what it meant to you. Try to show how childhood impressions can be distorted/different.

- Write a story with a character in it called 'Old Meg'.

Further development

This poem is set in the 1950s, and it mentions quite a few issues of the day. Choose one of them to investigate further, e.g. mushroom clouds; the Cold War; the Iron Curtain; Kruschev; Bulgarin.

Sir David Lyndsay

The Justing Betwix James Watsoun and Jhone Barbour

In Sanct Androis on Witsoun Monnunday,
Twa campionis, thare manheid did assay.
Past to the barres, enarmit heid and handis
(Wes never sene sic justing in no landis),
In presence of the kingis grace and quene,
Quhare mony lustie lady mycht be sene.
Mony ane knight, barroun, and baurent
Come for to se that aufull tornament.
The ane of thame was gentill James Watsoun,
And Johne Barbour, the uther campioun.
Unto the king thay war familiaris
And of his chalmer boith cubicularis.
James was ane man of greit intelligence,
Ane medicinar, ful of experience.
And Johne Barbour, he was ane nobill leche;
Crukit carlingis he wald gar thame get speche.
From tyme thay enterit war in to the feild,
Full womanlie thay weildit spear and scheild
And wichtlie waiffit in the wynd thare heillis,
Hobland lyke cadgeris rydand on thare creillis.
Bot ather ran at uther with sic haist
That thay could never their spear get in the reist!
Quhen gentil James trowit best with Johne to meit,
His spear did fald amang his horssis feit.
I am rycht sure gude James had bene undone,
War not that Johne his mark tuke by the mone.
Quod Johne, 'Howbeit thou thinkis my leggis lyke
    rokkis,
My speir is gude; now keip the fra my knokkis!'
'Tary,' quod James, 'ane quhyle, for, be my thrift,
The feind ane thing I can se bot the lift.'
'Nor more can I,' quod Johne, 'be Goddis breid!
I se no thing except the steipill heid!
Yit, thocht thy braunis by lyk twa barrow trammis,
Defend the, man!' Than ran thay to, lyk rammis.
At that rude rink, James had bene strykin doun,
Wer not that Johne, for feirsnes, fell in swoun.

And rychtso James to Johne had done gret deir,
Wer not amangis hors feit he brak his spear.
Quod James to Johne, 'Yit, for out ladyis saikis,
Lat us to gidder straik thre market straikis.'
'I had,' quod Johne, 'that sall on the be wrokin!'
Bot or he spurrit his hors, his spear was brokin.
From tyme with speiris none could his marrow
    meit.
James drew ane sweird with ane rycht auful spreit
And ran til Johne til haif raucht him ane rout;
Johnis swerd was roustit and wald no way cum
    out.
Than James leit dryfe at Johne with boith his
    fystis;
He mist the man and dang upon the lystis.
And, with that straik, he trowit that Johne was
    slane,
His swerd stak fast and gat it never agane.
Be this, gude Johne had gottin furth his swerd,
And ran to James with mony aufull word:
'My furiousnes, forsuith, now sall thow find!'
Straikand at James his swerd flew in the wind,
Than gentill James began to crak greit wordis:
'Allace,' quod he, 'this day, for falt of swords!'
Than ather ran at uther with new raicis;
With gluifis of plait thay dang at utheris facis.
Quha wan this feild no creature could ken.
Till at the last, Johne cryit, 'Fy! Red the men!'
'Ye, red,' quod James, 'for that is my desyre.
It is ane hour sen I began to tyre.'
Sone be thay had endit that royall rink
Into the field mycht no man stand for stink.
Than every man that stude on far cryit, 'Fy!'
Sayand, 'Adew!' – for dirt partis company.
Thare hors, harnes, and all geir was so gude,
Loving to God, that day was sched no blude.

Sir David Lyndsay

The Justing Betwix James Watsoun and Jhone Barbour

Introduction

Sir David Lyndsay was responsible for many of the major pageants and state events during the reign of James V. This poem may very well derive from the court entertainment arranged at St Andrews to celebrate the marriage of James V and Mary of Guise. The joust described, far from being the usual well-rehearsed encounter of champion knights, is between two doctors, who are incompetence with weapons personified. They cannot hold their long lances without getting them tangled in their horses' feet, they are hopeless with swords at close combat, and the only good thing to say about them as fighters is that at least they don't hurt each other. Presumably they are attempting to make a good job of their joust, but they could only be seen as the comic prelude to the real event. Although the language looks challenging, an honest attempt to read it aloud as it is written will make it much more easily understood. (*Quh–* is pronounced *wh–*)

> **THIRD LEVEL**
> **Related texts:**
> William Dunbar, '**Sir Jhon Sinclair Begowth to Dance**' (p. 80)
>
> **KEY WORDS:**
>
> **Battles**
>
> **Character**
>
> **History**
>
> **Humour**

Some key questions for class/group discussion

- Examine the form of the poem in terms of rhyme and rhythm. It is written in rhyming couplets, and the rhythm is da-dum, da-dum, da-dum, da-dum, da-dum, where the stress is on the second, fourth, sixth, eighth and tenth syllables of the line (which is properly called iambic pentameter). You will find that the words ending *–is* have to be pronounced *–s* to fit the rhythm, but where you find that the line seems to be a syllable short, it is filled by pronouncing *–is* as a separate syllable. Practise reading a few lines of the poem to get used to the language and you will find that it is not very different from modern Scots.

- These two 'champions' are very unlikely fighters. Pick out all the various elements of Lyndsay's descriptions of them which makes them ridiculous.

- The fight itself develops in comic fashion. What do the two men do wrong, which makes it impossible for either of them to achieve the points they desire?

- The fight ends with no-one being hurt, which is seen as a blessing. But what contributed to the fact that neither could lay a lance, sword or glove on the other?

Imaginative/creative writing

- Imagine you were in the audience at this performance (if you need some help to picture it, think of the knights that Shrek defeats in various films) and write your account of what you saw.

- Alternatively, imagine a particularly useless fight between schoolboys who have been egged into it but don't really want to take part, and describe how they manage to get through it without getting hurt.

Further development

See what you can find out about Lyndsay's role as Lyon King of Arms, and also see if you can find the rules of jousting of the time, which will point out clearly how useless these two combatants were – and how many rules they broke in the course of their contest.

Brian McCabe

Seagull

We are the dawn marauders.
We prey on pizza. We kill kebabs.
We mug thrushes for bread crusts
with a snap of our big bent beaks.
We drum the worms from the ground
with the stamp of our wide webbed feet.
We spread out, cover the area –
Like cops looking for the body
of a murdered fish-supper.
Here we go with our hooligan yells
loud with gluttony, sharp with starvation.
Here we go bungee-jumping on the wind,
charging from the cold sea of our birth.
This is invasion. This is occupation.
Our flags are black, white and grey.
Our wing-stripes are our rank.
No sun can match the brazen
colour of our mad yellow eyes.

We are the seagulls.
We are the people.

Brian McCabe

Seagull

Introduction

In this poem, McCabe celebrates the seagulls which are often reviled, while also concentrating on the villainous aspect of them. He has clearly spent some time watching their behaviour, as this is very closely observed. There is a rather comic note in the way he describes the detritus the humans leave as if it were alive, and the seagulls as murderers, but, in a quick switch of perspective, they become the law-enforcers. There is a very human aspect to the descriptions, which suggests various pictures in the mind of the reader. The second half of the poem looks more closely at the birds as birds, and at why they have invaded the human world to become urban rather than seashore birds.

KEY WORDS:

   Birds

   Bullying

   Nature

   Seagulls

Some key questions for class/group discussion

- In the first four lines, comment on the verbs used.

- What is the effect of the alliteration in 'big bent beaks' in line four?

- How have the seagulls changed in lines seven to nine compared to the description in the first four lines?

- How does the description of the seagulls in lines ten and eleven recall a rowdy football crowd (for example)?

- Comment on the effect of the repeated 'Here we go' in lines ten and twelve.

- How is the image of an invading army developed in lines fifteen to seventeen? And where was the image originally suggested in the poem?

- The poem ends 'We are the seagulls./We are the people.' Why is the poem itself called 'Seagull' in the singular, do you think?

Imaginative/creative writing

- Seagulls are generally disliked and sometimes feared because of their size and the numbers in which they descend on a feeding site. Another bird which suffers the same dislike is the feral or town pigeon, often described as a flying rat. Think about the way pigeons flock and feed in towns, and write your own short poem in McCabe's style celebrating their lives.

- Taking the image of the invading army which McCabe employs in this poem, imagine you are a smaller bird feeding quietly on the previous night's rubbish when the seagulls descend to take over. Write, either in poetry or prose, a short account of your experiences of being under attack by the seagulls.

Further development

It used to be said that seeing seagulls in towns indicated that there was a storm at sea, but the birds are now permanent residents rather than visitors. What has brought them, and foxes and other 'countryside' animals into the towns and cities, and is this a worrying development?

There have been stories in the news recently about attacks on people by seagulls, with some very real injuries being reported. Use online newspaper websites to investigate these, and identify what the issues are, before writing a report about the realities of the situation and what people can do to protect themselves.

Norman MacCaig

Toad

Stop looking like a purse. How could a purse
squeeze under the rickety door and sit,
full of satisfaction, in a man's house?

You clamber towards me on your four corners –
right hand, left foot, left hand, right foot.

I love you for being a toad,
for crawling like a Japanese wrestler,
and for not being frightened.

I put you in my pure hand, not shutting it,
and set you down outside directly under
every star.

A jewel in your head? Toad,
you've put one in mine,
a tiny radiance in a dark place.

Norman MacCaig

Toad

Introduction

Norman MacCaig divided his life and the attention of his poetry between Assynt in the West Highlands, and the city of Edinburgh, and wrote with a passion for clarity. 'Toad' illustrates perfectly MacCaig's distinctive way of looking at the natural world, where an unexpected aspect of the creature is foregrounded, and then developed. The poet describes the toad as a purse, a box, a Japanese wrestler, and finally as a little miracle which has brought him joy. He alludes to the legend that every toad has a hidden jewel in its head, the *toadstone*, also known as *bufonite*, supposed to be an antidote to poison.

THIRD LEVEL
Related texts:
J. M. Caie, 'The Puddock' (p. 44)
Norman MacCaig, **'Praise of a Collie'** (p. 134)
Kenneth McKellar, 'Midges'
Edwin Muir, **'The Late Wasp'** (p. 176)
Paul Muldoon, 'The Hedgehog'

KEYWORDS:

Amphibians

Animals

Myths

Nature

Some key questions for class/group discussion

- Can you see why the poet compares the toad to a purse in the first stanza? (It might be a good idea to find some illustrations of toads for this.)

- What impression of the toad is given by 'full of satisfaction'?

- The image in the second stanza, although on the surface very simple, is actually quite complex. Can you tease it out fully?

- The verbs 'clamber' and 'crawling' are not at first sight particularly attractive, but how does MacCaig make the picture of the toad moving appealing?

- Why should it be important to him that the toad is not frightened? Would it have had a different effect had he used 'afraid' rather than 'frightened'?

- Comment on the use of 'pure' to describe his hand in the fourth stanza.

- Why should the toad be put down 'directly under/every star' rather than 'under the stars'? What is significant about the distinction?

- The legend of the toadstone is the basis for the final stanza. What is the jewel that the toad has put in the poet's head?

Imaginative/creative writing

Try to write your own poem in MacCaig's style where you look at a generally disliked creature (a spider, slug, snail, etc.) in a more positive light with the aim of persuading readers that the creature is not as ugly and hateful as believed (for instance, the slug's slimy trail could be seen as a silver highway, or the spider's web as a jewelled hairnet in the morning mist). Note that you do not have to worry about rhyme or rhythm – it is the picture created which is important.

Further development

Research the belief in the toadstone, and see if you can find the earliest mentions of it. You should also be able to find some other references in literature, as in Shakespeare's *As You Like It*.

Hugh MacDiarmid

The Bonnie Broukit Bairn

Mars is braw in crammasy,
Venus in a green silk goun,
The auld mune shak's her gowden feathers,
Their starry talk's a wheen o' blethers,
Nane for thee a thochtie sparin',
Earth, thou bonnie broukit bairn!
– *But greet, an' in your tears ye'll droun*
The haill clanjamfrie!

Hugh MacDiarmid

The Bonnie Broukit Bairn

Introduction

Hugh MacDiarmid drew on his own Border dialect, words from other dialects and quarried sources such as Jamieson's *Etymological Dictionary of the Scottish Language* to create his own distinctive version of a Scots literary language, which was called 'Synthetic Scots'. 'The Bonnie Broukit Bairn' is generally recognised as one of his greatest lyric poems, squeezing the solar system into eight lines, and using quite dense Scots dialect, some of which will require a dictionary to understand. Mars, Venus and the Moon are described as if they were characters at a ball, all dressed up and talking nonsense, filled with their own self-importance, not understanding that Earth is the most important of the heavenly bodies.

> **THIRD LEVEL**
> **Related Texts:**
> Iain Crichton Smith, 'The Planets'
> Hugh MacDiarmid, 'The Watergaw'
> Hugh MacDiarmid, 'Empty Vessel'
>
> **KEY WORDS:**
>
> Clothes
>
> Myths
>
> Science
>
> Space

Some key questions for class/group discussion

- From the title of the poem, what did you expect the poem to be about? Why?

- How do the other planets compare with planet Earth in the poem?

- MacDiarmid personifies the planets. Do they seem attractive or unattractive to you? Why?

- Do you think the poet wants us to see these planets differently from how they have often been viewed by humans in the past? Why?

- What does he mean by saying 'their starry talk's a wheen o' blethers'? What is he now suggesting about them or how we have worshipped them and is it attractive?

- Why do you think he says about the Earth, 'nane for thee a thochtie sparin'?

- What is the poet saying in these last two lines? Does it imply something unattractive about earthly life, or is it maybe even celebrating life on our planet in some way? What? How?

- Who or what has made the Earth neglected or caused all the suffering?

- Do you think the image of a 'bonnie broukit bairn' is an appropriate or effective one for planet Earth?

Imaginative/creative writing

Imagine a real 'broukit bairn' in a family where he/she is not considered – a kind of Cinderella story – until it is discovered that the bairn has a very special power which threatens to destroy the rest.

Further development

- What did Mars and Venus represent in ancient times and which of their god-like qualities have humans worshipped?

- What qualities are associated with the moon that have been celebrated or worshipped in past (and perhaps present) times?

Calum MacDhòmhnaill / Calum MacDonald

Cearcall a'Chuain / Circle of Ocean

Tha sinn uile air cuan
stiùireadh cuairt tro ar beatha,
a' seòladh geòla dhorch
air chall an grèim na mara.
Tha a' ghaoth air ar cùl,
Tha a' gheòl' a' cumail roimhe
's cha dèan uair no an cuan
toinisg dhuinn no rian.

A' mhuir, tha i ciùin,
Tha i fiadhaich, tha i farsaing.
Tha i àlainn, tha i diamhair,
Tha i gamhlasach is domhainn.
O, ach sinn, tha sinn dall
's chan eil againn ach beatha,
tog an seòl, tog an ràmh
gus am faigh sinn astar ann.

Ach tha mi 'n dùil, tha mi 'n dùil,
nuair a bhitheas a' ghrian dol fodha,
chì iad mi a' stiùireadh 'n iar
null a dh' Uibhist air a' chearcall:
cearcall a' chuain
gu bràth bithidh i a' tionndadh
leam gu machair geal an iar
far an do thòisich an là.

We try to find a course
on the broad open sea,
sailing a dark ship lost
in the grip of the sea.
The winds push from behind,
Driving us on and on;
neither time passing nor the ocean
brings wisdom or order.

The sea may be calm,
may be wild, may be wide.
The sea may be beautiful,
may be secret, may be tumultuous, deep.
We see so little,
but have only one life.
Raise up the sail; pull on the oar;
let's be moving onwards.

I can see the time is coming
when the sun is going down,
when I'll be steering westwards,
with Uist on the horizon.
May the circle of the horizon
keep turning for me
until I reach the white sands of the West
where day first began.

Calum MacDhòmhnaill / Calum MacDonald

Cearcall a'Chuain / Circle of Ocean

Introduction

This song vividly evokes the power and mystery of the sea which can drive ships off course but equally provide a pathway home for the weary sailor. It works also as an extended metaphor for life's journey. Just as a sailor, governed by the ceaseless turning of the tides, must navigate the storms and steer for home, human life is a spiritual journey in the face of trials and tribulations. The first stanza vividly describes the sailors' predicament, blown off course and lost. The second verse is a reflection on the many aspects of the sea, especially its mystery, and by extension the mystery of life. We must, nevertheless, voyage on. In the third verse the singer grounds his philosophical thoughts in the specific: his hope that the tides and winds will help to steer him westwards home to Uist in the Outer Hebrides, which to him has a primal innocence and beauty.

> **THIRD LEVEL**
> **Related Texts:**
> William Hershaw, **'Dysart Tide Sonnet'** (p. 100)
> Brian McCabe, **'Seagull'** (p. 130)
> Derick Thomson, **'The Herring Girls'** (p. 216)
>
> **KEY WORDS:**
>
> **Gaelic**
>
> **Hebrides**
>
> **Islands**
>
> **Music**
>
> **The sea**
>
> **Ships**
>
> **Uist**

Questions for group/class discussion

- What situation does the sailor describe in verse one?

- Is the sailor referring solely to the sailors' predicament in the last two lines of verse one?

- In stanza two, the sailor describes the constantly changing aspects of the sea. Why, therefore, do you think he says 'We see so little'?

- In the third verse the sailor speaks more personally. Where does he wish to go?

- 'May the circle of the horizon/keep turning for me'. What does he mean by these lines?

- Why do you think he wishes to reach the white sands of the west?

- Thinking about the song as a whole, is it only about the sea and a sailor's journey?

Imaginative/creative writing

Choose a selection of words which vividly describe the sea in its many moods and go on to develop your own sea poem which evokes the sights and sounds of the sea.

Further development

Find another popular song which you think has something very important to say. Name the song and its writer and describe its message. You could also explain why it is important to you.

Johnny McEvoy

The Wee Magic Stane

The Dean o' Westminster was a powerful man
He held a' the strings o' the State in his hand
But wi' a' his great business it flustered him nane
When some rogues ran away wi' his wee magic stane
Wi' a too-ra-li-oo-ra-li-oo-ra-li-ay

The Stane had great powers that could dae sic a thing
That withoot it it seemed we'd be wantin' a king
So he sent for the polis and made this decree
Go hunt oot the Stone and return it tae me
Wi' a too-ra-li-oo-ra-li-oo-ra-li-ay

So the polis went beetlin' away up tae the North
They hunted the Clyde and they hunted the Forth
But the wild folk up yonder just kidded them a'
For they didnae believe it was magic at a'
Wi' a too-ra-li-oo-ra-li-oo-ra-li-ay

Noo the Provost o' Glesca, Sir Victor by name
Wis awfy put oot when he heard o' the Stane
So he offered the statues that stan' in George Square
That the High Church's masons might mak' a few mair
Wi' a too-ra-li-oo-ra-li-oo-ra-li-ay

When the Dean o' Westminster wi' this was acquaint
He sent for Sir Victor and made him a saint
But it's no good you sending your statues down heah
Said the Dean, But it gives me a jolly good ideah
Wi' a too-ra-li-oo-ra-li-oo-ra-li-ay

So they quarried a stane o' the very same stuff
And they dressed it all up till it looked like enough
Then he sent for the press and announced that the Stane
Had been found and returned tae Westminster again
Wi' a too-ra-li-oo-ra-li-oo-ra-li-ay

But the cream o' the joke still remains tae be telt
For the bloke that wis turnin' them aff on the belt
At the peak o' production was so sorely pressed
That the real yin got bunged in alang wi' the rest
Wi' a too-ra-li-oo-ra-li-oo-ra-li-ay

So if ever ye cam' on a stane wi' a ring
Just sit yersel' doon and proclaim yersel' king
There's nane will be able tae challenge yer claim
That ye've crooned yersel' King on the Destiny Stane
Wi' a too-ra-li-oo-ra-li-oo-ra-li-ay

Johnny McEvoy

The Wee Magic Stane

Introduction

This song was one of many which was written to celebrate the removal and return to Scotland of 'the Stone of Destiny' from Westminster Abbey by a group of young Scottish nationalist students on Christmas Day 1950. Their action was in protest against the fact that the post-war Labour Government had included home rule for Scotland in their election manifesto but had done nothing about it. Known in England as the coronation stone, it had been looted from Scone Abbey by Edward I of England in 1296 because Scottish kings had long been crowned on the stone and therefore it symbolised Scotland's political independence. According to legend, it was the stone on which Jacob of the Old Testament had rested his head and had been brought to Scotland via Spain and Ireland. According to another legend, the monks of Scone had hidden the real one before Edward had arrived and replaced it with a fake. In 1996 the stone (or a copy of it) was returned to Scotland and it is now kept in Edinburgh Castle, 'on loan'. The songwriter plays with the idea of a fake stone or stones to comic effect.

THIRD LEVEL
Related Texts:
    Other songs on the same subject can be found in *The Sangs of the Stane*, a booklet compiled by the Bo'ness Rebels Literary Society.

KEY WORDS:

Folk song

History

Humour

Music

Myths

Nationalism

Politics

Royalty

Some key questions for class/group discussion

- What 'magic' power was the stone supposed to have and what is funny or ironic about this?

- How did the Dean react when he heard about its disappearance?

- What was the Provost of Glasgow afraid of and what steps did he take?

- What idea did the Dean devise when he heard about the Provost's plan and what does this suggest about the Dean?

- How did people in Scotland react when they heard about this and which expressions suggest the quantities involved?

- Considering the size of the stone, why do you think the song refers to it as the '*wee* magic stane'?

- What do you think was the songwriter's attitude to the whole business and how does he show this, especially in the last verse?

Imaginative/creative writing

Write a song of your own which describes a contemporary event in a humorous way.

Further development

Research the facts about the stone's removal in 1950 and the legends surrounding it. Then prepare a short presentation outlining the key aspects of your research.

Matt McGinn

The Ballad of the Q4

The Mary and the Lizzie they were made right here,
But you'll never see the likes of them I fear.
They were the finest ever sailed the sea.
They were built by the hands of men like me.

Chorus
Thank you, Dad, for all your skill
But the Clyde is a river that'll no stand still.
You did gey well, but we'll do more,
Make way for the finest of them all, Q4.

We have an order we'll fulfil
Wi a touch o' the master and a bit more skill.
Now the backroom boys are under way
And the pens will be rolling till the launching day.
Chorus

There's big Tam O'Hara wi his burning gear
The plumber and the plater and the engineer
There's young Willie Wylie wi his welding rod
They're waiting at the ready for the backroom nod.
Chorus

We'll burn and cut and shape and bend
We'll be welding and riveting and in the end
When the painter's dabbed his final coat
We'll be launching the finest ever ship afloat.
Chorus

We've worked and sweated and toiled and now
See the expert's hand from stern to bow
She's ready for the torments o' the sea
She's a credit to the Clyde and you and me.
Chorus

Matt McGinn

The Ballad of the Q4

Introduction

Matt McGinn was a one-man folk song workshop, creating hundreds of songs – some funny, some serious, and some sad. This song commemorates the building of the last great ocean liner to be built at John Brown's shipyard, Clydebank. The *Queen Elizabeth 2*, or QE2, as she was better known, was launched in 1967 and completed in 1968. The song also celebrates the skill of the workers and the proud Clydeside tradition of building many of the best ships in the world, especially the *Queen Mary* and the first *Queen Elizabeth* (the Mary and the Lizzie of the song), both completed just before the Second World War. The name Q4, however, was unrelated to the name of the ship and was simply the reference number the shipyard gave to the quotation for the job. This is what she was referred to at the time of her building, and in later years shipyard workers often said with pride, 'We built yer actual Q4'.

<table>
<tr><td>

SECOND/THIRD LEVELS

Related Texts:

Jim Brown, 'The Waverley Polka'

Archie Fisher and Bobby Campbell, 'The Shipyard Apprentice'

Matt McGinn, 'Yes Yes UCS'

Jimmie Macgregor, 'Pack Yer Tools and Go'

</td></tr>
<tr><td>

KEY WORDS:

Art & Design

Folk song

Glasgow

History

Music

The sea

Ships

Work

</td></tr>
</table>

Some key questions for class/group discussion

- What are the different shipyard jobs mentioned in the song?

- Who are the 'backroom boys' and why would their pens be 'rolling'?

- How does the speaker feel about what their fathers achieved?

- How does he celebrate the importance of teamwork in the song?

- How does he show the men's sense of commitment in verse two, and how does he show in verses four and five how hard they have worked?

- Look at the final verse. What feelings do the men express about the completed ship?

- Matt McGinn uses repetition and gives the song a strong rhythm. Give some examples and say why you think he does this.

Imaginative/creative writing

Design your own fantastic ship of the future and describe what it will look like and what it will be able to do. Write your own song in praise of a ship and/or the people who built it.

Further development

Research the history, stories or memories of shipyard workers or research the history of the QE2 or another famous Clyde-built ship, possibly after a visit to, for example, the Riverside Museum in Glasgow or a famous ship like the *Discovery* in Dundee. Language work could involve learning more about terms used in shipbuilding and researching the stories, jokes or idioms frequently used by the workers, either by interviewing older people who had worked in the yards or by researching archive material or songs.

William McGonagall

The Tay Bridge Disaster

Beautiful Railway Bridge of the Silv'ry Tay!
Alas! I am very sorry to say
That ninety lives have been taken away
On the last Sabbath day of 1879,
Which will be remember'd for a very long time.

'Twas about seven o'clock at night,
And the wind it blew with all its might,
And the rain came pouring down,
And the dark clouds seem'd to frown,
And the Demon of the air seem'd to say—
'I'll blow down the Bridge of Tay.'

When the train left Edinburgh
The passengers' hearts were light and felt no
    sorrow,
But Boreas blew a terrific gale,
Which made their hearts for to quail,
And many of the passengers with fear did say—
'I hope God will send us safe across the Bridge of
    Tay.'

But when the train came near to Wormit Bay,
Boreas he did loud and angry bray,
And shook the central girders of the Bridge of
    Tay
On the last Sabbath day of 1879,
Which will be remember'd for a very long time.

So the train sped on with all its might,
And Bonnie Dundee soon hove in sight,
And the passengers' hearts felt light,
Thinking they would enjoy themselves on the
    New Year,
With their friends at home they lov'd most dear,
And wish them all a happy New Year.

So the train mov'd slowly along the Bridge of Tay,
Until it was about midway,
Then the central girders with a crash gave way,
And down went the train and passengers into
    the Tay!
The Storm Fiend did loudly bray,
Because ninety lives had been taken away,
On the last Sabbath day of 1879,
Which will be remember'd for a very long time.

As soon as the catastrophe came to be known
The alarm from mouth to mouth was blown,
And the cry rang out all o'er the town,
Good Heavens! the Tay Bridge is blown down,
And a passenger train from Edinburgh,
Which fill'd all the people's hearts with sorrow,
And made them for to turn pale,
Because none of the passengers were sav'd to tell
    the tale
How the disaster happen'd on the last Sabbath
    day of 1879,
Which will be remember'd for a very long time.

It must have been an awful sight,
To witness in the dusky moonlight,
While the Storm Fiend did laugh, and angry did
    bray,
Along the Railway Bridge of the Silv'ry Tay.
Oh! ill-fated Bridge of the Silv'ry Tay,
I must now conclude my lay
By telling the world fearlessly without the least
    dismay,
That your central girders would not have given
    way,
At least many sensible men do say,
Had they been supported on each side with
    buttresses,
At least many sensible men confesses,
For the stronger we our houses do build,
The less chance we have of being killed.

William McGonagall

The Tay Bridge Disaster

Introduction

The poem is a graphic account of the violent storm on 28 December 1879 when the first Tay Rail Bridge collapsed while a train was passing over it from Wormit to Dundee, killing all aboard. It is a very good example of McGonagall's style, which is 'so bad it's good', and shows a genuine response to a dreadful disaster. Stanzas of various lengths and a less-than-standard rhyme scheme throughout show the way the poet's mind was working. This is a story which needed to be told, even if in a very inept way. The amalgamation of factual detail such as would be found in a newspaper report with classical allusion is hopelessly comic. Perhaps McGonagall has been vindicated through time, however, as Dundee has taken him to its heart, and some of his lines have been incised in the Riverside walkway beside the river Tay.

THIRD LEVEL
Related texts:
William McGonagall, 'The Railway Bridge of the Silvery Tay'
William McGonagall, 'The Newport Railway'
William McGonagall, 'Address to the New Tay Bridge'
William McGonagall, 'The Famous Tay Whale'

KEY WORDS:

Death

Disaster

Dundee

History

Humour

Railways

Weather

Some key questions for class/group discussions

- In what way do the first two stanzas give all the essential information on the disaster described?

- The poet imagines the weather conditions personified in 'the Demon of the air' and 'Boreas'. Why do you think he does this?

- Rhyme, classical reference, personification and repetition are used in the poem to heighten the effect. Pick out examples of each technique and explain whether you find it effective or not.

- The poet refers in the fifth stanza to 'Bonnie Dundee' coming in sight. This is the nickname usually given to the Marquis of Montrose rather than to the city. Why is it appropriate to apply it to the city in this context?

- What is the effect of the final nine lines of the poem? Why do you think McGonagall chose to end the poem in this way?

Imaginative/creative writing

McGonagall has given you all the details you need to write either a newspaper report or a formal report for the Court of Inquiry on the Tay Bridge Disaster. Imagine that you have been sent to Dundee on the day after the catastrophe to interview those most directly affected. Who would you want to interview, and what do you think they would say?

Further development

- McGonagall wrote around two hundred poems in collections called *Poetic Gems*. These include more poems about the Tay disaster, and 'The Clepington Catastrophe', a description of a fire in a store in Clepington, on the outskirts of Dundee. He does seem to be drawn to destruction and death, perhaps because these themes allowed full rein to his predilection for pathos (which frequently descends into bathos). Pupils might be interested in finding more or these poems.

- Another poet, Archibald McKay, was knocked down by the gale-force wind that swept across Scotland on the night of the Tay Bridge Disaster, and never completely recovered. He could be an interesting topic for study.

Donnchadh Bàn Mac an t-Saoir / Duncan Bàn Macintyre

Cead Deireannach nam Beann (cuibhreann) / Final Farewell to the Bens (extract)

Bha mi 'n-dè 'm Beinn Dòbhrain
'S 'na còir cha robh mi aineolach;
Chunna mi na gleanntan
'S na beanntaichean a b' aithne dhomh:
B' e sin an sealladh èibhinn
Bhith 'g imeachd air na slèibhtean,
Nuair bhiodh a' ghrian ag èirigh
'S a bhiodh na fèidh a' langanaich.

I was on Ben Dorain yesterday,
no stranger in her bounds was I;
I looked upon the glens
and the bens that I had known so well;
this was a happy picture –
to be tramping on the hillsides,
at the hour the sun was rising,
and the deer would be a-bellowing.

'S togarrach a dh' fhalbhainn
Gu sealgaireachd nam bealaichean,
Dol mach a dhìreadh garbhlaich
'S gum b' anmoch tighinn gu baile mi;
An t-uisge glan 's am fàile
Th' air mullach nam beann àrda,
Chuidich e gu fàs mi,
'S e rinn dhomh slàint' is fallaineachd.

Blithely would I set out
for stalking on the hill passes,
away to climb rough country,
and late would I be coming home;
the clean rain and the air
on the peaks of the high mountains
helped me to grow, and gave me
robustness and vitality.

Bha mi 'n-dè san aonach
'S bha smaointean mòr air m' aire-sa,
Nach robh 'n luchd-gaoil a b' abhaist
Bhith siubhal fàsaich mar rium ann;
'S a' bheinn as beag a shaoil mi
Gun dèanadh ise caochladh,
On tha i nis fo chaoraibh,
'S ann thug an saoghal car asam.

Yesterday I was on the moor,
and grave reflections haunted me:
that absent were the well-loved friends
who used to roam the waste with me;
since the mountain, which I little thought
would suffer transformation,
has now become a sheep-run,
the world, indeed, has cheated me.

Mo shoraidh leis na frìthean,
O 's mìorbhailteach na beannan iad,
Le biolair uaine 's fìor-uisg',
Deoch uasal, rìomhach, ceanalta;
Na blàran a tha prìseil,
'S na fàsaichean a tha lìonmhor,
O 's àit a leig mi dhìom iad,
Gu bràth mo mhìle beannachd leò.

Farewell to the deer forests –
O! they are wondrous hill-country,
with green cress and spring water,
a noble, royal, pleasant drink;
to the moor plains which are well beloved,
and the pastures which are plentiful,
as these are the parts of which I've taken leave,
my thousand blessings aye be theirs.

Donnchadh Bàn Mac an t-Saoir / Duncan Bàn Macintyre
Cead Deireannach nam Beann (cuibhreann) / Final Farewell to the Bens (extract)

Introduction

'Final Farewell to the Bens' was composed on 19 September 1802. An old man of seventy-eight, Donnchadh Bàn returned to pay a final visit to the area of his childhood and earlier life in the mountainous area near Bridge of Orchy in Argyllshire dominated by Ben Dorain. The poem, which is also a song, is a series of poignant and nostalgic recollections of nature, of the deer and of the happy times he spent with the people he knew when he was a gamekeeper there. He also registers his disapproval of the destruction of the deer forests to make way for sheep, a practice which caused the Highland Clearances. (It is important to know that 'deer forest' is the technical description of areas of hillside where deer are free to roam. There are no trees in deer forests.)

SECOND/THIRD LEVEL
Related Texts:
John Cameron, **'The Mist-Covered Mountains of Home'** (p. 46)
James Kennedy, **'The Highland Crofter'** (p. 118)
Derick Thomson, 'Strathnaver'

KEY WORDS:

Animals

Argyll

Clearances

Deer

Exile

Gaelic

Geography

Highlands

History

Memory

Nature

Some key questions for class/group discussion

- What does the word nostalgia mean?

- The poet has returned as an old man to the mountainous area where he was brought up and was employed as a gamekeeper whose job was to manage the deer on the estate. In verse one, what memories of his earlier life does he treasure?

- In verse two he remembers setting out to stalk deer and climbing the high hills to do this. What is the overall feeling he experienced in his work? Why?

- In verse three, what two things upset him on coming back to his old home? Why does the presence of so many sheep upset him?

- As he takes his final farewell of his old homeland, what is the tone of the last verse?

Imaginative/creative writing

- Imagine that you have moved house to another part of the country and have returned to visit the area in which you were brought up. What changes do you think you will notice? Do you think you could comfortably fit back in there? Write a short essay describing what you think your feelings would be at such an experience.

- Write an adventure story set in a desolate mountainous area of Scotland.

Further development

- Using a map of the Highlands (e.g. Ordnance Survey Landranger No. 50) try to find the village of Bridge of Orchy in Argyllshire. Looking at the mountains near it see if you can find Ben Dorain. See if you can identify other mountains in the vicinity where Donnchadh Bàn would have stalked the deer. (On some maps you will see 'beinn' rather than 'ben'. 'Beinn' is the Gaelic spelling of 'ben'.)

- Research 'The Highland Clearances'. Once you have found out what they were and why they happened do you think they were justified?

Ewart Alan Mackintosh

In Memoriam

*Private D. Sutherland killed in action in the German
trench, May 16, 1916, and the others who died*

So you were David's father,
And he was your only son,
And the new-cut peats are rotting
And the work is left undone,
Because of an old man weeping,
Just an old man in pain
For David, his son David,
That will not come again.

Oh, the letters he wrote you,
And I can see them still,
Not a word of the fighting
But just the sheep on the hill
And how you should get the crops in
Ere the year got stormier,
And the Bosches have got his body,
And I was his officer.

You were only David's father,
But I had fifty sons
When we went up in the evening
Under the arch of the guns,
And we came back at twilight –
O God! I heard them call
To me for help and pity
That could not help at all.

Oh, never will I forget you,
My men that trusted me,
More my sons than your fathers',
For they could only see
The little helpless babies
And the young men in their pride.
They could not see you dying,
And hold you when you died.

Happy and young and gallant,
They saw their first-born go,
But not the strong limbs broken
And the beautiful men brought low.
The piteous writhing bodies,
The screamed 'Don't leave me, Sir,'
For they were only your fathers
But I was your officer.

Ewart Alan Mackintosh

In Memoriam

Introduction

On the evening of 16 May 1916, Lieutenant Ewart Alan Mackintosh and Second Lieutenant Mackay of the 5th Battalion Seaforth Highlanders led a raid on the German trenches in the sector of the front line north-west of Arras. By the end of the night there were sixteen British casualties, which included fourteen wounded and two killed. One of the two dead soldiers was Private David Sutherland, who has no known grave. His name is commemorated in Bay 8 of the Arras Memorial to the Missing at Faubourg d'Amiens military cemetery in Arras.

This very emotional poem unexpectedly contrasts the feelings of the soldiers' natural fathers with their 'battlefield fathers', the officers who commanded them and often sent them to their deaths. Although it appears in the first stanza that the writer is actually talking to David's father, this is unlikely, and it is more likely that he is preparing to write the letter he must send to the father telling him of his son's death. The emotive impact of the poem is enhanced by the direct address combined with third person description.

THIRD LEVEL
Related texts:
> Violet Jacob, 'Glory'
> Pittendrigh MacGillivray, 'In Memoriam'
> Ewart Alan Mackintosh, 'Cha Till MacCruimein'
> Ewart Alan Mackintosh, 'Recruiting'
> Ewart Alan Mackintosh, **'On Vimy Ridge'** (p. 152)
> Mary Simon 'The Glen's Muster-Roll'

KEYWORDS:

Battles

Death

Fathers

First World War

History

War

Some key questions for class/group discussion

- How do you think the officer knows about the content of David's letters, and what is the effect on you when you read the juxtaposition of the horrors of the battlefield and the thoughts of the home farm?

- Explain fully what the writer means by 'And the Bosches have got his body,/And I was his officer.'

- What does 'You were only David's father,/But I had fifty sons' in stanza three tell you about the relationship between the officer and his men? Does this surprise you in any way?

- What does the increasingly personal address in stanzas four and five tell you about the relationship between officer and men? How does the officer feel about his men? How do the men feel about their officer? What particular words and phrases bring out these feelings most strongly?

- This is an extremely moving poem although written very simply. What gives it its emotional impact?

Imaginative/creative writing

- Write one of David's letters home to his father, using the brief details you are given in the poem of the content.

- Write, either in first or third person, an account of a day for David's father as he tries to cope with the croft on his own, thinking about his hopes and fears for his son serving abroad.

Further development

There is obviously considerable scope for a collaboration with the History department on the First World War, and pupils could find out more about the career of Mackintosh himself (he received the Military Cross) and the events which led to the writing of this poem.

Ewart Alan Mackintosh

On Vimy Ridge

On Vimy Ridge four months ago
We lived and fought, my friends and I,
And watched the kindly dawn come slow.
Peace bringing from the eastern sky.
Now I sit in a quiet town
Remembering how I used to go
Among the dugouts up and down,
On Vimy Ridge four months ago.

And often sitting here I've seen,
As then I saw them every night.
The friendly faces tired and keen
Across the flickering candle-light.
And heard their laughter gay and clear,
And watched the fires of courage glow
Above the scattered ash of fear,
On Vimy Ridge four months ago.

Oh, friends of mine, where are you now?
Somewhere beneath the troubled sky.
With earth above the quiet brow,
Reader and Stalk for ever lie.
But dead or living out or here
I see the friends I used to know,
And hear the laughter gay and clear,
On Vimy Ridge four months ago.

Ewart Alan Mackintosh

On Vimy Ridge

Introduction

The poem recalls the Battle of Vimy Ridge, part of the Battle of Arras, which took place from the ninth to the twelfth of April 1917. The poet-soldier is haunted by the memory of the men who did not return from the recent battle, and continually sees and hears them as they were in life. The reminiscences do not include overt scenes of battle, fear, injury or death, although there are very subtle references to weariness, fear and the demands of battle. What the speaker wants to recall is the comradeship enjoyed in the trenches. The refrain 'On Vimy Ridge four months ago' highlights both how long ago the events happened, and how recent they are in his mind. Perhaps because now he is out of the battle he has time to grieve and to remember the lost men. The mood of the poem is sombre and calm, but with an undercurrent of grief unexpressed. It is written in three eight-line stanzas, rhymed *ababcdcd*.

THIRD LEVEL
Related texts:
   Ewart Alan Mackintosh, **'In Memoriam'** (p. 150)
   Ewart Alan Mackintosh, 'Cha Till MacCruimein'

KEY WORDS:

Battles

Death

First World War

History

Memory

War

Some key questions for class/group discussion

- The poet uses the phrase 'On Vimy Ridge four months ago' as the first line and as a refrain. How does this emphasise the memory?

- Another word which is repeated is 'friend', and its variants. What does this tell you about the relationships amongst the men?

- Look in detail at the second stanza and how the men are described. Do you find this surprising in the circumstances?

- What does the poet mean by lines nineteen and twenty? And who are Reader and Stalk?

Imaginative/creative writing

The scene in the second stanza is very clear. Imagining you are one of the soldiers (perhaps Reader or Stalk?), write a diary entry where you describe an evening during a lull in the battle where the men can forget some of the horror and talk about their past (and future) lives.

Further development

This poem would be an ideal introduction for a comparative study with the History department looking at the First World War. Vimy Ridge is not the best-known of the battles of the war in this country, but it is the site of Canada's largest and principal war memorial, indicating its importance to the soldiers of that country.

George Mackay Brown

The Hawk

On Sunday the hawk fell on Bigging
And a chicken screamed
Lost in its own little snowstorm.
And on Monday he fell on the moor
And the Field Club
Raised a hundred silent prisms.
And on Tuesday he fell on the hill
And the happy lamb
Never knew why the loud collie straddled him.
And on Wednesday he fell on a bush
And the blackbird
Laid by his little flute for the last time.
And on Thursday he fell on Cleat
And peerie Tom's rabbit
Swung in a single arc from shore to hill.
And on Friday he fell on a ditch
But the rampant rat,
The eye and the tooth, quenched his flame.
And on Saturday he fell on Bigging
And Jock lowered his gun
And nailed a small wing over the corn.

George Mackay Brown

The Hawk

Introduction

In this poem George Mackay Brown creates a series of vivid, dramatic descriptions of the hawk's search for food and subsequent death. The poet's repetition of the phrase 'fell on', which describes the speed of its rapid descent, further heightens his portrayal of the predatory bird relentless in its pursuit of prey. The precision of his descriptions of the hawk's hunting in the Orkney landscape has a terrible beauty, which intensifies our feelings for the vulnerable creatures he kills – the image of the screaming chicken 'lost in its own little snowstorm' of feathers as the hawk snatches and shakes it prey; the pathos evoked by the silencing of the blackbird, which has 'laid by his little flute for the last time' and the drama of the alliterative description of the hawk's action as it swings 'peerie Tom's rabbit/in a single arc from shore to hill'. Only 'the rampant rat' deters the hawk and the poet's use of the phrase 'the eye and the tooth' reinforces the theme of nature red in tooth and claw. The farmer at Bigging is at first unsuccessful in shooting the hawk but there is no sense of triumph, no Gotcha! in the final kill – rather an acknowledgement that the hawk has also become a vulnerable creature in the relentless cycle of nature in common with the creatures it has preyed upon and killed.

> **THIRD LEVEL**
> **Related texts:**
> J. K. Annand, 'Heron'
> George Hardie, 'Herrin Gull'
> Brian McCabe, **'Seagull'** (p. 130)
> Ian MacFadyen, 'The First Hoolet's Prayer'
> Edwin Morgan, 'Hyena'
>
> **KEY WORDS:**
> **Animals**
> **Art & Design**
> **Birds**
> **Hawks**
> **Islands**
> **Orkney**
> **Nature**
> **Science**

Some key questions for class/group discussion

- How does the poet organise his descriptions of the hawk's hunting to create a clear structure for the poem?

- Why does he repeat the phrase 'fell on' seven times?

- Choose two descriptions of the hawk's attacks on vulnerable creatures and, by examining the literary techniques used by the poet, explain why they are so vivid and dramatic.

- Why does the poet use the phrase 'the eye and the tooth'?

- What do the last two lines suggest about the poet's attitude to the death of the hawk?

- Why do you think he refers to the hawk as 'he'?

- What do you think is the theme of the poem?

Imaginative/creative writing

Using a structure similar to the one the poet used in 'The Hawk', create your own animal or bird poem which describes key happenings in its life. You could choose either a pet or a wild animal or bird.

Further development

Find out about the different types of hawk which inhabit the British Isles then create your own hawk booklet and illustrate it.

Jim McLean

Farewell to Glasgow

Oh where is the Glasgow I used to know?
The tenement buildings that let in the snow.
Through cracks in the plaster the cold wind did blow
And the water we washed in was fifty below.

We read by the gaslight, we had nae T.V.,
Hot porridge for breakfast, cold porridge for tea,
Some weans had rickets and some had T.B.,
Ay, that's what the Glasgow of old means to me.

Noo the neighbours complained if we played wi' a ba'
Or hunch-cuddy-hunch against somebody's wa'
If we played kick-the-can we'd tae watch for the law
And the polis made sure we did sweet bugger a'.

Noo ye've heard o' the closet that stood on the stair,
Oors had tae accommodate fifteen or mair,
An' the broken wee windae let in the fresh air,
An' I sometimes went in, aye, but just for a dare.

And we huddled together to keep warm in bed.
We had nae sheets or blankets, just auld coats instead,
And a big balaclava to cover your head,
And 'God but it's cold' was the only prayer said.

Noo there's some say that tenement living was swell.
That's the wally-close toffs who had doors wi' a bell,
Two rooms and a kitchen and a bathroom as well.
While the rest of us lived in a single-end hell.

So wipe aff that smile when you talk o' the days
Ye lived in the Gorbals or Cowcaddens ways.
Remember the rats and the mice ye once chased.
For tenement living was a bloody disgrace.

Jim McLean

Farewell to Glasgow

Introduction

This song was written in response to Adam McNaughtan's famous song, 'The Glasgow That I Used to Know', which is a nostalgic celebration of many good things about a Glasgow childhood of the past. In contrast, Jim McLean, who was brought up in the slums, shows us the grim reality of poverty and squalor in many city tenements of that period. McNaughtan's song focuses more on childhood experiences he recalls fondly, whereas Jim McLean's viewpoint is more that of an adult looking back on the worst aspects of slum life that he remembers from his childhood. Both these songs and others give us a memorable picture of the many changes that have taken place in Glasgow over the past half century or so, especially the effects of post-war slum clearance on a massive scale, the disappearance of many traditional industries along with the close-knit communities that accompanied them.

THIRD LEVEL
Related Texts:

Anon., 'The Broom Blooms Brawly'
Billy Connolly, 'I Wish I Was in Glasgow'
Ian Davison, 'Going Home to Glasgow'
Alex Jamieson, 'The People's Palace'
Matt McGinn, 'Big Sammy'
Adam McNaughtan, 'The Glasgow That I Used to Know'

KEY WORDS:

Art & Design

Drama

Folk song

Geography

Glasgow

History

Memory

Music

Some key questions for class/group discussion

- What do you think would have been the worst part of living in the sort of building Jim McLean describes? What was the worst thing for them as children and why?

- What were the other health problems and what do you think caused them?

- How did they try to amuse themselves and what problems did they sometimes have?

- Why would some people object to what they were doing and what impression does he give us of the police?

- Why would he only go into the stair closet (toilet) for 'a dare'?

- What does he think of the people who lived in better houses with 'wally closes'? Why do you think he might have felt this way?

- How does he create an effective contrast in verse five between the better houses and his own?

- Which verse of the song do you think shows his strongest feelings and why?

- How would you describe the mood or tone of the whole song? Do you find any parts of it funny? Why?

- Do you think he maybe exaggerates how bad things were in any way? Can you find any examples to back up your opinion and think of a reason why he does this?

Imaginative/creative writing

- Imagine a scene with Jim's neighbours complaining to his parents about what their children have been doing. Script the conversation or script the conversation of the children in bed some night, fighting for covers and trying to get warm.

- Write your own song about where you live, showing the good or bad things about it, or a poem about your town or village past and present.

Further development

- A version of this kind of house can be seen in the Tenement House Museum in Buccleuch Street in the Garnethill area of Glasgow.

- A number of street games are mentioned in both songs and some research could be done on these, with illustrations and explanations provided, plus maybe a short survey to find out how many such games are still played, plus the favourite outdoor games that are played by children today.

Somhairle Mac Gill-Eain / Sorley MacLean

Glac a' Bhàis / Death Valley

*Thuirt Nàsach air choreigin gun tug am Furair
    air ais do fhir na Gearmailte 'a' chòir agus
    an sonas bàs fhaotainn anns an àraich'.*

*Some Nazi or other has said that the Führer
    had restored to German manhood the 'right
    and joy of dying in battle'.*

'Na shuidhe marbh an 'Glaic a' Bhàis'
fo Dhruim Ruidhìseit,
gill' òg 's a logan sìos ma ghruaidh
's a thuar grìseann.

Sitting dead in 'Death Valley'
below the Ruweisat Ridge,
a boy with his forelock down about his cheek
and his face slate-grey;

Smaoinich mi air a' chòir 's an àgh
a fhuair e bho Fhurair,
bhith tuiteam ann an raon an àir
gun èirigh tuilleadh;

I thought of the right and the joy
that he got from his Führer,
of falling in the field of slaughter
to rise no more;

air a' ghreadhnachas 's air a' chliù
nach d' fhuair e 'na aonar,
ged b' esan bu bhrònaiche snuadh
ann an glaic air laomadh

of the pomp and the fame
that he had, not alone,
though he was the most piteous to see
in a valley gone to seed

le cuileagan mu chuirp ghlas'
air gainmhich lachdainn
's i salach-bhuidhe 's làn de raip
's de sprùillich catha.

with flies about grey corpses
on a dun sand
dirty yellow and full of the rubbish
and fragments of battle.

An robh an gille air an dream
a mhàb na h-Iudhàich
's na Comannaich, no air an dream
bu mhotha, dhiùbhsan

Was the boy of the band
who abused the Jews
and Communists, or of the greater
band of those

a threòraicheadh bho thoiseach àl
gun deòin gu buaireadh
agus bruaillean cuthaich gach blàir
air sgàth uachdaran?

led, from the beginning of generations,
unwillingly to the trial
and mad delirium of every war
for the sake of rulers?

Ge b' e a dheòin-san no a chàs,
a neoichiontas no mhìorun,
cha do nochd e toileachadh 'na bhàs
fo Dhruim Ruidhìseit.

Whatever his desire or mishap,
his innocence or malignity,
he showed no pleasure in his death
below the Ruweisat Ridge.

Somhairle Mac Gill-Eain / Sorley MacLean

Glac a' Bhàis / Death Valley

Introduction

Sorley MacLean fought in the Desert Campaign during the Second World War and was severely wounded at the Battle of El Alamein in Egypt. The poem 'Glac a' Bhàis'/'Death Valley' comes from personal experience and the English translation is his own. The poet comes upon the body of a young German soldier, lying in a fly-infested hollow in the desert. He shows no bitterness towards him, enemy though he be. Rather, his anger is aimed at those politicians and rulers who are responsible for war.

THIRD LEVEL
Related Texts:

George Campbell Hay, 'Bizerta'
Keith Douglas, 'Vergissmeinnicht'
Wilfred Owen, 'Dulce et Decorum Est'

KEY WORDS:

Battles

Death

Deserts

History

Second World War

Soldiers

War

Some key questions for class/group discussion

* What does the phrase 'slate-grey' suggest about the length of time the young soldier has been dead?

* Look at verses two and three. Find out what *Führer* means. Who was he? How do you think young German soldiers have been told by him to look upon fighting in war? Do you think the poet is using sarcasm here?

* Describe the surroundings in which the poet sees the young dead German soldier sitting. How do these suggest the pity he feels for the youth?

* Although the young soldier may have done terrible things under orders during the war, whom does the poet suggest is really to blame?

* What does the poet mean by the 'mad delirium of every war'?

* Look at the epigraph and then look at the last two lines of the poem. What is the poet telling us about war?

Imaginative/creative writing

* In pairs, discuss the conditions in which soldiers were forced to live when fighting in the Desert Campaign.

* Imagine you are a soldier in the Desert Campaign. Write an essay describing the conditions you have to live in and an attack to which you are subjected.

Further development

George Campbell Hay and Hamish Henderson are two other Scottish poets who took part in the Second World War. Research one of them, and then write a brief report on his part in the war and on his poetry.

Coinneach MacLeòid / Kenneth MacLeod

Holiday na Caillich / The Old Lady's Holiday

Thug mi cead dom chaillich dhol thairis air chuan
'S i 'n còmhnaidh a' gearan le cnatan 's le fuachd,
'S gun cumainn an dachaigh 's gach nì bh' air mun
    cuairt
'S gun dèanainn dhi cruach de mhòine.

Ach 's mise tha duilich bho dhealaich rium Mòr,
Toirt biadh dha na cearcan is deoch dhan a' bhò,
Càradh mo leap' 's cur na dachaigh air doigh –
Tha mis' ann an ceò bho dh'fhàg i.

An àm èirigh sa mhadainn tha 'n dachaigh cho fuar;
Cha lèir dhomh a' chagailt 's na th' oirre de luath;
Poitean is praisean cho dubh ris a' ghual
'S gun duine bheir sguab air làr dhomh.

Ach, fhearaibh, nam faiceadh sibh mise 's a' bhò,
Ise ri breabail 's a sinean nam dhòrn –
Am bainn' tha i frasadh chan fhaigh mi ri òl,
Tha mo bhriogais 's mo bhrògan làn dheth.

Thuirt cailleach bheag bheannaicht' rium 'n-diugh
    anns a' bhùth,
'Cuimhnich air d' anam 's bi lùbadh do ghlùin':
Is beag a bha dh'fhios aic' gu robh m' iosgaidean
    ruisgt'
Le cho tric 's tha mi sgùradh an làir orr'.

Ach nam bitheadh duine agams' a dh'ullaicheadh
    biadh,
Chan fhairichinn cho fad' e ged bheireadh i mìos;
Thug mi ionnsaigh air lit' nach do dh' itheadh
    a-riamh –
Bha cnapan a lìonadh an spàin ann.

Nuair thig i air ais bidh rud agam ri inns':
Chan eil cupan air sgeul, chan eil sgian ach a trì;
Bhàsaich an coileach 's chaidh na cearcan a dhìth;
Is bhris a' phoit-tì bho dh'fhàg i.

Cha troid mi rim bhean ged a throideadh i rium –
'S ann an-diugh tha mi coimhead a' chunnairt a th'
    ann:
Far nach bi bean, cha bhi dachaigh no clan,
'S chan fhaic duine a call 's i làthair.

I gave leave to my old lady to go over the sea –
She's always complaining of her cough and the cold;
I'd look after the house and all things around
And I'd make her a peat stack.

But oh I am sad since Marion departed from me:
I'm feeding the hens and giving drink to the cow,
I'm making my bed and tidying the house –
I'm in a daze since she left me.

When I rise in the morning the house is so cold,
I can't see the hearth for the ashes in it;
The pots and the pans are as black as coal
And there's no one to sweep the floor for me.

But, boys, if you could see me and the cow,
She kicking and her teats in my fist –
She's spraying her milk, I can't get it for drinking,
My breeks and my shoes are full of it.

A holy wee *cailleach* said to me today in the shop,
'Remember your soul and be bending your knee':
It's little she knew that I got my shins skint
From scrubbing the floor so often.

But if only I had someone who would cook my food
I wouldn't feel it so long if Marion were away for a
    month.
I tried making porridge but it could never be eaten –
There were lumps in it as big as the spoon.

When Marion comes back I'll have something to tell
    her:
There's no sign of a cup, only three knives are left;
The cock died and the hens disappeared;
And the teapot broke since she departed.

I'll not scold my wife though she would scold me –
Today I can see the danger in that:
Where there's no wife there'll be no house or kids,
A man can't see her loss when she's with him.

Coinneach MacLeòid / Kenneth MacLeod

Holiday na Caillich / The Old Lady's Holiday

Introduction

The speaker in this comic poem (which is also a song) bemoans his plight when left to cope with the house and croft on a Hebridean island after he has magnanimously, in his opinion, allowed his wife to go on holiday to recuperate from a series of colds. The first verse reveals his lack of sympathy for her and his arrogant self-confidence that he will cope. The rest of the poem is a catalogue of the disasters which befall him in her absence. He confesses he is in a daze since she left and he seems to revel in his misery as one disaster follows another. He reveals that he has gone down so often on his knees to scrub the floor that he has chronically skint shins. The penultimate verse ends with a comic anti-climax – even the teapot has not survived Marion's absence! The poem is a comic take on the stereotype of the hapless male who cannot cope without a strong woman's help and hard work.

SECOND LEVEL
Related texts:
Norman MacCaig, **'Aunt Julia'** (p. 132)
Norman MacCaig, **'Praise of a Collie'** (p. 134)
Lady Nairne, **'The Laird o' Cockpen'** (p. 182)

KEY WORDS:

Art & Design

Farming

Gaelic

Geography

Hebrides

History

Humour

Islands

Marriage

Some key questions for class/group discussion

- What does the line 'I gave leave to the old wife to go over the sea' tell us about the speaker?

- What does he promise to do while she is away?

- In verse two he says he is sad that Marion has gone away. What reason does he give for this? What does this tell us about him?

- He gives a catalogue of all the disasters that have happened to him since she left. Do you think he is exaggerating these disasters? Do you think he is deliberately making them seem comical to amuse his audience?

- Why would he be frequently scraping his shins?

Imaginative/creative writing

- Write a short story in which the main character (unlike the speaker in the poem) copes with a difficult situation and overcomes the problems it has caused.

Further development

Peat was traditionally used in crofting communities and is still used by many crofters as an essential fuel. Find out some facts about peat, make notes and then design a poster (with drawings) entitled The Story of Peat. Say what it is, how it was formed, where in Scotland it is most commonly found, how it was extracted and transported, and how a peat stack was built.

Adam McNaughtan

Yellow on the Broom

Well, I ken ye dinna like it, lass, tae winter here in toun
For the scaldies they all cry us, aye, and they try to bring us doon,
And it's hard to raise three bairnies in a single flea-box room,
And I'll tak' ye on the road again when the yellow's on the broom.

When the yellow's on the broom, when the yellow's on the broom,
Oh, I'll tak' ye on the road again when the yellow's on the broom.

Oh, the scaldies cry us 'tinker dirt' and they sconce our bairns at school,
But who cares what a scaldy says for a scaldy's but a fool.
They never hear the yarlin's sang nor see the flax in bloom,
For they're aye cooped up in hooses when the yellow's on the broom.

When the yellow's on the broom, when the yellow's on the broom,
For they're aye cooped up in hooses when the yellow's on the broom.

Nae sales for pegs and baskets noo, so just to stay alive
We've had tae work at scaldy jobs frae nine o'clock 'til five.
But we ca nae man oor master, for we own the warld's room,
And we'll bid farewell to Brechin, when the yellow's on the broom.

When the yellow's on the broom, when the yellow's on the broom,
And we'll bid farewell to Brechin, when the yellow's on the broom.

I'm weary for the springtime, when we'll tak' the road aince mair
Tae the plantin' and the pearlin', aye, and the berry fields o Blair,
There we'll meet wi all our kinfolk, frae a' the country roon',
When the ganaboot folk tak' the road, and the yellow's on the broom.

When the yellow's on the broom, when the yellow's on the broom,
When the ganaboot folk tak' the road, and the yellow's on the broom.

Adam McNaughtan

Yellow on the Broom

Introduction

Adam McNaughtan's song is a tribute to Betsy Whyte, whose memoir *The Yellow on the Broom* gives a vivid account of her early years growing up as a member of a travelling family and her longing, after living in a house in Brechin over the winter, to get back on the road again in springtime when the broom is in blossom. It celebrates the freedom of the open road and a love of nature, and expresses contempt for the ignorance and prejudice that travelling families have to deal with from town dwellers. In this song he imagines Betsy's mother promising to take the family on the road again in the spring. No longer able to survive on the sale of pegs and baskets, they have to take 'scaldy jobs' during the winter months. It is only when the spring comes that they can be free again to take the open road, find work in the countryside and be part of the wider community of travelling people.

It is important to hear a good recording of the song, especially a version which has not anglicised the original text or spelling. There are several available online, such as the version sung by the author or by Arthur Johnstone.

SECOND/THIRD LEVEL
Related texts:
Liz Lochhead, 'The Metal Raw' (p. 126)

KEY WORDS:

Drama

History

Music

Prejudice

Seasons

Travellers

Some key questions for class/group discussion

- Who is the speaker in the song and who is being addressed?

- What are the problems the speaker and her family face when they spend the winter months in Brechin?

- What does the speaker value about the travellers' way of life?

- What does the speaker think the townsfolk are missing in their way of life?

- Why do the travellers have 'tae work at scaldy jobs' during the winter months?

- What do the lines 'But we ca nae man oor maister/for we own the warld's room' reveal about the travellers' feelings about their way of life?

- What work do they find during the spring and summer months?

- What do they particularly enjoy about the times they spend working and travelling in the countryside?

- What gives the words of the chorus such emotional power?

Imaginative/creative Writing

Using the information you are given about the life of the 'ganaboot' folk, dramatise a dialogue between the parent and the child complaining about being cooped up 'in a single flea-box room'.

Further development

Pupils could research the different names that have been used for travelling people over the centuries, especially tinkers and gypsies. Further language work could be done on the Scots and 'cant' words used in the song. Pupils could then prepare a glossary or posters of other 'cant' terms.

Further research could involve finding out more about the traditional occupations and culture of the travellers and comparing this way of life with how they live today.

Angela McSeveney

Changing a Downie Cover

First: catch your downie.

They're big animals, sleep a lot of the time,
barely stirring as they snooze endlessly
loafing around on the beds.

But they only have to see
a clean cover –

suddenly you have six by three
of feathery incorporeality kicking and screaming
in your hands.
Wrestle them to the floor
and kneel on their necks:
you can't hurt them, no bones to break.

Pushing their head into the bag
keeps them quiet

but you're never sure
till each corner is flush inside the cover
securely buttoned shut.

They give up after that.
Pinioned in floral print polycotton
they lie back down and sleep.

Angela McSeveney

Changing a Downie Cover

Introduction

Angela McSeveney here presents in fantastic terms an everyday happening: the changing of a downie cover. The fun comes from her seeing this most domestic of activities in terms of a hunter coming upon, catching and then taming a wild beast. The first line of the poem suggests that it is going to be a 'How to …' instruction, but it turns out to be a fantastic and humorous description of wrestling the downie into its cover. It also teaches us a lot about two important figures of speech: personification and metaphor. It depends for its entire structure on an extended metaphor: the downie is not just personified as an animal (which would make it an ordinary metaphor); the poet extends the metaphor to show us the 'beast' in a *series* of extraordinary actions before it is brought under control.

SECOND LEVEL
Related texts:
Sheena Blackhall, 'Doric Reggae Spider Rap'
J. M. Caie, **'The Puddock'** (p. 44)
Helen B. Cruickshank, 'Beasties'

KEY WORDS:

Animals

Art & Design

Fantasy

Humour

Some key questions for class/group discussion

- Write down any words or phrases that suggest the downie is a lazy creature by nature.

- What exactly will bring these creatures to life?

- Write down all the words that suggest 'taming' a downie is a violent business.

- What does it take to get them to lie down and sleep again?

- The poet uses 'you' a lot here. What do you think is gained by doing this?

Imaginative/creative writing

- Try imagining some other domestic activities in this imaginative way. Hanging out jeans or a shirt on a washing line, for instance. How will they look as they fill with wind? Will they co-operate as you hang them up? Or imagine putting away a vacuum cleaner with its hose and cable. Write about your chosen activity as a poem.

- If you have read Sheena Blackhall's 'Doric Reggae Spider Rap' (in *The Kist*), write your own rap for a creature of your choice.

Further development

Although this poem does not offer a set of instructions, a lot of useful information is in fact given on how to get the downie into its cover. Find out the relevant facts and then create an attractive and informative illustrated leaflet containing a set of instructions for looking after a pet. Alternatively you could create a similar leaflet for a fantastical animal.

Ewan McVicar

Shift and Spin

Keep yer bobbins runnin easy,
Show ye're gallus, bright and breezy,
Waitin till Prince Charmin sees ye,
Workin in the mill.

Chorus
Shift and spin, warp and twine,
Making thread coarse and fine,
Dreamin o yer valentine,
Workin in the mill.

Oil yer runners, mend yer thread,
Do yer best until you're dead.
You wish you were a wife instead o
Workin in the mill.

Used to dream you'd be the rage,
Smilin on the fashion page.
Never dreamt you'd be a wage slave
Workin in the mill.

Used to think that life was kind.
No it isn't, never mind
Maybe some day love will find you
Workin in the mill.

He loves you not? So what?
Make the best of what you've got.
Win your pay, spin your cotton,
Workin in the mill.

Ewan McVicar

Shift and Spin

Introduction

Ewan McVicar's song is about the boredom of a young woman working in a large factory where the noise is so loud that she is alone with her machine and her thoughts. She dreams of romance and a better life but, although resigned to being 'a wage slave', puts on a brave, cheerful face to the world. 'Shift and Spin' began as a verse and chorus for a local history project in Paisley, documenting the lives of the workers in the cotton-thread mills of the town which once employed a substantial proportion of the population – especially women. The products of the mills became renowned worldwide. Ewan McVicar added additional verses and the song was popularised by Ray Fisher who sometimes suggested that the song was about the Dundee jute mills. The song could, however, apply to a girl working in a mill or factory anywhere.

SECOND/THIRD LEVELS
Related Texts:

Mary Brookbank, 'The Jute Mill Song'
Dorsey Dixon, 'Babies in the Mill'
Woody Guthrie, 'Weaverly Life'
Joe Hill, 'Down in the Old Dark Mills'
Dave McCarn, 'Poor Man, Rich Man'
James Taylor, 'Millworker'

KEY WORDS:

Drama

Factories

Folk song

Geography

History

Music

Work

Key questions for class/group discussion

• What are 'bobbins' and 'runners', and what does the expression 'shift and spin, warp and twine' mean?

• Who is speaking in the song?

• What impression does she try to give to others, and why do you think she does this?

• What did she used to dream about becoming?

• What did she think would never happen to her?

• Why does she say 'never mind'?

• Why do you think she says 'so what?', and what does this tell us about her?

• How would you describe the mood of this song?

Imaginative/creative writing

Imagine you are a young person in a boring job today, dreaming about doing something or becoming someone very different. Script the conversation you have with your friends about your dreams of a different life during the lunchbreak or on the way home.

Further development

Research the history, living conditions and stories or memories of Paisley mill-workers or any other important industry which used to employ many people in your local area. Give a short presentation about your findings. The Anchor Mill in Paisley houses an archive about the mills and there is also a Thread Mill Museum nearby.

Elizabeth Melville

My Lady Culros to Mr Andro Melville

Anagrame

Meik men ar vexed just saulls ar taine away
And *wel wer myne* to flit among the rest
Now lord mak haist and call me from this clay
Deir Jesus cum, how long sall troubill lest?
Resave my spreit with paine it is opprest
Evill is the aige the faithfull now dois faill
Wp lord, how long? Thy sanctts ar soir distressed
Mainteine thy treuth, let not the proud prevail
End out my fecht. How can this hart be haill,
Lord sall I leive to se thy spows in paine?
Why sleipis thow so? Thow seis thy secret seill,
In thee we trust althocht we sould be slaine
Now souls do schyne who luik unto thy licht
And wel were myne to sie that blissed sicht.

Elizabeth Melville

My Lady Culros to Mr Andro Melville

Introduction

Elizabeth Melville, Lady Culross, became, in 1603, the first Scottish woman to put her work into print, and once there her work was recognised and appreciated by generations of Scots. Her topic was invariably religious faith as the only means of living in the fallen world, and she expresses powerful thoughts boldly and seriously.

This poem is addressed to a Mr Andrew Melville (no relation), who was at the time jailed in the Tower of London by James VI and I, apparently for his 'treasonable' attitude to the King's support for the English form of worship. Lady Culross's sonnet offers the prisoner and his supporters spiritual consolation at a time of persecution and possible martyrdom.

The sonnet is subtitled 'Anagrame' but it is in fact also an acrostic, where the initial letters of each line spell out the name of the subject (with some leeway!). The anagram is shown in italics with the acrostic (M Andrew Melwin) in bold.

The Scots in this poem may look odd, but if it is read out loud, it is quite straightforward. The spelling has been lightly modernised to make it easier to understand.

THIRD LEVEL
Related texts:

Margaret Cunningham, 'What greater wealth then a contented mind'
Elizabeth Melville, 'Cast cair on Chryst, with courage bair his Cross'
Elizabeth Melville, 'A Call to Come to Christ'

KEY WORDS:

Character

Faith

History

Religion

Sonnets

Some key questions for group/class discussion

- Although the poem is addressed to a minister of the church it is also a plea to God to act. Pick out the words which show this aspect.

- What is the writer actually asking in this poem? Look particularly at lines three, five, nine, thirteen and fourteen for the evidence.

- There are two appeals to God to act – 'Wp (Up) lord, how long' (line seven) and 'Why sleepis thow so?' (line eleven) which are almost accusatory. What picture does this give you of Elizabeth Melville's personality?

- Look at the rhyme scheme. What do you notice that is unusual?

Imaginative/creative writing

Try writing your own acrostic poem addressed to someone you know or admire. If you can include an anagram of their name as well, bravo!

Further development

Find out what you can about Elizabeth Melville. She is a very interesting character who certainly did not behave as women of her time were expected to, meek and silent. If you can find any of her letters to her sons, you are in for a treat. Women poets of this period are unjustly ignored or completely unknown. Another worthy voice is Margaret Cunningham.

Edwin Morgan

Canedolia: an Off-Concrete Scotch Fantasia

oa! hoy! awe! ba! mey!

who saw?
rhu saw rum. garve saw smoo. nigg saw tain. lairg saw lagg.
rigg saw eigg. largs saw haggs. tongue saw luss. mull saw yell.
stoer saw strone. drem saw muck. gask saw noss. unst saw cults.
echt saw banff. weem saw wick. trool saw twatt.

how far?
from largo to lunga from joppa to skibo from ratho to shona from
ulva to minto from tinto to tolsta from soutra to marsco from
braco to barra from alva to stobo from fogo to fada from gigha to
gogo from kelso to stroma from hirta to spango.

what is it like there?
och it's freuchie, it's faifley, it's wamphray, it's frandy, it's
sliddery.

what do you do?
we foindle and fungle, we bonkle and meigle and maxpoffle. we
scotstarvit, armit, wormit, and even whifflet. we play at crossstobs,
leuchars, gorbals, and finfan. we scavaig, and there's aye a bit of
tilquhilly. if it's wet, treshnish and mishnish.

what is the best of the country?
blinkbonny! airgold! thundergay!

and the worst?
scrishven, shiskine, scrabster, and snizort.

listen! what's that?
catacol and wauchope, never heed them.

tell us about last night
well, we had a wee ferintosh and we lay on the quiraing. it was
pure strontian!

but who was there?
petermoidart and craigenkenneth and cambusputtock and
ecclemuchty and corriehulish and balladolly and altnacanny and
clauchanvrechan and stronachlochan and auchenlachar and
tighnacrankie and tilliebruaich and killieharra and invervannach
and achnatudlem and machrishellach and inchtamurchan and
auchterfechan and kinlochculter and ardnawhallie and
invershuggle.

and what was the toast?
schiehallion! schiehallion! schiehallion!

Edwin Morgan

Canedolia: an Off-Concrete Scotch Fantasia

Introduction

The title signals the humorous tone and playful, unconventional nature of this poem. The poet was very interested in concrete poetry – a form of poetry developed by avant-garde writers in the twentieth century which emphasised the visual shape of a poem and often moved words and letters about the page in unconventional ways. Edwin Morgan wrote a number of concrete poems, but in 'Canedolia' he wittily subverts the conventional definition of concrete poetry as visual poetry and creates an inventive, exuberant sound poem which celebrates Scottish place-names in all their linguistic variety and, by extension, Scotland itself. The poem does have, however, some characteristics of concrete poetry. The poet uses a specific semantic field, the place-names of Scotland, and, by exploiting their alliterative and onomatopoeic qualities and giving them new meanings and associations, he creates a dramatic narrative which ends with a toast to Scotland.

> **THIRD LEVEL**
> **Related Texts:**
> Ian Hamilton Finlay, 'The Boat's Blue Print'
> Ian Hamilton Finlay, 'Great Frog Race'
> Ian Hamilton Finlay, 'Lullaby'
> Edwin Morgan, 'The Chaffinch Map of Scotland'
> Edwin Morgan, 'The Computer's First Christmas Card'
> Edwin Morgan, '**The First Men on Mercury**' (p. 172)
> Edwin Morgan, '**The Loch Ness Monster's Song**' (p. 174)
>
> **KEY WORDS:**
>
> Art & Design
>
> Geography
>
> History
>
> Humour
>
> Language
>
> Place-names
>
> Scotland

Some key questions for class/group discussion

- What do the words of the title suggest to you about the subject matter and tone of the poem?

- What do you notice about the expressions in the first line of the poem? Why do you think the poet used them?

- How does the poet structure the poem into a dramatic narrative?

- Why did the poet use the names *Scrabster* and *Snizort* and *Treshnish* and *Mishnish*?

- The name *Freuchie* is used as an adjective to describe an aspect of Scotland. What do you think it might suggest?

- The poet describes the best of the country as *blinkbonny* and *airgold*. What do these words suggest to you?

- The poet ends the poem with a toast. What is he celebrating?

Imaginative/creative writing

- Choose some of the questions the poet uses to give a narrative structure to his poem and write your own off-concrete sound poem using the place names of your own area. Use your own local knowledge of official and unofficial place-names and a detailed map of your area.

- Create a visual and sound poem of your own to suggest, for example: a wild storm, a noisy city street, a sports event in a large stadium.

Further development

Working in pairs or small groups, research the origins of place-names in your own area using a detailed map. Create your own illustrated booklet of local place-names giving the language of origin and their meanings.

Edwin Morgan

The First Men on Mercury

– We come in peace from the third planet.
Would you take us to your leader?

– Bawr stretter! Bawr. Bawr. Stretterhawl?

– This is a little plastic model
of the solar system, with working parts.
You are here and we are there and we
are now here with you, is this clear?

– Gawl horrop. Bawr. Abawrhannahanna!

– Where we come from is blue and white
with brown, you see we call the brown
here 'land', the blue is 'sea', and the white
is 'clouds' over land and sea. We live
on the surface of the brown land,
all around is sea and clouds. We are 'men'.
Men come –

– Glawp men! Gawrbenner menko.
    Menhawl?

– Men come in peace from the third planet
which we call 'earth'. We are earthmen.
Take us earthmen to your leader.

– Thmen? Thmen? Bawr. Bawrhossop.
Yuleeda tan hanna. Harrabost yuleeda.

– I am the yuleeda. You see my hands,
we carry no benner, we come in peace.
The spaceways are all stretterhawn.

– Glawn peacemen all horrabhanna tantko!
Tan come at'mstrossop. Glawp yuleeda!

– Atoms are peacegawl in our harraban.
Menbat worrabost from tan hannahanna.

– You men we know bawrhossoptant. Bawr.
We know yuleeda. Go strawg backspetter
    quick.

– We cantantabawr, tantingko backspetter
    now!

– Banghapper now! Yes, third planet back.
Yuleeda will go back blue, white, brown
nowhanna! There is no more talk.

– Gawl han fasthapper?

– No. You must go back to your planet.
Go back in peace, take what you have gained
but quickly.

– Stretterworra gawl, gawl …

– Of course, but nothing is ever the same,
now is it? You'll remember Mercury.

Edwin Morgan

The First Men on Mercury

Introduction

The title of Edwin Morgan's 1973 collection, *From Glasgow to Saturn*, suggests the enormous range of his subject matter, epitomised in this poem. The poem is an imagined meeting between astronauts from Earth and the indigenous inhabitants of Mercury (interestingly not Mars, as would usually have been expected). Morgan here is using his love of languages and translation to humorous, but ultimately devastating effect, in his account of the effect of the meeting on both Earthmen and Mercurians. The poem is written as a conversation and has to be read out loud (or listened to) for the full effect, as on the page it can look quite intimidating. The Earthmen adopt a rather patronising tone, clearly thinking themselves superior in having the technology to get to Mercury, and use clichés that we are used to from science fiction. Although the Mercurian language is invented, it is relatively easy to 'translate' what is being said. The Earthmen are completely transformed by the experience (as are the Mercurians) and 'nothing is ever the same' again.

THIRD LEVEL
Related texts:

Robert Crawford, **'Alba Einstein'** (p. 60)
Hugh MacDiarmid, **'The Bonnie Broukit Bairn'** (p. 138)
Edwin Morgan, **'Canedolia'** (p. 170)
Edwin Morgan, **'The Loch Ness Monster's Song'** (p. 174)

KEY WORDS:

Humour

Language

Science

Space

Some key questions for class/group discussion

- How would you describe the way the astronauts talk to the people on Mercury? Why do you think they do this? What does the punctuation of the Mercurian speech suggest to you about the feelings of the Mercurians towards the astronauts?

- Look at the third Mercurian response. What is happening now?

- From the ninth stanza (beginning 'I am the yuleeda') the astronauts' language changes significantly. Can you explain the change?

- As you know what happens at the end of the poem, what is the significance of the Mercurian's advice that the astronauts 'go back … quickly'?

- What has happened to the languages of the two groups by the end of the poem?

- Who are the first men on Mercury?

Imaginative/creative writing

- What do you think will happen when the astronauts return to Earth? Will they be able to communicate? If not, what is likely to happen to them?

- Write a short conversation in which the leading astronaut tries to explain what they have discovered, using the language of the poem and inventing some additional Mercurian vocabulary of your own.

- Construct an English–Mercurian glossary from the poem.

Further development

Research the past and current human explorations of the solar system, whether manned or unmanned. What is your opinion of governments spending vast sums on space exploration when there are so many problems to be solved on our own planet?

Edwin Morgan

The Loch Ness Monster's Song

Sssnnnwhuffffll?
Hnwhuffl hhnnwfl hnfl hfl?
Gdroblboblhobngbl gbl gl g g g g glbgl.
Drublhaflablhaflubhafgabhaflhafl fl fl –
gm grawwwww grf grawf awfgm graw gm.
Hovoplodok-doplodovok-plovodokot-doplodokosh?
Splgraw fok fok splgrafhatchgabrlgabrl fok splfok!
Zgra kra gka fok!
Grof grawff gahf?
Gombl mbl bl –
blm plm,
blm plm,
blm plm,
blp.

Edwin Morgan

The Loch Ness Monster's Song

Introduction

'The Loch Ness Monster's Song' belongs to a long tradition of poems which give animals a voice, but it is also inspired by twentieth century avant-garde poets who experimented with the sound patterns of words or letter clusters and the shape of a poem on the page. It needs to be read out loud.

Through his playful use of the onomatopoeic and alliterative sounds of the letter clusters, and punctuation, the poet invites us to find a meaning in the monster's song. The first two lines suggest the snuffling sounds the monster makes as it emerges from the depth of the loch. Perhaps it wants to play on the surface of the loch but is disturbed by Nessie-watchers on the bank. It seems to be asking itself, 'What are they?' The dash at the end of line four signals a change of mood from curiosity to anger. The next four lines with their harsh /gr/ sounds and hard /k/ sounds, building to a climax in the explosive utterance, 'Zgra kra gka fok!' suggest that the monster is trying to frighten the watchers away. Perhaps it does! The final four lines suggest that, having vented its indignation and anger at this unwelcome intrusion into its territory, it slowly disappears into the loch and the only sounds are the repeated sounds, 'blm plm', of the bubbles created as it submerges, culminating in the final 'blp' once it has completely disappeared under the surface of the loch.

> **SECOND/THIRD LEVEL**
> **Related Texts:**
> Carol Ann Duffy, **'The Loch Ness Monster's Husband'** (p. 70)
> Edwin Morgan, 'The Chaffinch Map of Scotland'
> Edwin Morgan, 'The Computer's First Christmas Card'
> Edwin Morgan, 'Siesta of a Hungarian Snake'
>
> **KEY WORDS:**
>
> **Animals**
>
> **Art & Design**
>
> **Humour**
>
> **Language**
>
> **Loch Ness**
>
> **Monsters**
>
> **Myths**
>
> **Science**

Some key questions for class/group discussion

- Why do you think the poem is called 'The Loch Ness Monster's Song' rather than 'Nessie's Song'?

- In the first four lines what do you think the monster is doing and saying?

- Look at the next four lines and sound them out loud. What kind of sounds are they? What do they suggest about the monster's mood and what do you think it is saying? Which is the most dramatic line of the four? Give a reason for your choice.

- Which line marks the last utterance of the monster? What might it be saying?

- What do the last four lines suggest is happening?

- Why does the poem end with the single 'blp' sound?

Imaginative/creative writing

Write a sound poem of your own. Choose an animal or object or machine which makes a noise or noises. Imagine what it might be saying and choose your own clusters of letters to create its feelings and mood. What message might it be sending out to its human audience? You might also want to give the poem a shape.

Further development

Conduct your own research into the legend of the monster and the newspaper history of its reported sightings, or research the scientific theories about the kind of species it might be. Create an attractive, informative notebook presenting your research and illustrate it.

Edwin Muir

The Late Wasp

You that through all the dying summer
Came every morning to our breakfast table,
A lonely bachelor mummer,
And fed on the marmalade
So deeply, all your strength was scarcely able
To prise you from the sweet pit you had made, –
You and the earth have now grown older,
And your blue thoroughfares have felt a change;
They have grown colder;
And it is strange
How the familiar avenues of the air
Crumble now, crumble; the good air will not hold,
All cracked and perished with the cold;
And down you dive through nothing and through despair.

Edwin Muir

The Late Wasp

Introduction

'The Late Wasp' comes from the collection called *One Foot in Eden*, which looks at the natural world in a rather uncomfortable way, with reflections on the human condition. The wasp has lived through the summer, sharing the people's food, apparently without bothering them or being bothered, but now in autumn the air is colder, and death is imminent. There is a distinct echo of 'Things fall apart; the centre cannot hold' from W. B. Yeats's 'The Second Coming' in the line 'Crumble now, crumble; the good air will not hold', which is a point worth investigating further.

THIRD LEVEL
Related Texts:
Alexander Gray, **'On a Cat, Ageing'** (p. 90)
Brian McCabe, **'Seagull'** (p. 130)
Edwin Muir, 'The Late Swallow'

KEY WORDS:

Animals

Death

Insects

Old age

Seasons

Some key questions for class/group discussion

- Note that the poet uses the phrase 'dying summer' in the very first line of the poem. Why do you think he does this?

- The wasp is described as 'lonely', a 'bachelor' and a 'mummer'. What significant aspects do these words add to the description?

- Do you think the wasp's summer existence was a good one? What evidence can you find?

- What are the 'blue thoroughfares', and how are they connected to the 'avenues of the air'?

- Why do you think the poet repeats 'crumble' towards the end of the poem? What does he make the air sound like?

- What do you think the last line of the poem really means?

- Look at the rhyme scheme of the poem. How has it been constructed? Does it follow a particular formal form? How does the rhyme reinforce the meanings of the rhyming words?

Imaginative/creative writing

Take another creature which you associate with summer (or with any other particular season), and write your own poem celebrating its short time with us.

Further development

Find W. B. Yeats's 'The Second Coming' and make a study of the poem which can then be contrasted with Muir's poem. Although they are very different, what can you find that they have in common?

Neil Munro

John o' Lorn

My plaid is on my shoulder and my boat is on the shore,
And it's all bye wi' auld days and you;
Here's a health and here's a heartbreak, for it's hame my dear, no more,
To the green glens, the fine glens we knew!

'Twas for the sake o' glory, but oh! wae upon the wars,
That brought my father's son to sic a day;
I'd rather be a craven wi' nor name, nor fame, nor scars,
Than turn a wanderer's heel on Moidart Bay.

And you, in the day-time, you'll be here, and in the mirk,
Wi' the kind heart, the open hand, and free;
And far awa' in foreign France, in town or camp or kirk,
I'll be wondering if you keep a thought for me.

But never more the heather nor the bracken at my knees,
I'm poor John o' Lorn, a broken man;
For an auld Hielan' story I must sail the swinging seas,
A chief without a castle or a clan.

My plaid is on my shoulder and my boat is on the shore,
It's all bye wi' auld days and you;
Here's a health and here's a heartbreak, for it's hame my dear no more,
To the green glens, the fine glens we knew!

Neil Munro

John o' Lorn

Introduction

'John o' Lorn' is set on the coast of the West Highlands (Moidart) and is a poem of exile. The narrator, John o' Lorn, laments that, as a Jacobite whose cause was lost at Culloden, his boat awaits him and he must now take his leave forever of his homeland and of someone very dear to him, perhaps a sweetheart. He asks her if she will remember him once he is in exile in France. No more will he enjoy his native countryside. He was once a clan chieftain with his own castle but his loyalty to the Stuart cause has cost him everything. He is now, sadly, a 'broken man'. This simple poem has genuine pathos. It was later set to music and has been sung and recorded by Norman Stewart.

THIRD LEVEL
Related Texts:
Robert Burns, '**The Battle of Sherra-moor**' (p. 38)
Robert Burns, 'Ye Jacobites by Name'
James Hogg, '**Cam Ye by Atholl**' (p. 102)
Adam Skirving, '**Johnnie Cope**' (p. 204)

KEY WORDS:

Exile

Highlands

History

Jacobites

Love

War

Some key questions for class/group discussion

- Where is John o' Lorn when he tells us his story? What is about to happen to him?

- Why does he find himself in this sad situation?

- Whom do you think he is speaking to?

- Where does he think he will be forced to live?

- What status and property did he have before things went wrong for him?

Imaginative/creative Writing

- Imagine you were a Highlander forced to leave Scotland for France after the defeat of Bonnie Prince Charlie at Culloden in 1746. Describe your journey in a sailing ship and the sort of life you had to lead in France until you were finally allowed to return home.

- Write a story about a young person of today who is forced into exile from his/her own country because of war.

Further development

Find out who the Jacobites were, and how the cause was finally ended at the Battle of Culloden in 1746.

Charles Murray

The Whistle

He cut a sappy sucker from the muckle rodden-tree,
He trimmed it, an' he wet it, an' he thumped it on his knee;
He never heard the teuchat when the harrow broke her eggs,
He missed the craggit heron nabbin' puddocks in the seggs,
He forgot to hound the collie at the cattle when they strayed,
But you should hae seen the whistle that the wee herd made!

He wheepled on't at mornin' an' he tweetled on't at nicht,
He puffed his freckled cheeks until his nose sank oot o' sicht,
The kye were late for milkin' when he piped them up the closs,
The kitlins got his supper syne, an' he was beddit boss;
But he cared na doit nor docken what they did or thocht or said,
There was comfort in the whistle that the wee herd made.

For lyin' lang o' mornin's he had clawed the caup for weeks,
But noo he had his bonnet on afore the lave had breeks;
He was whistlin' to the porridge that were hott'rin' on the fire,
He was whistlin' ower the travise to the baillie in the byre;
Nae a blackbird nor a mavis, that hae pipin' for their trade,
Was a marrow for the whistle that the wee herd made.

He played a march to battle, it cam' dirlin' through the mist,
Till the halflin' squared his shou'ders an' made up his mind to 'list;
He tried a spring for wooers, though he wistna what it meant,
But the kitchen-lass was lauchin' an he thocht she maybe kent;
He got ream an' buttered bannocks for the lovin' lilt he played.
Wasna that a cheery whistle that the wee herd made?

He blew them rants sae lively, schottisches, reels an' jigs,
The foalie flang his muckle legs an' capered ower the rigs,
The grey-tailed futt'rat bobbit oot to hear his ain strathspey,
The bawd cam' loupin' through the corn to 'Clean Pease Strae';
The feet o' ilka man an' beast gat youkie when he played –
Hae ye ever heard o' whistle like the wee herd made?

But the snaw it stopped the herdin' an the winter brocht him dool,
When in spite o' hacks an' chilblains he was shod again for school;
He couldna sough the catechis nor pipe the rule o' three,
He was keepit in an' lickit when the ither loons got free;
But he aften played the truant – 'twas the only thing he played,
For the maister brunt the whistle that the wee herd made!

Charles Murray

The Whistle

Introduction

The poetry of Charles Murray celebrates the Doric, the Scots dialect of the north-east of Scotland. 'The Whistle' is rich in words which vividly describe farming life in the late nineteenth century and the natural world. The story of the young farm boy, who carves a whistle from the wood of a rowan tree and delights all around him, evokes a vanished way of life with humour and pathos. The boy is so absorbed in his task that he is oblivious to the sights and sounds of nature around him and completely neglects his herding duties. With humour and vivid description the poet describes the effect of his whistling on the farm workers and the animals around the farm. The poem builds to a dramatic climax in the penultimate verse with the rhetorical question, 'Hae ye ever heard o' whistle like the wee herd made?' There is an abrupt change of mood in the final verse when the herd must attend school during the winter months and is punished severely for being unable to recite the Catechism. It is a cruel blow for the boy when the schoolmaster, a disciplinarian and killjoy, burns the whistle.

SECOND/THIRD LEVEL
Related Texts:
Robert Burns, 'Song Composed in August'
Adam McNaughtan, **'Yellow on the Broom'** (p. 162)

KEY WORDS:

Farming

History

Music

Nature

North-east Scotland

School

Scots language

Seasons

Some key questions for class/group discussion

- What did the boy fail to notice or attend to as he went about carving the whistle?

- What actions were involved in the making of the whistle?

- Once he had finished making the whistle, how did his behaviour change?

- What comparison does the poet make to emphasise that the wee herd's whistle was the best?

- How did the music he made with his whistle affect the people and animals around him? Comment on two or three examples which you think are particularly effective in conveying the power of his music.

- Why did the teacher burn his whistle?

- What does this action suggest about the school experience and education of children at that time?

Imaginative/creative writing

Imagine that the boy's mother, having heard that the teacher had burned her son's whistle, goes to see the teacher. Script a scene in which the mother and the teacher discuss why this action had been taken. The mother would use the Doric version of Scots and the teacher would probably use Standard English. Try your hand at the two kinds of language as you bring their dialogue alive.

Further development

Find out about farming life in the north-east of Scotland in the late nineteenth century. What was life like for farm workers (herdsmen, ploughmen, kitchen servants, halflins)?

Carolina Oliphant, Lady Nairne

The Laird o' Cockpen

The Laird o' Cockpen, he's proud an' he's great,
His mind is ta'en up wi' the things o' the State;
He wanted a wife, his braw house to keep,
But favour wi' wooin' was fashious to seek.

Down by the dyke-side a lady did dwell,
At his table head he thocht she'd look well,
M'Leish's ae dochter o' Clavers-ha' Lea,
A penniless lass wi' a lang pedigree.

His wig was weel pouther'd and as gude as new,
His waistcoat was white, his coat it was blue;
He put on a ring, a sword, and cock'd hat,
And wha could refuse the Laird wi' a' that?

He took the grey mare, and rade cannily,
And rapp'd at the yett o' Clavers-ha' Lea;
'Gae tell Mistress Jean to come speedily ben, –
She's wanted to speak to the Laird o' Cockpen.'

Mistress Jean she was makin' the elderflower wine;
'An' what brings the Laird at sic a like time?'
She put aff her apron, and on her silk goun,
Her mutch wi' red ribbons, and gaed awa' doun.

An' when she cam' ben, he bowed fu' low,
An' what was his errand he soon let her know;
Amazed was the Laird when the lady said 'Na',
And wi' a laigh curtsie she turned awa'.

Dumfounder'd was he, nae sigh did he gie,
He mounted his mare – he rade cannily;
An' aften he thought, as he gaed through the glen,
She's daft to refuse the laird o' Cockpen.

Carolina Oliphant, Lady Nairne

The Laird o' Cockpen

Introduction

The Laird o' Cockpen is a busy important person, perhaps a politician, who requires a wife mainly to look after his house and grace his table. Love is not a consideration. A local girl, Jean McLeish, daughter of an impoverished aristocratic family – and therefore socially acceptable – will meet his requirements. He attires himself in his finest clothes and, certain of acceptance, sets off to propose to her. The laird is pompous and arrogant, believing that wealth and social status will secure the hand of Jean. She, on the other hand, even although a match with the laird could help to redeem the fortunes of her family, will not be bought. She has her pride and shows her strong character by rejecting him with a single word, 'Na'. In his complacency he is astounded that she rejects him, and concludes that she must be 'daft'. The use of colourful vibrant Scots words reminds us that Scots was still spoken by many in the aristocracy in the nineteenth century.

SECOND LEVEL

Related Texts:
Sir Walter Scott, **'Jock o' Hazeldean'** (p. 198)
Sir Walter Scott, **'Lochinvar'** (p. 200)

KEY WORDS:

Drama

History

Love

Marriage

Music

Scots language

Some key questions for class/group discussion

- Why does the laird think that McLeish's only daughter would make him a suitable wife?

- What does the line 'And wha could refuse the laird wi' a' that?' reveal about the narrator's opinion of the laird's attitude to marriage?

- Who might be speaking in verse four?

- How does Jean show her annoyance at the laird's arrival?

- Why do you think she put on her good clothes?

- Why was the laird amazed that she had refused his offer of marriage?

- What does her one-word refusal suggest about her personality?

- Which word suggests the laird's continuing amazement and incomprehension?

- Why do you think he continues to puzzle over her refusal?

Imaginative/creative writing

The poem lends itself to conversion into a short comic play. Other characters may be introduced to enrich the story and to bring out the laird's actions, for example, a clumsy well-meaning butler, Jean's father at Clavers-ha' Lea, and perhaps also a horse. The play could have five short scenes: The laird's study; The laird's dressing room; The journey to Clavers-ha' Lea; The interview with Jean; The journey home.

Further development

Find out about marriage customs in Scotland in the eighteenth and nineteenth centuries. Compare and contrast them with marriage customs today.

William Neil

Despatches Home

At last we have them all well fooled, well tamed;
they use our baths and lard themselves with oil,
truss up their souls and bodies in the toga.

The squireens speak school-Latin and affect
Misunderstanding of the kerns from their estates
(less slaves these than their masters
whom we have flattered into Roman ways).
Now, when our swords save them from their own kin
And mind plays traitor, there's no need for gyves.

Up in the hills, I grant you, there are those
whose hides are dun with peat-reek and who keep their arms
tough as our own with 'Parry! Thrust! Recover!'
who watch and watch, and hope that we grow weak.

Ungovernable these, growling in their own speech;
Lean as the wolves they prowl their bracken dales,
dream vengeance as the bards sing round their fires.
They curse their former lords – lost to Catullus –
and snarl like tigers when we bay them up.

Holding for the most part, then, to the Pax Romana,
out from the hills some few
attempt their bloody mischief on dark nights.
These demons armoured in enamelled bronze
hate us as we hate them.

                    We both despise
The Latin-lisping traitors of the town.

William Neil

Despatches Home

Introduction

William Neil wrote poetry in Gaelic, Scots and English. This poem deals with the Roman conquest of Britain and is a report by a Roman officer to his superiors. He explains how they have softened up the British ruling classes by introducing them to Roman dress and luxuries, so much so that they imitate the Roman way of life, try to speak Latin and even read the Latin love poetry of Catullus. There is no need to intimidate them by force for their minds and habits have now become decadent and enslaved to Rome. In the hills, however, are the resistance fighters who will not succumb. They are disciplined and practise military manoeuvres, watching for any weakness in the army of occupation. They continue to speak their own British language (Old Welsh). Occasionally they confront the Roman army and the Romans hate, yet respect, them. But the Romans and the freedom fighters both despise the British ruling classes who have surrendered their bodies and souls to Rome.

THIRD LEVEL
Related texts:
Sheena Blackhall, 'The Eruption of Vesuvius' (p. 34)

KEY WORDS:

Conquest

Geography

History

Romans

War

Some key questions for class/group discussion

- Why is the poem called 'Despatches Home'?

- What does the poet mean when he says the British ruling class 'truss up their souls and bodies in the toga'?

- Can you work out the meaning of 'squireen'? Why do you think the poet added '-een'?

- 'Kern' means 'peasant'. Why do the squireens pretend not to understand the peasants on their own estates?

- Look up the meaning of 'gyve'. Why do the Romans have no need for such things?

- How, then, have the Romans succeeded in conquering the British ruling classes who live in the towns?

- Who are the people who live in the hills? Describe their behaviour.

- What is the attitude of the Romans and the British hill-folk to 'the Latin-lisping traitors of the town'?

Imaginative/creative writing

- Imagine you are one of the British resistance fighters. Describe a night raid on a Roman fort.

- Transfer the situation of the poem to the future. Imagine this country had been invaded by aliens. Imagine you are a resistance fighter and describe a crucial raid on their headquarters.

Further development

When the Romans invaded Britain the furthest point of their conquest was marked by the Antonine Wall in Central Scotland. The Latin word for a fort is *castra* and is a clear sign of the existence of Roman rule in areas where it can be spotted. *Castra* shows itself in place-names as *-chester*, *-cester*, *-caster*, e.g. Chester, Manchester, Leicester, Doncaster. See how many place-names you can find containing this element.

Nancy Nicolson

Listen tae the Teacher

He's five year auld, he's aff tae school
Farmer's bairn wi a pencil and a rule.
His teacher scoffs when he says 'hoose';
'The word is house, you silly little goose.'
He tells his ma when he gets back
He saw a mouse in an auld cairt track.
His faither laughs fae the stackyard dyke,
'Yon's a moose, ye daft wee tyke.'

Chorus:
Listen tae the teacher, dinna say dinna.
Listen tae the teacher, dinna say hoose.
Listen tae the teacher, ye canna say maunna.
Listen tae the teacher, ye maunna say moose.

He bit his lip an shut his mooth,
Which one could he trust for truth?
He took his burden o'er the hill
Tae auld grey Geordie o' the mill.
'An did they mock thee for thy tongue
Wi them sae auld an you sae young?
They werena makin a fool o' ye –
They were makin a fool o' themsels ye see.

'Say hoose tae the faither, house tae the teacher;
Moose tae the fairmer, mouse tae the preacher.
When yer young it's weel for you
Tae dae in Rome as Romans do.
But when ye grow an ye are auld
Ye needna dae as ye are tauld.
Don't trim yer tongue tae suit yon dame
That scorns the language o' her hame.'

Then teacher thocht that he was fine;
He kept in step, he stayed in line.
Faither says that he was gran –
He spoke his ain tongue like a man.
An when he grew and made his choice
He chose his Scots, his native voice.
And I charge ye tae dae likewise.
Spurn yon pair misguided cries.

Nancy Nicolson

Listen tae the Teacher

Introduction

When Nancy Nicolson was in school in Caithness she was 'corrected' in front of the whole class for saying 'hoose' rather than 'house'. Although the correction was done fairly gently, Nancy felt a deep sense of humiliation and hurt that remained with her and which undermined her own self-worth and confidence. Like generations of Scottish children, this led her to adopt a code-switching tactic as a means of coping with the conflict between the culture of home and the education system, which for generations has perpetuated linguistic snobbery and ignorance about Scots being 'bad English' or 'slang'. Yet although this song is rooted in the Scottish experience of cultural and linguistic discrimination, this also happens in many cultures across the world, as various dominant groups or elites inflict a process of cultural colonisation which deprives children of the right to value and respect their own language and culture. It is a therefore a song that could be enjoyed and studied right across the age range.

SECOND/THIRD LEVEL
Related Texts:
  Jim Douglas, 'The New Teacher' (p. 68)
  Jackie Kay, 'In My Country' (p. 114)
  Liz Lochhead, 'The Metal Raw' (p. 126)
  Adam McNaughtan, 'Yellow on the Broom' (p. 162)

KEY WORDS:

  Identity

  Music

  Prejudice

  School

  Scots language

Some key questions for class/group discussion

- What is the attitude of the teacher to the way the child speaks, and how do we know this?

- How does the child feel, and which expressions describe this?

- What advice is he given, and what does this mean? What do you think of this advice?

- What is he advised to do when he has grown up? Do you think this is good advice?

- What is auld Geordie's opinion of the teacher and her advice, and how is his opinion supported by the narrator in the last two lines of the song? Which expressions reveal this?

- In the past Scottish children were often made to feel that their native languages were 'wrong' or inferior. What do you think of this attitude? Does this still sometimes happen?

- Do some people still think that Scots is 'bad' English or somehow not as 'proper'? Why? Should this be acceptable today?

- Do you change the way you talk for different audiences and do you think you need to be able to speak both Scots and English? Why?

Imaginative/creative writing

- Transform the poem into a script where the language used by the teacher and the pupil and his friends and family are clearly distinguished.

- Write a letter from the boy's father to the teacher complaining that he is being made to 'talk posh'.

Further development

- Undertake a linguistic study and survey of attitudes in school and amongst parents today regarding the issues raised.

- Research other cultures if there is a multi-ethnic population in the school. Does this kind of snobbery happen in other languages?

Liz Niven

Feart

In the pit mirk nicht at the fit o the stairs,
A heard a wee noise that jist made the hairs
oan the back o ma neck, staun straight up oan end,
ma teeth start tae chatter, ma hert fair bend.

A cocked ma lugs an strained fir tae hear.
Wis it ghaists or folk? Wir they faur or near?
Wid they be freenly craturs or murderers foul?
Wir they here fir a blether or a bluidthirsty prowl?

Wi a flash o lichtnin, an a rattle o thunner,
the storm fair brewed an A coontit tae a hunner.
Then A gaithert ma courage an stertit tae climb
When oot o the shaddas twae fit at a time,

a wee black baw o fur an fluff
came trottin doon the stairs, fair in a huff.
Ma new wee kitten jist gied me a look,
an walkt strecht past, fair famisht fir her food.

Liz Niven

Feart

Introduction

This poem is a vivid account of an incident which threw the narrator into a state of fear but which ends with a humorous anti-climax when the source of the noise is revealed as her new kitten. Liz Niven's skilful use of rhyme, rhythm and alliteration brings the incident vividly to life. Her use of questions adds drama to the poem and the description of the storm mirrors her fear. The use of the phrases 'a wee black baw o fur and fluff' and 'fair in a huff' creates a reassuring, familiar tone and brings the poem to a humorous conclusion.

> **SECOND LEVEL**
> **Related Texts:**
> J. K. Annand, 'Heron'
> Anon., **'The Twa Corbies'**
> (p. 28)
> J. M. Caie, **'The Puddock'**
> (p. 44)
> Brian McCabe, **'Seagull'**
> (p. 130)
> Norman MacCaig, **'Toad'**
> (p. 136)
> Kenneth McKellar, 'Midges'
> William Soutar, 'Wullie
> Waggle Tail'
>
> **KEY WORDS:**
>
> Animals
>
> Cats
>
> Fear
>
> Humour

Some key questions for class/group discussion

- Read this poem aloud to get the rhythm of it. Which Scots words emphasise the feeling of fear that she has?

- Show how the mood of the poem changes in the last stanza and pick out the phrases which convey this change of mood.

- Choose two examples of alliteration and explain how they add to the tone of the poem.

Imaginative/creative writing

- Write an account of a time when you were 'feart'.

- Write a poem about a pet showing how it gets up to mischief.

Further development

Liz Niven uses the Scots language to vivid effect in this poem. Using a Scots dictionary, find Scots words for animals, their movements and the sounds they make.

Catrìona NicÌomhair Parsons / Catriona McIvor Parsons

Cuimhne / Memory

'Nam shuidh' am bucas cairt mo sheanar
'S mi beag bìodach, air mo bhrùthadh a-null's a-nall
'S na rothan a' leum air clachan a' rathaid
'S an làir a' toirt céim gu trom's gu mall.

Bha an dithis againn—mi-fhìn's e-fhéin
(Mise 'faireachdainn cho mór!) – 'dol an tòir
    air gainmhich bho'n tràigh;
Os ar cionn adhar breac gorm, 's a' cionacrachadh
        ar sròintean
Fàileadh cùbhraidh na seamraig bhàin.

Mi coiseachd eadar muir is achadh
Air mór-thìr eile, 's gaoth bhlàth na mara
A' gluasad tarsainn air a' raon, geal le seamragan,
'S a' toirt mo sheanar – glan, geur, gràdhaichte –
        gu m' aire.

Sitting in the box of my grandfather's cart
When I was tiny wee, jostled back and forth
As the wheels bounded over the rocks in the road
And the mare stepped heavily and slowly.

The two of us – myself and himself –
(I feeling so big!) were going
    to fetch sand from the beach.
Above us a blue speckled sky, and hugging
        our noses
The fragrant smell of white clover.

Walking between sea and field
On another continent, and the warm sea-wind
Moving across the meadow, white with clover,
(And) bringing my grandfather – clear, etched, beloved –
        to my attention.

Catrìona NicÌomhair Parsons / Catriona McIvor Parsons

Cuimhne / Memory

Introduction

Catriona McIvor Parsons wrote this poem in memory of her grandfather. As a young girl, she helped her grandparents on their croft in Aignish, a small village in the district of Point out on the Eye peninsula on the island of Lewis. 'Eye' is an English corruption of 'Aoidh', the Gaelic word for a peninsula. Her evocative poem brings vividly to life her experience of riding in her grandfather's cart as they went to fetch sand from the beach. It was an uncomfortable ride over the rocky road but she felt privileged to be included in this expedition. Years later, as an adult living and working in Nova Scotia, she remembers this experience when the scent of clover in a field by the sea triggers her particular memory of the clover-scented ride in her grandfather's cart. It is a touching tribute to him.

> **SECOND LEVEL**
> **Related Texts:**
> Jackie Kay, **'Grandpa's Soup'** (p. 112)
> Liz Lochhead, **'For My Grandmother Knitting'** (p. 124)
> Norman MacCaig, **'Aunt Julia'** (p. 132)
> Alan Riach, **'A Short Introduction to My Uncle Glen'** (p. 196)
>
> **KEY WORDS:**
> Family
> Farming
> Grandparents
> Hebrides
> History
> Islands
> Lewis
> Memory

Some key questions for class/group discussion

- Why do you think the poet describes herself as 'tiny wee'?
- How do we know it was not a comfortable ride?
- What does the line 'The two of us – myself and himself' suggest about the girl's feelings as she rides to the beach?
- Why is she 'feeling so big'?
- How would you describe 'a blue speckled sky' in your own words?
- What does the word 'hugging' suggest about the smell of white clover?
- Looking at stanza three, what most of all brings back her memories of her grandfather?

Imaginative/creative writing

Write an account of a particularly happy time you spent with a grandparent or older relative or friend which remains vividly in your mind.

Further development

Catriona McIvor Parsons' grandfather worked a croft many years ago on the island of Lewis. Find out about crofting on the island and prepare a short talk on the life of a crofting family. You could choose to research what crofting is like now or many years ago.

Allan Ramsay

The Twa Cats and the Cheese

Twa cats anes on a cheese did light,
To which baith had an equal right;
But disputes, sic as aft arise,
Fell oot a-sharing of the prize.
'Fair play,' said ane, 'ye bite o'er thick,
Thae teeth of yours gang wonder quick!
Let's part it, else lang or the moon
Be changed, the kebuck will be doon.'
But wha's to do't? they're parties baith,
And ane may do the other skaith.
Sae with consent away they trudge,
And laid the cheese before a judge:
A monkey with a campsho face,
Clerk to a Justice of the Peace.
A judge he seemed in justice skill'd,
When he his master's chair had fill'd:
Now umpire chosen for division,
Baith sware to stand by his decision.
Demure he looks; the cheese he pales;
He prives, it's good; ca's for the scales:
His knife whops throw't, in twa it fell;
He put ilk haff in either shell:
Said he, 'We'll truly weigh the case,
And strictest justice shall have place.'
Then lifting up the scales, he fand
The tane bang up, the other stand:
Syne out he took the heaviest haff,

And ate a knoost o't quickly aff,
And tried it syne: – it now proved light: –
'Friend cats,' said he, 'we'll do ye right.'
Then to the ither half he fell,
And laid till 't teughly tooth and nail,
Till weigh'd again, it lightest prov'd.
The judge, wha this sweet process lov'd,
Still weigh'd the case, and still ate on,
Till clients baith were weary grown;
And tenting how the matter went,
Cried, 'Come, come, Sir we're baith
    content.'—
'Ye fools,' quoth he, 'and justice too
Maun be content as well as you.'
Thus grumbled they, thus went he on,
Till baith the halves were near-hand done.
Poor pussies now the daffin saw
Of gaun for nignyes to the Law;
And bill'd the Judge, that he wad please
To give them the remaining cheese.
To which his worship grave reply'd,
'The dues of Court maun first be paid. –
Now Justice pleas'd, what's to the fore
Will but right scrimply clear your score;
That's our decreet: – gae hame and sleep,
And thank us ye're win aff sae cheap.'

Allan Ramsay

The Twa Cats and the Cheese

Introduction

Allan Ramsay enthusiastically pioneered a revival of interest in older Scottish poetry and song, and made lively use of Scots in his own writings. As a poet, one of the ways in which he demonstrated the versatility of the language was by rendering French animal fables into Scots.

Like the fox (see 'The Fox and the Salmon Fisher', p. 32), the monkey is presented in animal lore as a nimble trickster. As the cats cannot decide between themselves how to divide the cheese fairly, they go to a lawyer, where they find the monkey-clerk adopting the position of his employer. He cuts the cheese in half, but, unsurprisingly, the two parts are uneven, whereupon he eats a bit of the larger portion to make it match. He gradually eats all of the cheese while making the parts equal, and then charges the silly cats for the privilege. The moral of this tale is that you should be wary of the glib-tongued greed of lawyers.

SECOND/THIRD LEVEL
Related Texts:
John Barbour, 'The Fox and the Salmon Fisher' (p. 32)
Robert Henryson, 'The Wolf and the Lamb' (p. 98)

KEY WORDS:

Animals

Cats

Fables

Justice

Monkeys

Moral

Some key questions for class/group discussion

- Try to work out the meaning of words which have now dropped out of use completely, such as 'campsho', 'knoost' and 'nignyes', and then check how accurate your guess was using a Scots dictionary.

- Clarify the cause of the dispute between the cats.

- Why can they not solve the problem themselves?

- How does the monkey convince the cats to let him make the division of the cheese?

- Explain what happened to the cheese in the course of the monkey's 'trial'.

- What did the cats learn by going to law? What is the meaning of the final two lines?

Imaginative/creative writing

- Use the poem to construct and act out a playscript of the episode. You may need to add some dialogue for the cats as they see their cheese disappear.

- Write your own story where two people who cannot agree on something are tricked out of it by the person they go to for advice or arbitration.

Further development

The monkey is being asked to make what is sometimes called a 'Judgement of Solomon'. You will find the original story in the Bible, I Kings 3.16–28. Read the story and write your own version of it.

Alastair Reid

My Father, Dying

At summer's succulent end,
the house is green-stained.
I reach for my father's hand

and study his ancient nails.
Feeble-bodied, yet at intervals
a sweetness appears and prevails.

The heavy-scented night
seems to get at his throat.
It is as if the dark coughed.

In the other rooms of the house,
the furniture stands mumchance.
Age has engraved his face.

Cradling his wagged-out chin,
I shave him, feeling bone
stretching the waxed skin.

By his bed, the newspaper lies furled.
He has grown too old
to unfold the world,

which has dwindled to the size of a sheet.
His room has a stillness to it.
I do not call it waiting, but I wait,

anxious in the dark,
to see if the butterfly of his breath
has fluttered clear of death.

There is so much might be said,
dear old man, before I find you dead;
but we have become too separate

now in human time
to unravel all the interim
as your memory goes numb.

But there is no need for you to tell –
no words, no wise counsel,
no talk of dying well.

We have become mostly hands
and voices in your understanding.
The whole household is pending.

I am not ready
to be without your frail and wasted body,
your miscellaneous mind-way,

the faltering vein of your life.
Each evening I am loth
to leave you to your death.

Nor will I dwell on
the endless, cumulative question
I ask, being your son.

But on any one
of these nights soon,
for you, the dark will not crack with dawn,

and then I will begin
with you that hesitant conversation
going on and on and on.

Alastair Reid

My Father, Dying

Introduction

Alastair Reid was a Scottish poet who spent only approximately a third of his life in Scotland. For the rest of the time he lived in Spain, France, Switzerland, the United States and South America. 'My Father, Dying' is a quietly emotional poem about the imminent death of his father, written in a very loose *terza rima*, three-line stanzas with assonant rhyme. Reid paints a portrait of a man who has lived a long life, and whose aged body shows the weight of time, a man with whom he has perhaps lost touch over the years, as there is a feeling of conversations unspoken, questions unasked. Throughout the poem, there is a linking of the father with the natural world, sometimes in quite unexpected ways.

THIRD LEVEL
Related texts:

James Copeland, **'Black Friday'** (p. 56)
W. N. Herbert, 'The Land o' Cakes'
William McIlvanney, 'Grandmother'
Edwin Muir, **'The Late Wasp'** (p. 176)

KEY WORDS:

Death

Family

Night

Old age

Parents

Some key questions for class/group discussion

- Throughout the poem there are several references to evening, night and the dark. Find these references and suggest what they contribute to the poem as a whole.

- The poem is autobiographical, dealing with the death of the poet's father in late summer. What is gained, however, by referring directly to 'summer's succulent end'? What does mentioning the ending of summer and its 'succulent' nature add to what the poet seems to be feeling at this time?

- Reading the poem carefully, detect references in the text which indicate the relationship the poet feels with his father.

- Explain in your own words: 'We have become mostly hands/and voices in your understanding.'

- The poem ends on a rather mysterious reference to a 'hesitant conversation' that will continue after the old man's death. What do you think the poet means by this and what do you think the subject of that conversation might be?

Imaginative/creative writing

The poet here uses the time of day to add to the atmosphere and mood of the events described. In a story of your own describing an incident in your life, bring in recurring references to the time of day to emphasise the mood of the events you are writing about. You might like to think about dawn, morning, noon, afternoon, evening and night.

Further development

Find a copy of William McIlvanney's 'Grandmother', W. N. Herbert's 'The Land o' Cakes', or James Copeland's 'Black Friday', which also look at the passing of a family member. Each deals with the event in ways which are very different from that of Alastair Reid here. Compare how the poems differ.

Alan Riach

A short introduction to my Uncle Glen

Glen was always building sheds, He'd buy
wood. He had a thing about building sheds. He built
six stables in his garden, then realised
he'd have to buy the horses for them (and did). He built at least
three aviaries and more kennels than I can remember.
He filled the aviaries with parrots and canaries
from Australia, Pacific Islands. He always
had dogs: Alsatians, a Great Dane he would dance with
around the kitchen, before he was married. Now,
his kitchen cupboards are full of his kids' litters of Jack Russells.
He used to like Lonnie Donegan.
He used to play the guitar and yodel like Frank Ifield.
At every piece of news today you tell him
he looks amazed and shakes his head and says: 'My, my!'
A couple of years ago some of the family took a week's
holiday in Tenerife. Glen was walking on the beach
with my father, talking. Apart from the army,
when he'd been in England and learned to be a chef
(and cook these great sweet yellow curries)
he had never been out of Scotland much. He said
to my father, 'Jimmie,' (which is his name) 'you've sailed about
the world a few times.' (Which is true.)
'Tell me,' he said,
'Where exactly are we?'
Surely,
it's the best way to travel.

Alan Riach

A short introduction to my Uncle Glen

Introduction

The poem 'A short introduction to my Uncle Glen' is an affectionate portrait of a man whose life clearly revolves round family and animals, and who finds the rest of the world a source of wonder and delight. Although short, there is a wealth of information in the poem, from which it would be possible to construct a fairly full biography. Although Glen appears to be connected to exotic parts of the world through his birds and dogs, and the curries he learned to cook in the army, he clearly is rooted to his home turf, and has a very localised outlook.

THIRD LEVEL

Related Texts:

Christopher Rush, 'My Grandmother'

Jackie Kay, **'Grandpa's Soup'** (p. 112)

Liz Lochhead, **'For my Grandmother Knitting'** (p. 124)

Norman MacCaig, **'Aunt Julia'** (p. 132)

Alastair Reid, **'My Father, Dying'** (p. 194)

KEY WORDS:

Childhood

Family

Memory

Some key questions for class/group discussion

- When you hear of someone building a shed, what kind of structure do you picture? What kind of sheds did Glen build?

- What do you notice about the types of birds and dogs Glen put in his aviaries and kennels?

- In what way are his children's dogs different?

- What does Glen's reaction to the news suggest about the way he lives and thinks?

- The anecdote about the holiday in Tenerife tells you something more about Glen, and about the poet's father. Why do you think the poet puts in the two parentheses here? What do they add to the tone of the writing?

- How do you think it was possible for Glen not to know where he was on holiday?

- Comment on the effect of the final sentence of the poem.

Imaginative/creative writing

Choose a member of your own family, or someone you know well. Construct a description, which can be in prose or verse, where you begin by concentrating on one particular aspect of his/her personality, as in this poem, and add little anecdotes which illustrate the person best.

Further development

Find out what you can about Lonnie Donegan and Frank Ifield, which will help you to locate Glen in time.

Sir Walter Scott

Jock o' Hazeldean

Why weep ye by the tide, lady
Why weep ye by the tide?
I'll wed ye to my youngest son
And ye shall be his bride
And ye shall be his bride, lady
Sae comely to be seen
But aye she loot the tears doon fa'
For Jock o' Hazeldean.

Now let this wilfu' grief be done
And dry that cheek sae pale
Young Frank is chief of Errington
And laird o' Langley-dale
His step is first in peaceful ha'
His sword in battle keen
But aye she loot the tears doon fa'
For Jock o' Hazeldean.

A chain of gold ye shall not lack
Nor braid to bind your hair
Nor mettled hound, nor managed hawk
Nor palfrey fresh and fair.
And you, the foremost o' them a'
Shall ride our forest queen
But aye she loot the tears doon fa'
For Jock o' Hazeldean.

The kirk was deck'd at morningtide
The tapers glimmer'd fair
The priest and bridegroom wait the bride
And dame and knight were there
They sought her baith by bower and ha'
The lady was na' seen
She's o'er the Border and awa'
Wi' Jock o' Hazeldean.

Sir Walter Scott
Jock o' Hazeldean

Introduction

'Jock o' Hazeldean' might be studied alongside Sir Walter Scott's poem 'Lochinvar' (p. 200). It deals with exactly the same situation – a young English woman is obliged to marry a man she does not want and is madly in love with a young Scot, in this case Jock o' Hazeldean. Unlike 'Lochinvar', however, all the emphasis is on the unnamed damsel. We do not meet Jock at all! In the first six lines of the first three stanzas the father of Frank, the groom-to-be, addresses the lady, urging her to marry his son. Why her own parents are not involved we never learn. What is clear is that Frank, unlike the wimpish bridegroom in 'Lochinvar', is a fine accomplished young man; the lady simply prefers Jock. Frank's father promises her comfort and prestige if she marries his son, but on the morning of the wedding she does not appear in church; she has eloped with Jock. The dramatic ending of the poem is emphasised by the change in the last two lines of the last stanza from the earlier: 'But aye she loot the tears doon fa' / For Jock o' Hazeldean' to 'She's ower the Border and awa' / Wi' Jock o' Hazeldean'.

> **SECOND/THIRD LEVEL**
> **Related Texts:**
> Anon., 'The Demon Lover'
> Carolina Oliphant, Lady
> Nairne, **'The Laird o'**
> **Cockpen'** (p. 182)
> Sir Walter Scott, **'Lochinvar'**
> (p. 200)
>
> **KEY WORDS:**
>
> **Borders**
>
> **History**
>
> **Love**
>
> **Marriage**
>
> **Middle Ages**
>
> **Music**

Some questions for class/group discussion

- Who speaks the first six lines in the first three stanzas?

- From the last two lines of the first three stanzas what can we tell about the lady's affections?

- Describe the character of Frank, the bridegroom.

- What sort of gifts and advantages are promised to the lady if she marries Frank?

- Why do you think the bride's parents are not there to support her?

- Describe the preparations in the kirk for the wedding.

- Where is the bride at the end of the poem?

- How effective is the change of wording in the last two lines of stanza four from the last two lines of the other stanzas?

Imaginative/creative writing

Imagine that Jock and his bride have lived into old age. Write the story of their elopement and marriage as told by either Jock or his bride to their grandchildren.

Further development

In May 1782, the Earl of Westmoreland and Sarah Anne Child decided to elope to Gretna Green to marry against her father's wishes. Why did young couples from England go to Gretna Green to get married after the Marriage Act of 1753 in England? Find out about the history of Gretna Green as the place where eloping couples from England married and prepare a short presentation about the history of Gretna Green marriages.

Sir Walter Scott

Lochinvar

O, young Lochinvar is come out of the west,
Through all the wide Border his steed was the best;
And save his good broadsword, he weapons had
  none,
He rode all unarmed, and he rode all alone.
So faithful in love, and so dauntless in war,
There never was knight like the young Lochinvar.

He stayed not for brake, and he stopped not for
  stone,
He swam the Esk river where ford there was none;
But, ere he alighted at Netherby gate,
The bride had consented, the gallant came late:
For a laggard in love, and a dastard in war,
Was to wed the fair Ellen of brave Lochinvar.

So boldly he entered the Netherby Hall,
Among bride's-men, and kinsmen, and brothers,
  and all:
Then spoke the bride's father, his hand on his
  sword,
(For the poor craven bridegroom said never a
  word,)
'O come ye in peace here, or come ye in war,
Or to dance at our bridal, young Lord Lochinvar?'

'I long woo'd your daughter, my suit you denied;
Love swells like the Solway, but ebbs like its tide;
And now am I come, with this lost love of mine,
To lead but one measure, drink one cup of wine.
There are maidens in Scotland, more lovely by far,
That would gladly be bride to the young Lochinvar.'

The bride kissed the goblet: the knight took it up,
He quaffed off the wine, and he threw down the
  cup.
She looked down to blush, and she looked up to
  sigh,
With a smile on her lips and a tear in her eye.
He took her soft hand, ere her mother could bar, –
'Now tread we a measure!' said young Lochinvar.

So stately his form, and so lovely her face,
That never a hall such a galliard did grace;
While her mother did fret, and her father did fume,
And the bridegroom stood dangling his bonnet
  and plume:
And the bride-maidens whispered, "Twere better
  by far
To have matched our fair cousin with young
  Lochinvar.'

One touch to her hand, and one word in her ear,
When they reached the hall-door, and the charger
  stood near;
So light to the croup the fair lady he swung,
So light to the saddle before her he sprung!
'She is won! we are gone, over bank, bush, and
  scaur;
They'll have fleet steeds that follow,' quoth young
  Lochinvar.

There was mounting 'mong Graemes of the
  Netherby clan;
Forsters, Fenwicks, and Musgraves, they rode and
  they ran:
There was racing and chasing on Cannobie Lee,
But the lost bride of Netherby ne'er did they see.
So daring in love, and so dauntless in war,
Have ye e'er heard of gallant like young Lochinvar?

Sir Walter Scott

Lochinvar

Introduction

'Lochinvar' is a free-standing poem embedded (as 'Lady Heron's Song') in Canto V of Scott's long poem *Marmion*. Set in medieval times in the border country of Scotland and England, it is highly romantic and full of action. Lochinvar, a gallant young Scottish knight of the Gordon family in Dumfriesshire, is deeply in love with Ellen, a young English lady. She, however, is about to be married – against her wishes – to a man of whom her family approves in Netherby, Cumberland, on the English side of the Border. Lochinvar gallantly rides to Netherby, hoping to stop the wedding. But he is too late; Ellen has already been married to an insipid bridegroom. When challenged by the bride's father, Lochinvar dupes him and succeeds in dancing a galliard with Ellen. When they reach the door of the hall, they escape to his waiting charger. He lifts her onto the horse and they ride away to be happy together. The poem, which is a development of the ballad form, is written with a simple *aabbcc* rhyme scheme, and moves at a rollicking pace.

SECOND AND THIRD LEVEL Related Texts:

Anon., 'The Demon Lover'
Carolina Oliphant, Lady Nairne, **'The Laird o' Cockpen'** (p. 182)
Sir Walter Scott, **'Jock o' Hazeldean'** (p. 198)

KEY WORDS:

Art & Design

Ballads

Borders

History

Love

Marriage

Middle Ages

Some key questions for class/group discussion

- How would you describe the personality and character of Lochinvar?

- What sort of obstacles does he encounter on his journey?

- How would you describe the character of the bridegroom? Consider, for example, the lines: 'For a laggard in love and a dastard in war / Was to wed the fair Ellen of brave Lochinvar'.

- How does Lochinvar persuade Ellen's father that he is not going to cause trouble? Consider the lines: 'There are maidens in Scotland, more lovely by far / That would gladly be bride to young Lochinvar'.

- What does the poet mean when he says: 'Love swells like the Solway, but ebbs like its tide'?

- Explain how the lovers escape. What, according to the last stanza, will happen after that?

- Listen to the sound of the poem. What do you think makes it move so quickly?

Imaginative/creative writing

- In your group consider how you might story-board this poem.

- Write your own sequel to the poem (in verse or prose) using the information you are given in the last stanza.

Further development

Using the ballad form Sir Walter Scott uses in 'Lochinvar', write your own ballad about the deeds of a hero in historic times (e.g. Robin Hood or Maid Marian) or a modern comic-strip hero (e.g. Superman or Wonder Woman).

Sir Walter Scott

Proud Maisie

Proud Maisie is in the wood
Walking so early
Proud Robin sits on the bush
Singing so rarely.

'Tell me thou bonnie bird
When shall I marry me?'
'When six braw gentlemen
Kirkward shall carry ye.'

'Who makes the bridal bed,
Birdie, say truly?' –
'The grey-headed sexton
That delves the grave duly.

'The glow-worm o'er grave and stone
Shall light thee steady.
The owl from the steeple sing,
"Welcome, proud lady."'

Sir Walter Scott

Proud Maisie

Introduction

'Proud Maisie' is sung by the pathetic and unstable character Madge Wildfire in Chapter 40 of Sir Walter Scott's great novel *The Heart of Midlothian*. In some ways it reflects her own life. The poem takes the form of a dialogue between Maisie and a robin. Maisie is a very proud woman and expects the very best in life. She confidently asks the bird to tell her when she will be married. The bird replies: 'When six braw gentlemen / Kirkward shall carry ye.'

Maisie, of course, does not see the ambiguity of this answer and assumes 'carry' to be understood in its older sense of 'escort'. She then asks who will be her bridegroom. When she is told it will be the sexton (the gravedigger), it becomes clear that she will die a spinster and the only big occasion for her in a church will be her funeral. There will be no candles or wedding bells. There will only be the dim shining of the glow-worms in the churchyard where she will be buried and the screech of the owl in the bell tower at night. Pride indeed comes before a fall, but at the same time we have pity for Maisie.

> **THIRD LEVEL**
> **Related texts:**
> J. M. Caie, 'The Puddock' (p. 44)
> Robert Henryson, 'The Two Mice'
> Carolina Oliphant, Lady Nairne, 'The Laird o' Cockpen' (p. 182)
>
> **KEY WORDS:**
>
> Birds
>
> Death
>
> History
>
> Marriage
>
> Pride

Some key questions for class/group discussion

- Maisie is described in this poem as 'proud'. What do you understand by the expression 'pride comes before a fall'?

- When Maisie asks the robin to tell her when she will get married and the robin replies 'When six braw gentlemen / Kirkward shall carry ye', what do you think 'carry' means and what do you think Maisie understands by it? (When a word can be understood in two different ways we call this 'ambiguity'.)

- Find out what a sexton is.

- What is the robin really telling Maisie about her future?

- What is being described in the last stanza and how would you describe the atmosphere in it?

- Do you think Maisie's pride deserves what is forecast for her? Do you feel sorry for her?

- Why do you think the poet has Maisie talking to a robin?

Imaginative/creative writing

Write a story in which the main character's pride comes before a fall.

Further development

Sir Walter Scott included a number of self-contained stories and poems within his novels. Find 'Proud Maisie' in *The Heart of Midlothian*, and examine its context within the novel. Find another example, such as 'Lucy Ashton's Song' from *The Bride of Lammermoor*, and contextualise it also.

William Soutar

Ae Nicht at Amulree

When Little Dunnin' was a spree,
And no a name as noo,
Wull Todd wha wrocht at Amulree
Gaed hame byordinar fou.

The hairst had a' been gether'd in:
The nicht was snell but clear:
And owre the cantle o' the mune
God keekit here and there.

Whan God saw Wull he gien a lauch
And drappit lichtly doun;
Syne stude ahint a frostit sauch
Or Wull cam styterin on.

Straucht oot He breeng'd, and blared: 'Wull Todd!'
Blythe as Saint Johnstoun's bell:
'My God!' gowp'd Wull: 'Ye'r richt,' says God:
I'm gled to meet yersel.'

William Soutar

Ae Nicht at Amulree

Introduction

William Soutar lived in Perth. For the last thirteen years of his life he was very ill and confined to his bed. His finest work was written in Scots, much of it for children. 'Ae Nicht at Amulree' is very amusing. It describes a sharp, cold, clear night in Highland Perthshire near the village of Amulree. One of the locals, Wull Todd, is making his unsteady way home, well under the influence of drink. God, looking down from behind the moon, spots him and decides to have some fun at his expense. He drops down to earth and hides behind a willow tree as Wull comes staggering along. Then he leaps out and greets Wull, shouting out his name. In fear Wull blurts out the mild oath 'My God!' – which God, good humouredly, takes literally and, no doubt shaking Wull's hand, exclaims that he is very glad to meet Wull too! The quandary, of course remains: did Wull meet God or was it only the drink talking? The poem gets much of its effect from the deftly handled colloquial Scots in which it is written, including particularly telling onomatopoetic words like 'snell', 'styterin' and 'breeng'd'.

SECOND LEVEL
Related Texts:
Robert Burns, 'Tam o' Shanter'

KEY WORDS:

Alcohol

God

Humour

Religion

Supernatural

Some key questions for class/group discussion

- Don't be afraid of the Scots words in this poem. Say them out loud and you will get most of their meanings. If you still can't work them out, the online Dictionary of the Scots Language can help you.

- In what sort of state is Wull when he is coming home this evening?

- What time of year is it? What is the weather like? Consider the words 'hairst' and 'snell'.

- Who spots Wull and laughs at him?

- What is Wull's reaction when this 'person' leaps out at him?

- Explain the joke in the last two lines.

Imaginative/creative writing

- Write a short story in which the main character has a 'supernatural' experience on his/her way home late one night.

- This poem can be dramatised very simply and effectively by pupils working in pairs. The performance should last only a few minutes.

Further development

Find some other poems written for children by William Soutar. Choose one which you like and in one paragraph write down what it is about and in the second paragraph why you like it.

The Scottish Poetry Library has a selection of William Soutar's poems online.

Alan Spence

Haiku

dark already –
the icy rain
incessant

bright winter morning –
how simple it all seems,
how clear

so cold –
tying my shoelaces
with gloved hands

december dusk –
the dog's harsh bark
deepens the cold

overnight snow
crystalized into
ice flowers

in the snow
the fox and I, startled
by each other

that winter smell –
old towel drying
on the radiator

it fades, it fades,
the last light
of the year

Alan Spence

Haiku

Introduction

Originally a Japanese poetic form, haiku poems had seventeen 'on', or sounds (interpreted in English as syllables), divided into three phrases in the order of five sounds, seven sounds and five sounds. Generally they did not rhyme and were written in one straight line with juxtaposed ideas separated by a 'cutting word'. They expressed the poet's intense sensory experience of an aspect of the natural world: the seasons, for example. Modern haiku, however, focus on different aspects of life, both human and natural. Poets writing in English write haiku poems in three separate lines. They often do not adhere strictly to the five–seven–five rule.

These eight haiku poems by Alan Spence focus on different aspects of winter in a series of sensory images. The individual poems distil, without directly expressing his feelings, his perceptions and experiences of winter: the bleak mood created by the phrase 'the icy rain / incessant'; the intensity of the cold expressed by the homely image of the poet tying his shoe laces 'with gloved hands'; the fragile beauty of the snow 'crystalized into ice flowers'; the sour smell of the 'old towel drying/on the radiator' and the melancholy music of the repeated 'it fades, it fades', the last light of the dying year.

THIRD LEVEL
Related Texts

Sheena Blackhall, 'Spring'
Edwin Morgan, 'Summer Haiku'
Alan Spence, 'Spring – Warming my feet'
Billy Watt, 'One pink sock, one blue'
Roseanne Watt, 'Haiku'

KEY WORDS:

Animals

Birds

Dogs

Foxes

Haiku

Nature

Seasons

Some key questions for class/group discussion

- In the first poem, what three facts does the poet state about a specific winter's day? Discuss his use of the dash after 'dark already' and the word 'incessant'. What might they convey of his feelings?

- In the fourth poem, which literary techniques does the poet use to evoke his experience of a December afternoon?

- What aspect of winter does the fifth poem evoke?

- In the seventh poem, what do you think is the purpose of the dash at the end of the first line?

- In the eighth poem, the poet describes the last day of the year. What mood or emotion does the poem evoke? What literary techniques does the poet use to heighten this experience?

Imaginative/creative writing

- Write two or three haiku poems of your own. Your teacher will give you the rules. Traditional Japanese haiku poems created striking images and often caught fleeting moments in the life of nature and the animal world. Your poems, however, can be on any topic which interests you.

- Write your own seasonal haiku poems. Try to avoid naming the season. Let the images you create 'speak'.

Further development

Find out more about haiku poems and their history, particularly the poems of Bashō, the great seventeenth-century Japanese poet.

Robert Louis Stevenson

Heather Ale – A Galloway Legend

From the bonny bells of heather
They brewed a drink long-syne,
Was sweeter far than honey,
Was stronger far than wine.
They brewed it and they drank it,
And lay in a blessed swound
For days and days together
In their dwellings underground.

There rose a king in Scotland,
A fell man to his foes,
He smote the Picts in battle,
He hunted them like roes.
Over miles of the red mountain
He hunted as they fled.
And strewed the dwarfish bodies
Of the dying and the dead.

Summer came in the country,
Red was the heather bell;
But the manner of the brewing
Was none alive to tell.
In graves that were like children's
On many a mountain head,
The Brewsters of the Heather
Lay numbered with the dead.

The king in the red moorland
Rode on a summer's day;
And the bees hummed, and the curlews
Cried beside the way.
The king rode, and was angry,
Black was his brow and pale,
To rule in a land of heather
And lack the Heather Ale.

It fortuned that his vassals,
Riding free on the heath,
Came on a stone that was fallen
And vermin hid beneath.
Rudely plucked from their hiding,
Never a word they spoke;
A son and his aged father –
Last of the dwarfish folk.

The king sat high on his charger,
He looked on the little men;
And the dwarfish and swarthy couple
Looked at the king again.
Down by the shore he had them;

And there on the giddy brink –
'I will give you life, ye vermin,
For the secret of the drink.'

There stood the son and father
And they looked high and low;
The heather was red around then,
The sea rumbled below.
And up and spoke the father,
Shrill was his voice to hear;
'I have a word in private,
A word for the royal ear.

'Life is dear to the aged,
And honour a little thing;
I would gladly sell the secret,'
Quoth the Pict to the King.
His voice was small as a sparrow's
And shrill and wonderful clear;
'I would gladly sell my secret,
Only my son I fear.

'For life is a little matter,
And death is nought to the young;
And I dare not sell my honour
Under the eye of my son.
Take him, O king, and bind him,
And cast him far in the deep;
And it's I will tell the secret
That I have sworn to keep.'

They took the son and bound him,
Neck and heels in a thong.
And a lad took him and swung him,
And flung him far and strong.
And the sea swallowed his body,
Like that of a child of ten; –
And there on the cliff stood the father,
Last of the dwarfish men.

'True was the word I told you:
Only my son I feared;
For I doubt the sapling courage
That goes without the beard.
But now in vain is the torture,
Fire shall never avail;
Here dies in my bosom
The secret of Heather Ale.'

Robert Louis Stevenson

Heather Ale – A Galloway Legend

Introduction

As is often the case with people who are far from home, in this instance in the Pacific island of Samoa, Robert Louis Stevenson's thoughts returned to his native Scotland, and he produced this ballad based on a legend from the south-west of Scotland. The tribe in the legend is said to be the Picts, but contrary to the traditional description of a well-built warrior race, here they are described as stunted and dwarfish, easily defeated by the Scottish king. However, with the Picts has gone the recipe for the delicious heather ale, until the current king finds the last two members of the tribe who hold the secret. The king hopes to bargain with them for the recipe, offering their lives in exchange, but by cunning trickery, the elder Pict sacrifices his son, and then shows his own courage by refusing to give the recipe.

SECOND/THIRD LEVEL
Related texts:
Robert Louis Stevenson, **'The Spaewife'** (p. 212)
Robert Louis Stevenson, **'Windy Nights'** (p. 214)

KEY WORDS:

Alcohol

Conquest

Family

History

Picts

Pride

South-west Scotland

Some key questions for class/group discussion

- What, according to the poem's first verse, did this race do once they had brewed the heather ale?

- What adjective would you use to describe the king who appears in the second verse?

- In verse two, what do we learn about the physical size of this race?

- Despite his victory in battle, this king seems very discontented. What appears to be upsetting him?

- How were the last two representatives of this 'dwarfish' race related?

- What deal did the king attempt to strike with these two men?

- What, according to the older man, do old people value and what do they not value so much?

- What exactly does the old man propose to the king?

- What does the old man say is the only thing stopping him doing a deal with the king?

- How does the old man propose getting around this problem? Does the king accept this solution?

- What is the old man's explanation for his proposal?

Imaginative/creative writing

Returning home, the king encounters his daughter who, in her nature, takes after her gentle mother rather than her father. He tells her the tale of the two Picts. Write a scene between father and daughter in which the incident is described by the king and commented on by his daughter.

Further development

- Find out as much as you can about the Picts. Were they a particularly small race? Why were they called Picts, and who gave them that name?

- Research recipes for heather ale.

Robert Louis Stevenson
The Spaewife

Oh, I wad like to ken – to the beggar-wife says I –
Why chops are guid to brander and nane sae guid to fry.
An' siller, that's sae braw to keep, is brawer still to gi'e.
It's *gey an' easy spierin'*, says the beggar-wife to me.

Oh, I wad like to ken – to the beggar-wife says I –
Hoo a' things come to be whaur we find them when we try,
The lasses in their claes an' the fishes in the sea.
It's *gey an' easy spierin'*, says the beggar-wife to me.

Oh, I wad like to ken – to the beggar-wife says I –
Why lads are a' to sell an' lasses a' to buy;
An' naebody for dacency but barely twa or three.
It's *gey an' easy spierin'*, says the beggar-wife to me.

Oh, I wad like to ken – to the beggar-wife says I –
Gin death's as shure to men as killin' is to kye,
Why God has filled the yearth sae fu' o' tasty things to pree.
It's *gey an' easy spierin'*, says the beggar-wife to me.

Oh, I wad like to ken – to the beggar-wife says I –
The reason o' the cause an' the wherefore o' the why,
Wi' mony anither riddle brings the tear into my e'e.
It's *gey an' easy spierin'*, says the beggar-wife to me.

Robert Louis Stevenson

The Spaewife

Introduction

Although one of our greatest writers of fiction, and also well known for *A Child's Garden of Verses*, Robert Louis Stevenson was also a fine poet in Scots as well as English.

The figure of the spaewife may not be familiar to children today, but that of the fortune teller with her crystal ball certainly is, while they will also be very familiar with horoscopes. However, note that Stevenson does not call the woman a spaewife in the poem, but a beggar-wife. The questions he asks are varied, from the banal: the best way to cook chops; through the personal: the matter of relationships; to the philosophical: why things are the way they are in the world. Some of these questions we may have asked ourselves, but none of them gets any answers, just a reiterated refrain that asking is easy.

> **SECOND/THIRD LEVEL**
> **Related texts:**
> Robert Louis Stevenson,
> 'From a Railway Carriage'
> Robert Louis Stevenson,
> **'Heather Ale'** (p. 210)
> Robert Louis Stevenson,
> **'Windy Nights'** (p. 214)
>
> **KEY WORDS:**
>
> History
>
> Questions
>
> Riddles
>
> Scots language
>
> Supernatural

Some key questions for class/group discussion

- Describe the structure of the poem using the conventional poetic terms. Why do you think it has been written in this way?

- A spaewife is a woman believed to have special powers to foretell the future, but the speaker is addressing a 'beggar-wife'. Do you think he expects answers?

- The Scots in this poem is not particularly dense, but there are some words that might cause difficulty. Using a Scots dictionary, make your own glossary of unknown words.

- The questions become more metaphysical as the poem progresses. Take the fourth stanza and explain in detail what the poet is asking.

- What do you think are the full implications of '*it's gey an' easy spierin*' in the context of the poem, and why do you think the expression is printed in italics?

Imaginative/creative writing

- Think of the questions you would like have answers to, and who you think would be able to answer them, then either write your own poem based on this one, or write a question-and-answer dialogue.

- The class could try reading the poem over in groups and take it in turns to read it back to others trying to capture the voices of the spierer and the spaewife. Each group could take it in turns to explain what they think each question or riddle means and then try to come up with their own answers to the questions, serious or funny.

Further development

Find out everything you can about spaewives, the powers they were believed to have, and how they were regarded by people.

Robert Louis Stevenson

Windy Nights

Whenever the moon and stars are set,
Whenever the wind is high,
All night long in the dark and wet,
A man goes riding by.
Late in the night when the fires are out,
Why does he gallop and gallop about?

Whenever the trees are crying aloud,
And ships are tossed at sea,
By, on the highway, low and loud,
By at the gallop goes he.
By at the gallop he goes, and then
By he comes back at the gallop again.

Robert Louis Stevenson
Windy Nights

Introduction
Robert Louis Stevenson's imagination had a fearful side, with darkness holding its own special fears. This we can perhaps see at work here.

Some readers may see the horseman of the poem simply as a rider; others may see him as being the young Stevenson's imaginative way of coping with the frightening noise made by a thunderstorm. The coming and going of the rider could perhaps be the coming and going of the rumbles of thunder as they first advance and then retreat.

SECOND/THIRD LEVEL
Related Texts:
Walter de la Mare, 'The Listeners'
Robert Louis Stevenson, 'From a Railway Carriage'

KEY WORDS:
Drama
Environment
Music
Mystery
Nature
Weather

Some key questions for class/group discussion
- This poem has been very successfully set to music and there are various performances on the internet which you might enjoy listening to once you have read and thought about the poem for yourself.
- What is the weather like when the poet hears the rider?
- Tap out the rhythm of the first two lines of the poem on your desk. Why do you think Stevenson chose this particular rhythm?
- The atmosphere of this poem describes sounds and events that might be frightening to a small child. Write down the words that make the poem noisy and/or scary.
- Do you think the horseman is a real man on a horse or is he young Stevenson's way of making the thunder sound less frightening?

Imaginative/creative writing
- Imagine this is truly a horseman, and not the poet's way of describing how a thunderstorm might be imagined by a small child. What is it that drives him to be riding about on such a wild night? Is he looking for someone or something? Is he trying to get away from someone or something?
- Write the story of the horseman and his situation, trying to bring in as much description of the night and weather as Stevenson does.
- This poem's effect comes from the sounds the poet creates. Write your own sound poem about a stormy journey by land or sea.

Further development
Listen to a recording of Modest Mussorgsky's 'A Night on the Bare Mountain' (also known as 'A Night on Bald Mountain'), which was originally composed as a 'musical picture' on the theme of a witches' sabbath. See if you can hear in the music the images the composer is picturing.

Ruaraidh MacThòmais / Derick Thomson

Clann Nighean An Sgadain / The Herring Girls

An gàire mar chraiteachan salainn
ga fhroiseadh bho 'm beul,
an sàl 's am picil air an teanga,
's na miaran cruinne, goirid a dheanadh giullachd,
no a thogadh leanabh gu socair, cuimir,
seasgair, fallain,
gun mhearachd,
's na sùilean cho domhainn ri fèath.

B' e bun-os-cionn na h-eachdraidh a dh'fhàg iad
'nan tràillean aig ciùrairean cutach,
thall 's a-bhos air Galldachd 's an Sasainn.
Bu shaillte an duais a thàrr iad
às na mìltean bharaillean ud,
gaoth na mara geur air an craiceann,
is eallach a' bhochdainn 'nan ciste,
is mara b' e an gàire
shaoileadh tu gu robh an teud briste.

Ach bha craiteachan uaille air an cridhe,
ga chumail fallain,
is bheireadh cutag an teanga
slisinn à fanaid nan Gall –
agus bha obair rompa fhathast
nuair gheibheadh iad dhachaigh,
ged nach biodh maoin ac':
air oidhche robach gheamhraidh,
ma bha siud an dàn dhaibh,
dheanadh iad daoine.

Their laughter like a sprinkling of salt
showered from their lips,
brine and pickle on their tongues,
and the stubby short fingers that could handle
    fish,
or lift a child gently, neatly
safely, wholesomely
unerringly,
and the eyes that were as deep as a calm.

The topsy-turvy of history had made them
slaves to short-arsed curers,
here and there in the Lowlands, in England.
Salt the reward they won
from those thousands of barrels,
the sea-wind sharp on their skins,
and the burden of poverty in their kists,
and were it not for their laughter
you might think the harp-string was broken.

But there was a sprinkling of pride on their
    hearts,
keeping them sound,
and their tongues' gutting knife
would tear a strip from the Lowlanders' mockery –
and there was work awaiting them
when they got home, though they had no wealth:
on a wild winter's night,
if that were their lot, they would make men.

Ruaraidh MacThòmais / Derick Thomson

Clann Nighean An Sgadain / The Herring Girls

Introduction

This modern Gaelic praise poem, written in free verse, powerfully combines the personal and the political. It describes the girls of Lewis who used to travel to fishing ports on mainland Scotland and England to gut herring. In the first stanza the poet uses sea imagery to describe the girls' ready laughter, their forthright speech and their skill in gutting herring. They were hard-working women with attitude, but they were unfailingly gentle and protective towards their children and possessed an inner strength and wisdom. The poet respects and admires them. He uses forceful language in stanza two to express his anger at the 'short-arsed curers' who employed and exploited them. He refers with bitter irony to their only 'reward': harsh working conditions and poverty. Such hardships could have broken their spirit but in their shared laughter they demonstrated that they had the strength and resilience to survive. In the final stanza the poet develops the theme of survival. He admires their pride and, with their sharp tongues, their ability to destroy the mockery of the Lowlanders. He concludes the poem by implying that, as wives and mothers, despite the hardship and poverty, they created not just any men, but strong hardy men with the qualities they themselves possessed.

THIRD LEVEL
Related Texts:
> Iain Crichton Smith, 'Do Mo Mhathair / To My Mother'
> Ewan MacColl, 'Come A Ye Fisher Lassies'
> Carolina Oliphant, Lady Nairne, 'Caller Herring'

KEY WORDS:

Fishing

Gaelic

History

Music

The sea

Work

Some key questions for class/group discussion

- Which aspects of the girls' characters does the poet describe in stanza one? Comment on the images he uses.

- What feelings does he express in stanza two about their working lives? Comment on the effectiveness of some of the expressions he uses.

- In stanza three he develops the theme of their survival in a harsh world. What qualities does he refer to which enable them to survive?

- Why do you think he concludes the poem with the lines 'on a wild winter's night / if that were their lot / they would make men'?

Imaginative/creative writing

Write a short story entitled either 'Looking for Work' or 'A Part-time Job'.

Further development

Research some of the history of the fishing industry in the early years of the twentieth century. Then imagine you were a herring girl or fisherman who had to leave home to find work. Write a letter home telling your family about your experiences.

Ruaraidh MacThòmais / Derick Thomson

Na Lochlannaich A' Tighinn Air Tìr An Nis / The Norsemen coming ashore at Ness

Nuair thainig a' bhirlinn gu tìr	When the galley touched the shore,
nuair a tharraing iad i	when they hauled her up
air gainmheach a' Phuirt,	on the sand at Port,
ged a bha am muir gorm,	though the sea was blue, and the sand white,
's a' ghainmheach geal,	though the flowers grew
ged a bha na sìtheanan a' fàs	on both banks of the burn, and green grass
air dà thaobh an uillt,	in the ditches,
is feur gorm as na claisean,	though the sun shone
ged a bha ghrian a' deàrrsadh	on the buckles of their shields,
air bucaill nan sgiath,	on their helmets,
air na clogadan,	and there was a grey-green haze of barley on
is àile liathghorm an eòrna air na	the fields
h-iomairean,	though that was how things were,
ged a bha sin mar sin	and the roar of the waves was behind them,
is sian nan tonn air an cùlaibh,	the solan plunging out of space,
an t-sùlaire a' tuiteam à fànas,	and foam on the warm milk of the sea,
is cop air bainne blàth na mara,	they were afraid.
bha eagal orra.	
	But they went up into the land,
Ach chaidh iad a-steach dhan an tìr,	and got houses,
is fhuair iad taighean	and women,
is boireannaich,	and families,
is teaghlaichean,	and they cut the barley,
is bhuain iad an t-eòrna,	and sowed the barley,
is chuir iad an t-eòrna,	took birds from the rock ledges,
fhuair iad eun as a' phalla,	and fish from the sea,
is iasg à fairge,	gave names to rocks and children,
thug iad ainmean air creagan 's air cloinn,	and filled the barns,
is lìon iad na saibhlean,	and their homesickness went away.
agus dh'fhalbh an cianalas.	

Ruaraidh MacThòmais / Derick Thomson

Na Lochlannaich A' Tighinn Air Tìr An Nis / The Norsemen coming ashore at Ness

Introduction

Rather than the stereotypical perception of the Vikings as bloodthirsty warriors who plundered and ravaged the communities and lands they reached, Derick Thomson presents a different image. He portrays the Norsemen as men who were afraid of what they might find when they landed on an island strange to them. Nevertheless, despite their fears and their homesickness, they become permanent settlers, building houses, marrying and founding families. The poet creates a positive picture of warriors becoming farmers, adapting to the way of life of the islanders on Lewis. Their influence can still be found in island place-names and people's names. The first stanza is structured as a series of images which describe the beauty and fertility of the island. It comes to a climax in a perhaps unexpected final line, 'they were afraid'. The second stanza has a similar structure, but emphasises their transformation from fierce Norse sea-raiders to peaceful, productive farmers. It culminates in the final affirmative statement, 'and their homesickness went away'. They have become an integral part of the island community and feel they belong there. The poem celebrates the Lewis islanders' Norse heritage.

> **THIRD LEVEL**
> **Related Texts:**
>   Christine De Luca, 'Viking Landfall'
>   Calum MacDhomhnaill / Calum MacDonald, **'Cearcall A' Chuain' / 'Circle of Ocean'** (p. 140)
>
> **KEY WORDS:**
>
> Gaelic
> Geography
> Hebrides
> History
> Islands
> Lewis
> Place-names
> Vikings

Some key questions for class/group discussion

- What kind of land do the Norsemen find when they reach the shores of the island of Lewis?

- Which line suggests that they were relieved to have arrived at the island?

- What other feelings did they have? Is this surprising?

- How does the structure of the first stanza help to emphasise the poet's portrayal of the Norsemen?

- What does the second stanza tell us about the Norsemen?

- How does the structure of the second stanza help to emphasise the poet's positive portrayal of the Norsemen?

Imaginative/creative writing

Imagine that one of the Norsemen who has settled on the island is now a grandfather. One of his grandchildren is curious to know the story of his life. Write the conversation/dialogue he might have had with the boy or girl.

Further development

Study a detailed map of the island of Lewis. Research the origins of the following place-names and choose some of your own to explore: Ness, Skigersta, Swainbost, Garbh Sgeir, North Tolsta, Barvas, Stornoway, Laxdale, Achmore, Beinn Mholach, Ceann Hulavig, Callanish, Carloway, Kirrival.

Valerie Thornton

Prospecting in Pa▲

It wasn't the dipping flight
of some departing finch,
nor an indeterminable trill
from a wee silhouette on a treetop,
nor a flash of olive and acid yellow
that might have been a greenfinch:

It was right here in White Street
on the pavement at St Peter's
exotic with its scarlet mask,
white cheeks and black cap.
Its eyes were shut, its head slack,
the black, white and gold wings folded.

I laid it in state under the fence
at number 48 and paid my respects
over the weeks as the mites
that burrow and chew spirited it away
leaving, as relics of treasure in Partick,
a tiny gold pinion or two.

Ruaraidh MacThòmais / Derick Thomson

Clann Nighean An Sgadain / The Herring Girls

Introduction

This modern Gaelic praise poem, written in free verse, powerfully combines the personal and the political. It describes the girls of Lewis who used to travel to fishing ports on mainland Scotland and England to gut herring. In the first stanza the poet uses sea imagery to describe the girls' ready laughter, their forthright speech and their skill in gutting herring. They were hard-working women with attitude, but they were unfailingly gentle and protective towards their children and possessed an inner strength and wisdom. The poet respects and admires them. He uses forceful language in stanza two to express his anger at the 'short-arsed curers' who employed and exploited them. He refers with bitter irony to their only 'reward': harsh working conditions and poverty. Such hardships could have broken their spirit but in their shared laughter they demonstrated that they had the strength and resilience to survive. In the final stanza the poet develops the theme of survival. He admires their pride and, with their sharp tongues, their ability to destroy the mockery of the Lowlanders. He concludes the poem by implying that, as wives and mothers, despite the hardship and poverty, they created not just any men, but strong hardy men with the qualities they themselves possessed.

THIRD LEVEL
Related Texts:
Iain Crichton Smith, 'Do Mo Mhathair / To My Mother'
Ewan MacColl, 'Come A Ye Fisher Lassies'
Carolina Oliphant, Lady Nairne, 'Caller Herring'

KEY WORDS:

Fishing

Gaelic

History

Music

The sea

Work

Some key questions for class/group discussion

- Which aspects of the girls' characters does the poet describe in stanza one? Comment on the images he uses.

- What feelings does he express in stanza two about their working lives? Comment on the effectiveness of some of the expressions he uses.

- In stanza three he develops the theme of their survival in a harsh world. What qualities does he refer to which enable them to survive?

- Why do you think he concludes the poem with the lines 'on a wild winter's night / if that were their lot / they would make men'?

Imaginative/creative writing

Write a short story entitled either 'Looking for Work' or 'A Part-time Job'.

Further development

Research some of the history of the fishing industry in the early years of the twentieth century. Then imagine you were a herring girl or fisherman who had to leave home to find work. Write a letter home telling your family about your experiences.

Ruaraidh MacThòmais / Derick Thomson

Na Lochlannaich A' Tighinn Air Tìr An Nis / The Norsemen coming ashore at Ness

Nuair thainig a' bhirlinn gu tìr
nuair a tharraing iad i
air gainmheach a' Phuirt,
ged a bha am muir gorm,
's a' ghainmheach geal,
ged a bha na sìtheanan a' fàs
air dà thaobh an uillt,
is feur gorm as na claisean,
ged a bha ghrian a' deàrrsadh
air bucaill nan sgiath,
air na clogadan,
is àile liathghorm an eòrna air na
        h-iomairean,
ged a bha sin mar sin
is sian nan tonn air an cùlaibh,
an t-sùlaire a' tuiteam à fànas,
is cop air bainne blàth na mara,
bha eagal orra.

Ach chaidh iad a-steach dhan an tìr,
is fhuair iad taighean
is boireannaich,
is teaghlaichean,
is bhuain iad an t-eòrna,
is chuir iad an t-eòrna,
fhuair iad eun as a' phalla,
is iasg à fairge,
thug iad ainmean air creagan 's air cloinn,
is lìon iad na saibhlean,
agus dh'fhalbh an cianalas.

When the galley touched the shore,
when they hauled her up
on the sand at Port,
though the sea was blue, and the sand white,
though the flowers grew
on both banks of the burn, and green grass
        in the ditches,
though the sun shone
on the buckles of their shields,
on their helmets,
and there was a grey-green haze of barley on
        the fields
though that was how things were,
and the roar of the waves was behind them,
the solan plunging out of space,
and foam on the warm milk of the sea,
they were afraid.

But they went up into the land,
and got houses,
and women,
and families,
and they cut the barley,
and sowed the barley,
took birds from the rock ledges,
and fish from the sea,
gave names to rocks and children,
and filled the barns,
and their homesickness went away.

Ruaraidh MacThòmais / Derick Thomson

Na Lochlannaich A' Tighinn Air Tìr An Nis / The Norsemen coming ashore at Ness

Introduction

Rather than the stereotypical perception of the Vikings as bloodthirsty warriors who plundered and ravaged the communities and lands they reached, Derick Thomson presents a different image. He portrays the Norsemen as men who were afraid of what they might find when they landed on an island strange to them. Nevertheless, despite their fears and their homesickness, they become permanent settlers, building houses, marrying and founding families. The poet creates a positive picture of warriors becoming farmers, adapting to the way of life of the islanders on Lewis. Their influence can still be found in island place-names and people's names. The first stanza is structured as a series of images which describe the beauty and fertility of the island. It comes to a climax in a perhaps unexpected final line, 'they were afraid'. The second stanza has a similar structure, but emphasises their transformation from fierce Norse sea-raiders to peaceful, productive farmers. It culminates in the final affirmative statement, 'and their homesickness went away'. They have become an integral part of the island community and feel they belong there. The poem celebrates the Lewis islanders' Norse heritage.

THIRD LEVEL
Related Texts:
Christine De Luca, 'Viking Landfall'
Calum MacDhomhnaill / Calum MacDonald, **'Cearcall A' Chuain'** / **'Circle of Ocean'** (p. 140)

KEY WORDS:

Gaelic

Geography

Hebrides

History

Islands

Lewis

Place-names

Vikings

Some key questions for class/group discussion

- What kind of land do the Norsemen find when they reach the shores of the island of Lewis?

- Which line suggests that they were relieved to have arrived at the island?

- What other feelings did they have? Is this surprising?

- How does the structure of the first stanza help to emphasise the poet's portrayal of the Norsemen?

- What does the second stanza tell us about the Norsemen?

- How does the structure of the second stanza help to emphasise the poet's positive portrayal of the Norsemen?

Imaginative/creative writing

Imagine that one of the Norsemen who has settled on the island is now a grandfather. One of his grandchildren is curious to know the story of his life. Write the conversation/dialogue he might have had with the boy or girl.

Further development

Study a detailed map of the island of Lewis. Research the origins of the following place-names and choose some of your own to explore: Ness, Skigersta, Swainbost, Garbh Sgeir, North Tolsta, Barvas, Stornoway, Laxdale, Achmore, Beinn Mholach, Ceann Hulavig, Callanish, Carloway, Kirrival.

Valerie Thornton

Prospecting in Partick

It wasn't the dipping flight
of some departing finch,
nor an indeterminable trill
from a wee silhouette on a treetop,
nor a flash of olive and acid yellow
that might have been a greenfinch:

It was right here in White Street
on the pavement at St Peter's
exotic with its scarlet mask,
white cheeks and black cap.
Its eyes were shut, its head slack,
the black, white and gold wings folded.

I laid it in state under the fence
at number 48 and paid my respects
over the weeks as the mites
that burrow and chew spirited it away
leaving, as relics of treasure in Partick,
a tiny gold pinion or two.

Valerie Thornton

Prospecting in Partick

Introduction

The first stanza of the poem evocatively describes the movements, colour and sound of various birds, but in the second stanza the poet's focus shifts to a bird lying dead on the pavement, describing the bright plumage of a goldfinch – a relatively uncommon bird to see in the city. The poet buries the bird 'in state' in a precise location, 'at number 48' in White Street. Her words 'I laid it in state' and 'paid my respects' are gently ironic, perhaps suggesting a degree of surprise that she had attached such importance to the death of the bird and an acknowledgement that it had affected her emotionally. By associating her discovery of the bird with prospectors finding precious metals or archaeologists discovering the bones of holy men or women, the poet shows both respect and compassion for the bird.

THIRD LEVEL
Related texts:
J. K. Annand, 'Heron'
Brian McCabe, **'Seagull'** (p. 130)
George Mackay Brown, **'Hawk'** (p. 154)
Flora Wilson, 'Owl'

KEY WORDS:

Birds

Death

Glasgow

Nature

Science

Some key questions for class/group discussion

- From what the poet has to say in the first stanza and the first line of the second stanza, what is it that seems to surprise her most about having her attention caught by this bird?

- Although the bird is dead, how does the poet seem to bring it 'alive' for us in stanza two?

- The poet says that she 'laid it in state'. Why does she use this expression in connection with a humble bird?

- How does she continue the idea of showing regard for the bird in the last stanza?

- 'a tiny gold pinion or two'. In what way does this expression link to the title of the poem?

Imaginative/creative writing

Write about a time when you were surprised by finding something unexpected in a familiar place. Write about the feelings it aroused in you as well as writing about the event itself.

Further development

Research the facts about a bird common to the British Isles, then create a poem which conveys its essential character in a precise and vivid way.

Margaret Tollick

Mairi's Sang

They were awfy braw an awfy grand
Three strangers frae afar
Speirin at ma faither
Fir a baby an a star.

Faither couldna unnerstaun
I kent fine by his face.
'I canna think that royalty
Wid bide in sic a place.

'Folk cryin oot fir wine an breid,
Folk dossin on the flair?
I canna stop tae listen!'
Then he showed them ower the door.

I wis runnin fir ma mither
Fetchin blankets, servin wine,
When o a sudden sic a thocht
Cam bleezin tae ma mind!

Fir I minded o the lassie
An her man, in oor oot-bye
An the bairnie in the barrie-coat
That times deeved us wi his cry.

Ma mither thocht I'd gone clean daft
When I drappit a, an ran
Tae try and find thae strangers
'Fore they moved their caravan.

They must hae thocht me daft an a
As they stood about their fire –
A wee lassie, rinnin, screechin
'It's thon laddie in oor byre!'

Margaret Tollick

Mairi's Sang

Introduction

'Mairi's Sang' by Margaret Tollick is a very Scottish version of the Adoration of the Magi told by the young girl narrator, Mairi. 'Three strangers frae afar' come to an inn looking for 'a baby an a star'. The girl explains that her father cannot understand why royalty should seek accommodation in his poor crowded establishment and shows them out. Suddenly Mairi, who is busy attending to the needs of customers, realises that the family the strangers are looking for have been accommodated in an outhouse at the back of the inn. She runs after them terrified that their caravan may have moved on, screeching that the laddie that they are looking for is in their byre! The story is beautifully and simply told. It has strong rhyme and rhythm and is all the more immediate for a Scottish audience because of its well-judged simple Scots vocabulary.

**SECOND/THIRD LEVEL
Related Texts:**

Alexander Gray, 'There Cam Thrie Kings'
Tom Leonard, **'The Good Thief'** (p. 122)
Edwin Morgan, 'Trio'
Josephine Neill, 'A Christmas Poem'

KEY WORDS:

Christmas

Drama

Religion

Scots language

Some key questions for class/group discussion.

- Who is telling the story?

- Who do you think the strangers are?

- Why does the father find it strange that the strangers want to visit his inn?

- What makes Mairi drop everything to run to catch the strangers before they leave?

- Who is 'thon laddie in oor byre'?

- Does it make any difference to you that the Christmas story is told in Scots? Why?

- What do 'bairnie', 'barrie-coat' and 'deeve' mean? And what does 'caravan' mean here?

Imaginative/creative Writing

- We are given an idea of what the strangers say, but not their actual words. Compose a script of the conversation between the strangers and Mairi's father, and try to include some appropriate noises off and stage directions.

- Write your version of the Christmas story in your own form of Scots.

Further development

Find the Christmas story in Lorimer's Scots translation of the Bible and compare it with both the King James Version in Matthew, and a modern English translation (e.g. the Good News Bible). Which do you prefer, and why?

Rab Wilson

Aye, He's the Big Man

Aye, he's the Big Man,
Or so they think,
Bowchin, blusterin,
Bullyin, blawin,
Aboot whit he wid dae,
Hou he wid sort them oot,
Wi aw his answers in his fists.

A forensic history,
Lang as yer airm,
An a jyle-hoose tattoo
Fir evri stretch he's duin,
The litany o a life lost
Etched upon his skin.
Aye, he's the Big Man.

But they dinnae see him
In the wee sma hours,
Curlt up ticht in a foetal ba,
When the ghaist o his faither
Veesits his room,
Baith hauns clampt grimly
Owre his face.
Aye, he's the Big Man.

Rab Wilson

Aye, He's the Big Man

Introduction

Rab Wilson never shies away from dealing with controversial subjects and this is no exception. In the three stanzas he builds up a vivid picture of this 'Big Man'. In the first two stanzas the alliterative use of verbs shows his actions and the last line, 'Wi aw his answers in his fists', summarises his character. The idea that the tattoos are a 'litany o a life lost' is particularly effective. But it is the final stanza that sums up the true reason for his behaviour: the way he has been mistreated by his father. He is still haunted by the 'ghaist o his faither' every night, and cowers in his bed from the vision.

THIRD LEVEL
Related Texts:
  Edwin Morgan, 'King Billy'

KEY WORDS:

Bullying

Character

Family

Fear

Justice

Some key questions/group discussions

- What does the second line of stanza one imply?

- Discuss the use of verbs in the third and fourth lines. Say what they add to the description of the man.

- Which words in the second stanza relate to prison and why are they effective?

- The tone of the last stanza is different. Which words show that the poet has some sympathy for the 'Big Man'.

- What does the repetition of 'Aye, he's the Big Man' add to the poem?

Imaginative/creative Writing

- Write about a bully who has another side to him.

- Try to write a poem in the same style with a repetitive line. You could use the same format but change 'Big Man' to 'joker' or 'wit'. See if you can use some Scots verbs to emphasise the kind of person you are describing.

Further development

Tattoos are increasingly popular these days. Look at why people get them. In this poem it is a sign of having been in jail, but what are some other reasons for getting tattoos?

Biographies

Marion Angus (1865–1946)

Marion Angus's family moved from Sunderland to Arbroath in 1876 when her father became the minister of Erskine United Free Church. From 1902 she and her sister, Emily, ran a private school in Cults but gave it up after the outbreak of the First World War. In 1930 she moved to the Glasgow area to be near Emily. Her first collection of poetry, *The Lilt*, was published in 1922, to be followed by *The Singin' Lass, The Turn of the Day* and *Lost Country and Other Verses*. Angus's continuing popularity is attested in the recent publication of *Voices from Their Ain Countrie* and *The Singin' Lass – Selected Works of Marion Angus*. Her poems were strongly influenced by the Scottish ballad and folk song traditions and many explored the experience of women.

J. K. Annand (1908–1993)

Born in Edinburgh, James K. Annand graduated from the University of Edinburgh in 1930 and subsequently taught History at schools in Edinburgh and Whithorn. He was a skilled translator of German poetry and fiction and of medieval Latin texts into Scots. He edited *Lallans*, the magazine for writing in Scots, published by the Scots Language Society, from its foundation in 1973 until 1983. His children's poetry collections *Sing it Aince for Pleisure; Twice for Joy; Thrice to Show Ye* and *A Wale o Rhymes* have become classics of their kind. A volume of *Selected Poems 1925–1990* was published in 1992. He was a champion of the Scots language and his children's poetry collections, with their skilful use of Scots and playful humour, have encouraged the use and enjoyment of the Scots language in schools.

Anon.

Many of the poems in the anthology have no known author. There are many reasons for an anonymous attribution, the most likely being that the poem, song or ballad derives from the oral tradition passed down through word of mouth, where the name of the originator has faded from memory. However, many political, scurrilous and potentially seditious poems and songs could be published anonymously to protect the author from prosecution. It is also worth bearing in mind that 'Anon.' may shelter a female writer in times where it was not considered 'proper' or permissible for women to be seen writing.

John Barbour (c. 1320–1395)

John Barbour, considered to be the father of Scots poetry, was the first named poet to write in the Scots language. He studied in Oxford and Paris and was made the archdeacon of the kirk of St Machar in Aberdeen in 1356. He was recorded as a clerk of audit in the royal household of Robert II in 1373. His historic verse romance, *The Brus*, focusses on the deeds of Robert the Bruce and Sir James Douglas in the first war of Scottish independence. The central episode describes the Battle of Bannockburn and the poem ends with the death of Douglas and the burial of the Bruce's heart in 1332. The Bruce and Douglas are celebrated as the finest flowers of Scottish chivalry. His verse style demonstrates the strength of Scots as a literary language.

Sheena Blackhall (1947–)

Sheena Blackhall studied at Gray's School of Art in Aberdeen. She became a primary school teacher and subsequently a special needs teacher. She gained a BSc Hons in Psychology from the Open University in 1995 and an M.Litt with distinction from the University of Aberdeen in 2000. As a poet, novelist, short story writer, illustrator, traditional storyteller and singer, she has tirelessly promoted Scots culture and language in the north-east. She was inaugurated as Makar for Aberdeen and the North-east in 2009 and has won awards for both her fiction and poetry. She has written two television plays for children, *The Nicht Bus* and *The Broken Heart,* and published the collection *Wittins: Selected Poems. The Space Between: New and Selected Poems* includes a selection of her poems.

Robert Burns (1759–1796)

Robert Burns, the eldest son of a tenant farmer, was born in Alloway. Although by the age of fifteen he was working on the farm, his father ensured that he had a formal education. In his short life, while working as a tenant farmer and latterly as an exciseman, he composed a multiplicity of poems and song lyrics. The pivotal event of his poetic career was the publication in 1786, to great acclaim, of his first collection of poetry, *Poems, Chiefly in the Scottish Dialect,* known as *The Kilmarnock Edition.* He contributed a third of the songs to James Johnson's *The Scots Musical Museum,* published between 1787 and 1803, and was a major contributor to George Thomson's *The Melodies of Scotland – A Select Collection of Original Scottish*

Airs for the Voice. He was a master of the love lyric, biting satire, comic mock-heroic narrative, the verse epistle, the dramatic monologue and radical political verse.

J. M. Caie (1878–1949)

James Morrison Caie was born in Banchory-Deverick in Kincardineshire. He studied at the University of Aberdeen and the North of Scotland College of Agriculture. From 1905 he lectured on agriculture in Ireland, Perthshire and the University of Aberdeen. He became Assistant Secretary of the recently formed Board of Agriculture for Scotland in 1918 and retained the post when the Board became the Department for Agriculture for Scotland in 1929. He wrote two books of poetry in English and Scots: *The Kindly North* and *Twixt Hills and Sea*. He wrote about farming from his knowledge and observation. There is no idealisation of that way of life and his poems reflect the realities of working on the land with perception and humour.

John Cameron (n.d.)

John Cameron was a native of Ballachulish, near the entrance to Glencoe in Argyllshire. He wrote 'Chì mi na Mòr-Bheanna' and *Dàn Spioradail*, a religious work. He was also bard to the Ossianic Society. Malcolm MacFarlane (1853–1931), a well-known writer and translator of Gaelic, produced the English version, 'The Mist-Covered Mountains of Home'.

Thomas Campbell (1777–1844)

Born in Glasgow, Thomas Campbell attended the High School of Glasgow and subsequently studied at the University of Glasgow. He spent holidays as a tutor in the West Highlands and his poems 'Glenara' and 'The Ballad of Lord Ullin's Daughter' were written at this time. *The Pleasures of Hope*, published in 1799, a didactic poem written in heroic couplets dealing with contemporary events and issues such as the French Revolution, the partition of Poland, and slavery, was an instant success. In 1800 he went abroad and was forced to seek refuge in a Scottish monastery in Regensburg three days before the city was taken by the French. His poems, 'Hohenlinden', 'Ye Mariners of England' and 'The Soldier's Dream' belong to this German period. He was Rector of the University of Glasgow from 1826 to 1829 and his statue stands in George Square in Glasgow.

W. D. Cocker (1882–1970)

Born in Rutherglen, William Dixon Cocker left school at thirteen and started work in his father's stationery business. He spent weekends and holidays at a small cottage at his mother's family's farming lands in the parish of Drymen and grew up with a good knowledge of farming life and the Scots spoken in that district. He enlisted in 1914, serving with the Highland Light Infantry and subsequently the Royal Scots. He was taken prisoner in 1917. His poems, 'Up the Line to Poelkapelle', 'The Sniper' and a five-part sonnet sequence, 'Sonnets in Captivity', come from his war experiences. After the First World War he worked in the accounts department of the *Daily Record* and served as its drama critic until his retirement. His poems of rural life in Strathendrick, written between the First and Second World Wars, portray that way of life with sympathy and humour.

Stewart Conn (1936–)

Born in Glasgow, Stewart Conn grew up in Kilmarnock. From 1977 until 1992 he worked as Head of Radio Drama at BBC Scotland. A prolific poet and dramatist, he has won three Scottish Arts Council (Creative Scotland) book awards and served as Edinburgh's first Makar from 2002 until 2005. Collections of his poetry include *In the Kibble Palace*; *Ghosts at Cockcrow*; *The Breakfast Room* and *The Touch of Time: New and Selected Poems*. His plays include *Hugh Millar*; *Play Donkey* and *I Didn't Always Live Here*. His poetry shows a keen observation of people and artworks and expresses the universal themes of love and loss, family life and the passage of time with sensitivity and humour.

James Copeland (1918–2002)

James Copeland was born in Helensburgh. During the Second World War he worked in Blackburn Aircraft Factory in Dumbarton and had been a policeman and a water bailiff. He studied at the Royal Scottish Academy of Music and Drama in Glasgow and his first acting engagement was at the Citizens' Theatre in Glasgow. In 1961 he began working as a presenter and continuity announcer at Grampian Television. He published two books of poetry: *Some Work* and *Jimmy Copeland's Shoogly Table Book of Verse*, and often read his own poems on radio. His poems, often humorous and poignant, have an enduring popularity.

Joe Corrie (1894–1968)

Joe Corrie was born in Slamannan, Stirlingshire. His family moved to Cardenden in the Fife coalfields and he began working in the pits in 1908. After the First World War he started to write articles, short stories and poems which were published in well-known socialist newspapers and journals, including *Forward* and *The Miner*. His full-length play, *In Time o' Strife*, depicted the effects of the General Strike in 1926 on the Fife mining community, He subsequently wrote plays for the Scottish Community Drama Association's annual festivals. The agitprop theatre group 7.84 republished *In Time o' Strife* after their 1982 staging of the play. His poetry is contained in three collections: *The Image o' God and Other Poems*; *Rebel Poems* and *Scottish Pride and Other Poems*.

Robert Crawford (1959–)

Robert Crawford was born in Bellshill and grew up in Cambuslang. After graduating M.A. from the University of Glasgow he achieved a PhD from Balliol College, Oxford. He is currently Professor of English at the University of St Andrews. He founded *Verse*, an international poetry magazine, in 1984, and served as poetry editor for Polygon in the 1990s. He was joint editor, with Mick Imlah, of *The New Penguin Book of Scottish Verse* and published *The Bard: Robert Burns*, a biography. His first collection of poetry, *A Scottish Assembly*, received the Eric Gregory Award. His collections of poetry include *Sharawaggi: Poems in Scots* and *Testament*. His poems encompass science, religion and the developing politics of modern Scotland. His interest in information technology is reflected in many of his poems.

Iain Mac a' Ghobhainn/Iain Crichton Smith (1928–1998)

Born in Glasgow, Iain Crichton Smith was brought up by his widowed mother in the crofting township of Bayble on the island of Lewis. He wrote in both English and Gaelic. A graduate of the University of Aberdeen, he taught English in secondary schools in Clydebank, Dumbarton and Oban. During this period he had novels and poems published. He retired from teaching to become a full-time writer in 1977. His best-known prose works are the novels *Consider the Lilies* and *The Last Summer* and his short stories *The Thoughts of Murdo*. Collections of his poems include *Collected Poems* and *New*

Collected Poems. Many of his poems reflect his dislike of religious dogma and often show a striving for grace and beauty. Other common themes are the effects of the Highland Clearances on individuals and communities and the suffering of elderly women and alienated individuals.

Christine De Luca (1947–)

Christine De Luca writes poetry in English and Shetlandic and translates other poets' work into Shetlandic. She is the founder of the Hansel Co-operative Press, which was established to promote artistic and literary work in Shetland and Orkney. She is a member of the Shore Poets group in Edinburgh and was appointed Edinburgh Makar in 2014. She has had six collections of poems published, among them *Voes and Sounds*; *Parallel Worlds*; *North End of Eden* and *Dat Trickster Sun*. She has encouraged dialogue between Palestinian and Scottish writers. Her poetry expresses subtle evocations of landscape and the history of communities through its people, artefacts and paintings, not only of her native Shetland but of Canada, France and India.

Jim Douglas (n.d.)

Jim Douglas, artist, poet and teacher, comes from a mining background in Fife. He was first encouraged to nurture his creative talents at the Glenfarg Folk Club and has been closely involved with the New Makars Trust as a singer and songwriter. The Trust was founded to encourage community songwriting and preserve the songs of local cultures. The Trust has run successful projects in Fife and South Lanarkshire and has produced CDs which celebrate local culture and traditions.

Carol Ann Duffy (1955–)

Born in Glasgow, Carol Ann Duffy moved with her family to Stafford when she was six years old. She achieved an Honours degree in Philosophy at the University of Liverpool in 1977 and received an Honorary Doctorate from Heriot-Watt University in 2009. She is currently Professor of Contemporary Poetry at Manchester Metropolitan University and was appointed Poet Laureate in 2009. She has received a number of literary awards including the T. S. Eliot Prize. Her collections of poetry include *Standing Female Nude*; *Selling Manhattan*; *Meantime*; and *Rapture*. She has written poetry collections for children: *Meeting Midnight*; *The Oldest Girl in the World* and *The Hat*. Her plays include *Take*

My Husband; *Little Women* and *Loss*. Her poetry encompasses a wide range of themes: oppression, gender, politics and everyday experience.

William Dunbar (c. 1459–1530)

William Dunbar first appears in the historical record in 1474 as a student of the Faculty of Arts at the University of St Andrews. Details from his later life suggest that he had been ordained as a priest. From 1500 he was employed at the court of James IV and it is from this period that the bulk of his poetry can be dated. In Sir David Lyndsay's 'The Testament and Complaynt of Papyngo', published in 1530, Dunbar is referred to as being deceased. The most recent collection of his work is *The Poems of William Dunbar*, edited by Priscilla Bawcutt. Writing in Scots, he demonstrates a mastery of different verse forms and language registers. His poetry has a broad range of themes encompassing religious devotional poetry, comic satires of courtly life and commissioned works to mark public events.

Jean Elliot (1727–1805)

Also known as Jane Elliot, she wrote one of the most famous versions of 'The Flowers of the Forest', a song lamenting the Scottish army's defeat in the Battle of Flodden. Published in 1776, it may be her only surviving work. The lyrics are set to a tune later collected into a melody by John Skene. During the Jacobite Rising of 1745, when a party of Jacobites came to arrest her influential father, Sir Gilbert Elliot, of Minto House in Teviotdale, she received and entertained the unwelcome officers with calmness and composure, convincing them that her father was long gone. From 1782 to 1804 she lived in Edinburgh, where she had many admirers, but never married. She returned to Teviotdale shortly before her death.

Alec Finlay (1966–)

Alec Finlay, the son of Ian Hamilton Finlay, is an artist, poet and publisher. He works with various forms and media including poetry, sculpture, collage, audio-visual and other technologies. He has exhibited at Tate Modern, Norwich Castle Museum and the Highland Institute for Contemporary Art. He set up the Morning Star, a small press which publishes his pocket-book series of poems. His collections include *Shared Writing*; *White Blown Clouds* and *Be My Reader*. His recent work *The Road North* is a book-length series of poems in haiku form describing a journey through Scotland guided by the seventeenth-century Japanese poet, Bashō.

Matthew Fitt (1968–)

Born in Dundee, Matthew Fitt is a poet, novelist and translator who writes in the Scots language. With the novelist and poet, James Robertson, he co-founded Itchy Coo, a publishing imprint and educational project to introduce schoolchildren to the Scots language. He is a Scots translator for the Scottish Parliament and has spoken on behalf of the Scots language at the United Nations in New York. He published *But 'n' Ben A-Go-Go*, a cyberpunk novel in Scots, in 2005. Among the books in Scots he has written for children are *The Hoose o Havers*, a loose retelling of the *Metamorphoses* of Ovid, and *Kate o Shanter's Tale and Other Poems*. He has translated a number of favourite children's stories into Scots, such as *The Eejits*; *Asterix the Gallus* and *The Dundee Gruffalo*.

Robert Garioch (1909–1981)

Robert Garioch (R. G. Sutherland) was born in Edinburgh and educated at the High School of Edinburgh and Edinburgh University. He served in the Royal Corps of Signals during the Second World War and endured three years as a prisoner in Italy and Germany from 1942 until 1945. On his return he worked as a teacher until his retirement in 1964. He subsequently worked on a number of Scottish literary magazines and in 1970 became writer in residence at the University of Edinburgh. Collections of his poems include: *Selected Poems*; *Collected Poems*; *Complete Poetical Works* and a new *Collected Poems*. He had great technical mastery of different verse forms and his knowledge and use of the Scots language was extensive. His shorter poems are sharply observant, often humorous commentaries on Scottish life. His translations into Scots of the Italian poet, G. C. Belli, and Pindar and Hesiod are highly regarded.

Sir Alexander Gray (1882–1968)

Born in Dundee, Alexander Gray was a distinguished academic, civil servant and poet. He achieved First Class Honours in both Mathematics (1902) and Economic Science (1905) at the University of Edinburgh. He was appointed Chair of Political Economy at the University of Aberdeen in 1921 and occupied the equivalent post at the University of Edinburgh from 1934 to 1956. In the 1920s he was a member of the Royal Commission on

National Health Insurance. His early poems were published in the third series of Hugh MacDiarmid's magazine *Northern Numbers* and later a volume of *Selected Poems*. He used the dialect of Angus for his own poems and for his translations of German and Danish poetry. His poems have a clarity and directness of expression and his best-known poem, 'Scotland', continues to resonate with both Scots at home and in the diaspora.

Margaret Green (n.d.)

Margaret Green lived in Argyll as a child, but has spent most of her adult life in Glasgow. She has had a varied career in medical research, science editing and college teaching. Later in her career she was secretary and administrator for courses in the teaching of English as a foreign language. While living briefly in Fife she travelled to a writers' group in Dundee where she was encouraged to write in Scots.

Ian Hamilton Finlay (1925–2006)

Ian Hamilton Finlay was born in Nassau in the Bahamas and educated at Dollar Academy in Clackmannanshire. In the Second World War he served in the Royal Army Service Corps. His first collection of poetry, *The Dancers Inherit the Party*, was published in 1960, but it was as a concrete poet that he first achieved wide renown. Through his magazine, *Poor.Old.Tired.Horse*, published by his own Wild Hawthorn Press, he published his own concrete poems and the works of other experimental writers. In 1966 he bought an upland farm, Stoneypath, near Dunsyre, and with his wife, Sue, and by using the expertise of sandblasters and engravers, he created an extensive garden, incorporating inscribed stones and sculptures which evoked classical themes of both beauty and destruction. He named the garden Little Sparta. He also produced landscape installations for many European and American clients.

Robert Henryson (c. 1435–c. 1500)

There is evidence to suggest that Robert Henryson was a teacher who had been trained in law and the humanities. In 1478 his name appears as a witness on Dunfermline Abbey charters and it may have been his duty to run the grammar school for Dunfermline abbatial burgh. His works are written in Middle Scots when this had become the language of court and state. He is best known for his three long poems,

The Morall Fabillis of Esope, the Phrygian; *The Testament of Cresseid* and *The Tale of Orpheus and Erudices his Quene*, and among his shorter poems, 'Robene and Makyne' and 'Ane Prayer for the Pest'. His narrative poems demonstrate inventive storytelling techniques and psychological insight. His use of Scots is masterful, showing his skill in the use of different tones and registers. He writes with both a medieval and early Renaissance sensibility and world view.

William Hershaw (1957–)

William Hershaw, poet, playwright, musician and songwriter, was born in Newport-on-Tay. His writing has been inspired by his own family's mining heritage, the Scots language and the songs of Bob Dylan and Neil Young. He began writing poems in English but soon found a form of Scots closer to his own speech. As a teacher of English, he is committed in his teaching and writing to passing on 'the decent and humane values of the people [I] was brought up with'. His collections include *The Cowdenbeath Man*; *Fifty Fife Sonnets* and *Makars*. His poems are vivid evocations of the people, landscape and history of Fife.

James Hogg (1770–1835)

Born on a small farm near Ettrick, James Hogg worked as a shepherd in the Borders and was largely self-educated. In 1801 he was recruited to collect ballads for Sir Walter Scott's *The Minstrelsy of the Scottish Border* and in 1802 he began working for the *Edinburgh Magazine*. He returned to the Borders in 1817 and in the following years he published major works including *Jacobite Reliques*, and three novels: *The Three Perils of Man*, *The Three Perils of Women*, and his best-known work, *The Private Memoirs and Confessions of a Justified Sinner*. His literary reputation suffered for many years after his death and it was not until André Gide discovered the power of *The Justified Sinner* in 1944 that his reputation began to grow again among scholars and the general public. He is now considered one of Scotland's major writers.

Kathleen Jamie (1962–)

Kathleen Jamie, poet, essayist and travel writer, was born in Perthshire. She lives in Fife and has been Professor of creative writing at Stirling University since 2011. Her poetry collections include *The Queen of Sheba*; *Jizzen*; *The Tree House* and *The Bonniest Companie*. Her travel writing includes *The Golden Peak – Travels in*

North Pakistan and *The Autonomous Region: Poems and Photographs from Tibet.* Her prose essays *Findings* and *Sightlines* are poetic evocations of the natural world and humanity's relationship with it. Her writing is often witty and inventive and her acute observations of nature are precise and subtle.

Jackie Kay (1961–)

Jackie Kay, poet, novelist and dramatist, was born in Edinburgh to a Scottish mother and a Nigerian father. She was adopted as a baby by Helen and John Kay and brought up in Bishopbriggs. Her first book of poetry, *The Adoption Papers,* based on her own experience of adoption, was published in 1991. Since then she has published collections of poetry, the novel *Trumpet* and poems and short stories for children. Her poetry collections include *Other Lovers*; *Off Colour* and *Darling.* Her memoir, *Red Dust Road,* explores her search for her birth parents and is a heartfelt tribute to her adoptive parents. She is currently Professor of Creative Writing at Newcastle University and became Scots Makar in 2016. In her work she confronts prejudice and human frailty with emotional honesty and often humour.

James Kennedy (n.d.)

The poem 'The Highland Crofter', which was originally published anonymously in *Punch* in 1903, was later acknowledged as having been written sixty years before and attributed to James Kennedy, an evicted crofter and blacksmith from Loch Tayside. It was intended as a bitter attack on John Campbell, the second Marquis of Breadalbane, who once owned half a million acres of Highland Perthshire and Argyllshire, for his ruthless eviction policies on some two and a half thousand people round Loch Tay between 1834 and 1850. It is not known whether Kennedy wrote any other poems, or, indeed, whether he was able to remain in Scotland after his eviction.

Tom Leonard (1944–2018)

Tom Leonard was born in Glasgow and worked at various jobs, including bus conductor and university bookshop assistant. Since the 1970s, Leonard has made his living as a writer. He is best known for his poems in Glasgow speech, epitomised in *Six Glasgow Poems*, highly compressed poems in a phonetic spelling, often attacking the various establishments of our time: educational, political, religious. Through the voice the speaker is made vividly present, and

the poems' physical arrangement on the page intensifies the scraps and gaps of vernacular speech. The poems are direct, often angry, but equally compassionate, and often very funny. While Writer in Residence at Renfrewshire Libraries he compiled an anthology of local poets, *Radical Renfrew.* In 2001 he was appointed, with Alasdair Gray and James Kelman, joint Professor in Creative Writing at the University of Glasgow, from which he retired in 2009.

Liz Lochhead (1947–)

Liz Lochhead was born in Motherwell, Lanarkshire. She entered Glasgow School of Art in 1965, where she attended an informal creative writing group. While working as an art teacher, Lochhead developed her writing talent, publishing her first two collections, *Memo for Spring* and *Islands.* As well-known nowadays as a playwright as a poet, Lochhead published *Dreaming Frankenstein & Collected Poems* and her monologues and performance pieces *True Confessions and New Clichés.* The collection *The Colour of Black and White – poems 1984–2003,* includes 'Kidspoem/Bairnsang', which has become one of her signature poems. Lochhead was appointed Poet Laureate for Glasgow in 2005 and held that post until 2011, when she succeeded Edwin Morgan as Scots Makar. She was awarded the Queen's Gold Medal for Poetry in 2015.

Sir David Lyndsay (c. 1490–c. 1555)

In the sixteenth to eighteenth centuries, a literate household in Scotland was likely to own two books: the Bible and the works of Sir David Lyndsay, Lord Lyon King of Arms under James V. Lyndsay is best known nowadays for his great morality play *The Thrie Estaitis.* One of his greatest strengths is his sense of the ridiculous, which is evident in *The Justing betwix James Watsoun and Jhone Barbour,* the description of a contest allegedly staged before James V and his queen. Instead of the usual knights, the two combatants are 'ane medicinar' and 'ane leche', and whatever their skills in treating illness, they are useless on the jousting field. Although Lyndsay had seen at first hand the fatal results of the joust, this poem is a parody, and by visual jokes, pokes fun at both the combatants and the formal nature of serious jousting.

Norman MacCaig (1910–1998)

Norman MacCaig was born in Edinburgh.

His mother was from Scalpay, Harris and her Gaelic language and heritage made an enduring impression on him. A graduate in Classics at the University of Edinburgh, for much of his career he was a primary school teacher. In 1967 he was appointed Fellow in Creative Writing at the University of Edinburgh and in 1970 he became a Reader in Poetry at the University of Stirling. A prolific writer, his collections include *Far Cry*; *Riding Lights*; *Surroundings*; *Old Maps and New Selected Poems*; *Voice Over*; *Collected Poems*; *Selected Poems of Norman MacCaig* and *The Poems of Norman MacCaig*. His poetry is notable for its lucid style, its use of striking metaphors, and wit. He observed individuals, places and animals with a sharp eye and a humane vision, qualities which have given his poems a lasting popularity.

Hugh MacDiarmid (1892–1978)

Christopher Murray Grieve was born in Langholm, in the Borders, and took the pen-name Hugh MacDiarmid when he started writing. He was a founder member of the National Party of Scotland in 1928, but in the 1930s was ejected for his left-wing views. Following his investigations into nationalism and nationhood he started writing in Scots, using words and phrases he knew from boyhood and acquired from reading in dictionaries and the works of Henryson and Dunbar. The poems of *Sangschaw*, *Penny Wheep* and *A Drunk Man Looks at the Thistle* were shockingly novel in their language and themes. He edited anthologies of poetry, three collections representing the traditionalists alongside younger generations, and positively encouraged women writers. He is strongly associated with the Scottish Renaissance of the 1920s.

Calum MacDonald (1953–)

Calum MacDonald was born in Lochmaddy, North Uist. His family subsequently moved to the Isle of Skye where he attended Portree High School. In 1973 he, his brother Rory, and Blair Douglas formed *Runrig*, the Celtic rock band. He was the primary songwriter and his brother Rory wrote the melodies. He worked as a PE teacher until the band went professional. The lyrics of his songs are deeply influenced by his and his brother's awareness of the history and way of life of Gaelic communities and, through the band's blend of folk and rock music, an understanding and appreciation of Gaelic culture has reached a national and international audience.

Donnchadh Bàn nan Òran/Duncan Bàn Macintyre (1724–1812)

Duncan Bàn Macintyre, known in Gaelic as Donnchadh Bàn nan Òran (Fair Duncan of the Songs) was born in Argyllshire near Bridge of Orchy. He first served as a soldier in the Argyll Militia and fought – reluctantly – against the Jacobites. He was then employed as a gamekeeper in his home area, managing the deer in Glen Lochay, on Ben Dorain and in Glen Etive. In 1766 he left the Highlands for Edinburgh and a post in the City Guard. Above all Donnchadh Bàn was a poet of nature as is well illustrated by his long poems 'Song to the Misty Corrie' and 'Praise of Ben Dorain'. He composed about six thousand lines of poetry but he could neither read nor write and these had to be noted down by others at his dictation. (The translation used here is from *The Songs of Duncan Bàn Macintyre*, edited by Angus MacLeod.)

George Mackay Brown (1921–1996)

George Mackay Brown was born in Stromness, Orkney. He was educated at Stromness Academy, Newbattle Abbey College (1951–1952) and Edinburgh University. Edwin Muir at Newbattle encouraged him to write poetry. Owing to a tubercular condition, he spent most of his life in Orkney writing poetry, short stories and articles and essays for the local newspaper. His themes were mainly religious and ceremonial, his verse forms traditional, and his sources and influences were Norse sagas, Catholic rituals and ceremonies, and island lore. His writing exhibits crystal-clear language and images. His second collection, *Loaves and Fishes*, was critically appreciated. He was awarded the James Tait Black Memorial Prize in 1987 for his volume of two short stories *The Golden Bird*, and was nominated for the Man Booker prize for his novel *Beside the Ocean of Time*.

Ewart Alan Mackintosh (1892–1917)

Ewart Alan Mackintosh was born in Brighton. His father's family came from Alness in Ross and Cromarty and during school holidays he studied Gaelic and learned to play the pipes. A classical scholar at Oxford University, he became a member of the university's Officers' Training Corps. A second lieutenant in the Seaforth Highlanders, he received the Military Cross in June 1916 for 'conspicuous gallantry', having led a successful raid on the German trenches. One of his men, David Sutherland, who did not survive the raid, inspired his powerful poem, *In Memoriam*. His other war poems, such as *Recruiting, On Vimy Ridge, The Waiting Wife* and *To the 51st Division – High Wood, July–August 1916* are equally powerful and evocative. He was killed in action in November 1917.

Somhairle MacGill-Eain/Sorley MacLean (1911–1996)

Sorley MacLean was born on the island of Raasay, studied at Edinburgh University and became headmaster of Plockton High School. His sequence of passionate and intellectual love poems *Dàin do Eimhir* (*Poems to Eimhir*) transformed Scottish Gaelic poetry. His war poems are of outstanding quality, as is 'Hallaig', one of the finest of his later works. His epic poem 'An Cuilithionn' ('The Cuillin'), originally written in 1939, was published in full for the first time in 2011. MacLean is the greatest Scottish Gaelic poet of the twentieth century, if not of all time. See Somhairle MacGill-Eain/Sorley Maclean, *Caoir Gheal Leumraich/White Leaping Flame: Collected Poems in Gaelic with English Translations*, edited by Christopher Whyte and Emma Dymock.

Coinneach MacLeòid/Kenneth MacLeod (1899–1977)

Coinneach MacLeòid/Kenneth MacLeod was born in the Point peninsula in Lewis and spent all his life there except for several years in Canada and the USA when he was a young man in the 1920s. He returned to live in Lower Bayble where he worked as crofter, fisherman, builder and shopkeeper. Like many people in Lewis he had a nickname and was usually known as 'Red'. His amusing songs, of which 'Holiday na Caillich' is one, proved very popular and are still sung today.

Brian McCabe (1951–)

Born in 1951 in Bonnyrigg, a small mining community near Edinburgh, Brian McCabe has been a freelance writer since 1980, and is also a tutor and editor. Alongside Rob Butlin, Andrew Greig and Liz Lochhead, McCabe was one of 'The Lost Poets', a collective who organised readings in central Scotland in the early 1970s. He has had various residencies and fellowships in Scotland and abroad, including the William Soutar Fellowship in Perth, and has worked at various universities as a creative writing tutor. He is the award-winning author of five collections of poetry, three short story collections and two novels, his most recent publications being *Body Parts*; *A Date With My Wife*; *Selected Stories* and *Zero*. He also writes radio drama.

Johnny McEvoy (1945–)

Johnny McEvoy is an Irish singer and entertainer of Country and Irish genre born in Banagher, County Offaly, Ireland. Although there is some dispute about the authorship, he is credited with the lyrics to 'The Wee Magic Stane' set to the tune of 'The Ould Orange Flute', about the 'liberation' of the Stone of Destiny from Westminster Abbey. The Scots thought this was pretty funny and enough songs appeared to honour the circumstances to be published in a small book, *Sangs o' the Stane*. 'The Wee Magic Stane' is by far the best known of them and may be the only one still sung. The song was banned by the BBC from 1959 to 1960, but was later re-popularised by The Corries.

Matt McGinn (1928–1977)

Born in the Calton district of Glasgow, Matt McGinn was a shipyard worker, teacher, folk-singer, song writer, novelist and poet, and actor and comedian. He created many memorable songs for children, such as 'The Red Yo-Yo', 'The Wee Kirkcudbright Centipede', and 'The Magic Shadow Show'. He produced many songs about his home city and social and political issues and events, among the best known of which are 'The Ballad of John Maclean', 'The Ibrox Disaster', and 'Three Nights and a Sunday'. He was very much at the heart of the Scottish folk-song revival from the late 1950s onwards and has been a source of inspiration for many folk musicians.

William Topaz McGonagall (1825–1902)

William McGonagall was born in Edinburgh. He became a handloom weaver in Dundee, but by the 1870s, the Industrial Revolution was making handloom weaving obsolete. He subsequently earned money by selling his poems in the street. Although his poems are considered some of the worst in the English language, his many listeners appreciated him as a comic music-hall performer and his work continues to inspire and entertain. He clearly saw himself as something of a public defender, commentating on fatal accidents caused by corner-cutting. He died penniless and was buried in an unmarked grave in Greyfriars Kirkyard in Edinburgh.

Jim McLean (1938–)

Born in Paisley, Jim McLean is a prolific song writer. Many of his songs deal with political issues and events, such as the anti-Polaris protest movement of the 1960s, the UCS work-in of the early 1970s and many songs about Glasgow and Scottish history. His songs have been recorded by many well-known singers and as a producer he has created a number of albums. Perhaps he is best known in Scotland for 'The Ballad of Glencoe'. He completed an MSc in Scottish Ethnology at the University of Edinburgh in 2008.

Adam McNaughtan (n.d.)

Adam McNaughtan, singer, songwriter, teacher and researcher, was involved in the Folk Revival of the 1950s. He sang with the folk group *Stramash* for many years. He is well-known for his songs about post-Second World War Glasgow, most notably the humorous 'The Jeely Piece Song' and the nostalgic 'Where is the Glasgow that I used to know?'. An Honorary Research Fellow in Scottish Studies at the University of Glasgow, he edited Volume V of the *Greig-Duncan Folk Song Collection*. The lives of communities and the social changes they experience are reflected in his research and provide inspiration for his song-writing.

Angela McSeveney (1964–)

Angela McSeveney was born in Edinburgh. She was brought up in Ross-shire, Livingston and the Borders, and is a graduate of the University of Edinburgh. She works as a personal care assistant in the city. Her collections of poetry are *Coming Out With It*, *Imprint* and *Slaughtering Beetroot*. Her inspiration comes from letting 'ideas happen – a metaphor, a phrase, a reflection'. Her poems explore emotional and physical frailty with sensitivity and wry humour.

Ewan McVicar (1941–)

Ewan McVicar was born in Inverness but later moved to Glasgow. He was employed in various areas of social work for over twenty years before becoming a self-employed storyteller and writer, performing many shows in Scotland and abroad. He has written songs for the Singing Kettle children's show and his study of playground songs for the School of Scottish Studies is documented in his book *Doh Ray Me, When Ah Wis Wee*. He is the author of *Scots Sangs Fur Schools* (traditional and new songs with support notes for teachers) and *One Singer One Song* (an anthology of old and new stories and songs of Glasgow).

Elizabeth Melville, Lady Culross (c. 1578–c. 1640)

In 1603, Elizabeth Melville, Lady Culross became the first Scotswoman to see her work in print when she published *Ane Godlie Dreame*. A large body of manuscript verse was discovered in 2002, and her extant poetry runs to some 4,500 lines, written in many different verse-forms. Melville was an active member of the presbyterian resistance to the ecclesiastical policies of both James VI and Charles I. She was a personal friend of leading figures in the presbyterian opposition, whose frustration eventually erupted in 1637 in the Edinburgh Prayerbook Riots, leading to the National Covenant of February 1638. Dr Jamie Reid Baxter has edited the first complete collection of Melville's shorter poems, which express a very strong Protestant faith, but also a strong sense of humour. Melville is the seventh woman commemorated by a stone in Makars' Court in Edinburgh, unveiled by Germaine Greer in 2014, and the only one so far who published work before 1900.

Edwin Morgan (1920–2010)

Scotland's first official Makar in modern times, Edwin Morgan was born in Glasgow's West End, and brought up in Pollokshields and Rutherglen. He attended Rutherglen Academy and Glasgow High School, and after his war service took a first-class Honours degree in English Language and Literature at Glasgow University. He took up the offer of a lectureship in the Department of English at Glasgow University, where he remained until he retired in 1980. For fifty years Morgan maintained a double poetic output, translations from Russian and Hungarian, Latin and French, Italian and Old English keeping pace with his own work, showing astonishing variety and technical skills in both. His first collection, *The Vision of Cathkin Braes and other poems* was followed by *The Second Life*, *Instamatic Poems*, and *From Glasgow to Saturn*. He won the Soros Translation Award in 1985. Poems celebrating Glasgow, Scotland, and celebrities of cinema, concrete poems, 'Instamatic' poems, love poems, science fiction, dramatic monologue, and polemic flowed from his pen. Morgan was awarded an OBE in 1982, the Queen's Gold Medal in 2000, and appointed the first Poet Laureate of Glasgow in 1999, and then of Scotland, as the Scots Makar, in 2004. His poem on the opening of the Scottish Parliament building is a model of public poetry, challenging and celebratory.

Edwin Muir (1887–1959)

Edwin Muir was born in Deerness, island of Wyre, Orkney. His father was a farmer but in 1901 he lost his farm and they left Orkney to live in Glasgow, and the teenage Muir had to find work; he was employed in a series of jobs in offices and factories. He taught himself German, and with his wife, Willa, worked on enormously influential translations from German. From the 1920s Muir was writing poetry as well as translating. Muir wrote his poems in English, and in his study *Scott and Scotland* famously opposed MacDiarmid's drive to Scots. His poems often reach for archetypes beneath the everyday. In 1950 he was appointed Warden of Newbattle Abbey College, where he met the younger George Mackay Brown whose work he was to encourage. Some major writings, *Collected Poems, 1921–1951* and *One Foot in Eden,* date from this period. From 1955 to 1956 he was Norton Professor of English at Harvard.

Neil Munro (1863–1930)

Neil Munro was born in Inverary, but left before his eighteenth birthday to seek work in Glasgow. He pursued a career in journalism, eventually becoming editor of the Glasgow *Evening News*. He was a popular novelist and short story writer, and his successful historical novels relate to the Highlands. During the First World War Munro visited the front line as a war correspondent, in 1914 and again in 1917. The war concentrated his poetic creativity, perhaps inevitably, as his son was killed during the Battle of Loos in 1915. Poems under the title 'Bagpipe Ballads' were published in *Blackwoods Magazine* in 1917, and in them the sad realities of war, as well as its humour, reflect the pipe-music themes of the Highland culture Munro knew so well. John Buchan edited *The Poetry of Neil Munro* after his death.

Charles Murray (1864–1941)

Charles Murray was born in Alford in north-east Scotland, and was a skilled and popular poet who wrote in the pure Scots of his native Aberdeenshire, despite spending his working lifetime as a civil engineer and senior civil servant in South Africa. He served in the second Boer War, and as Director-of-Works in the South African Defence Force in the First World War. He returned to Scotland upon retirement in 1924. Three volumes of poetry, *A Handful of Heather, Hamewith* and *The Sough o' War*, were published before his retirement. His poems on the war, written with a clear eye and without sentimentality, give a picture of the effects of the conflict upon ordinary country people.

William Neill (1922–2010)

William Neill was born in Prestwick, Ayrshire. After service in the RAF, he studied Celtic literatures as a mature student at the University of Edinburgh. He then taught English in Galloway, before retiring to the village of Crossmichael. He saw his poetry – in Scots, Gaelic and English – as 'a standing up for the small tongues against the big mouths', and made translations from various European languages, often exploring other minority European languages and attitudes to them. He took the National Mod's bardic crown at Aviemore in 1969, won the Grierson Verse Prize and the Sloan Prize in 1970, and received a Scottish Arts Council Book Award in 1985.

Nancy Nicolson (n.d.)

Nancy Nicolson is a native of Caithness, who worked as a teacher in Edinburgh. She describes herself as a writer, singer, storyteller and animateur, telling stories rooted in her childhood on a croft in wartime Caithness. She came late to singing, in her thirties at the Edinburgh Folk Club, but soon afterwards started to write songs and to play the melodeon. In 1996, while a primary teacher in Midlothian and Edinburgh, she was a contributor to *The Kist*, the Scottish Education Department's resource on Scots and Gaelic writing and song for schools, advising schools on its use. She then became a trustee of The New Makars Trust, a school/community song-writing project in Fife, acting as a tutor and tutor-trainer. She has contributed to many Celtic Connections Schools events, and presented 'Air Alba' ('About Scotland') at the 2012 Edinburgh Festival Fringe.

Liz Niven (1952–)

Liz Niven was born in Glasgow. She was educated at Glasgow University and Jordanhill College of Education. As a teacher, she has had a strong interest in Scots language in education, recognising that many Scots-speaking children and families should have the right to speak, and be respected for using, their native tongue. She has been Scots Language Development Officer for Dumfries and Galloway Education Department and Writer-in-Residence for Dumfries and Galloway Arts Association. Her poetry has been published in most major Scottish magazines, as well as along the River Cree in Galloway, in a commissioned collaboration with sculptors and wood-carvers. Her poetry collections include *Cree Lines, Stravaigin, Burning Whins and Other Poems,* and *The Shard Box.*

Carolina Oliphant, Lady Nairne (1766–1845)

Scotland's greatest songstress, Carolina Oliphant, Lady Nairne, was the author of many beautiful songs often today thought of as traditional. Born in the 'auld hoose' of Gask, Perthshire, the daughter of a staunchly Jacobite family (she was named for Prince Charles Edward Stuart), she wrote in sympathy to the cause, setting her songs to old tunes. Marriage to Major William Murray Nairne brought her to Edinburgh, where she carried on her 'queer trade of song-writing' under a pseudonym, Mrs Bogan of Bogan, keeping it secret even from her husband. Lady Nairne wrote poems about notable gentry characters, such as 'The Laird o' Cockpen', Jacobite songs like 'Charlie is my darling', and other songs of more general Scottish life, such as 'Caller Herrin". *Lays from Strathearn* appeared under her own name, posthumously, in 1846.

Catrìona Nic`Iomhair Parsons/Catriona McIvor Parsons (n.d.)

Born on the island of Lewis, Catriona McIvor Parsons is a highly respected educator in Nova Scotia. She teaches at St Francis Xavier University and at the Gaelic College, Cape Breton. A singer and a poet, she is a tradition bearer who has used her gifts to promote the Gaelic language and culture in the USA and Canada. She is co-founder with Donald F. MacDonald of Carolina of the US Mod.

Allan Ramsay (1686–1758)

Allan Ramsay was born at Leadhills, Lanarkshire, educated at the parish school of Crawford, and in 1701 was apprenticed to a wig-maker in Edinburgh. His eldest child was Allan Ramsay, the portrait painter. Ramsay's first efforts in verse-making were inspired by the meetings of the Easy Club (founded in 1712), where he took the pseudonym 'Gawin Douglas' to illustrate his boast that he was 'a poet sprung from a Douglas loin', and in 1715 he became the Club Laureate. In 1716 he published a transcript of *Christ's Kirk on the Green* from the Bannatyne Manuscript with supplementary verses of his own. By 1718 he had gained a reputation as a writer of occasional verse, and published a volume of his poems in 1721. He is celebrated for *The Tea-Table Miscellany* and *The Ever Green,* containing original and traditional poems and songs.

Alastair Reid (1926–2014)

Alastair Reid was born in Whithorn, Galloway but developed a sense of the possibilities of other lives and travel very early. He had a year at St Andrews University before he joined the Royal Navy, then returned to complete his degree in classics. In the early 1950s, when Reid was teaching at Sarah Lawrence College in New York State, he published some poems in the *New Yorker* and produced a slim volume, *To Lighten My House.* He undertook translations of the poetry of Jorge Luis Borges, Pablo Neruda, Herberto Padilla, and José Emilio Pacheco. He published more than forty books of poems, translations and travel writing, including *Ounce Dice Trice,* a book of word-play and literary nonsense for children. In Scotland, his best-known poem is 'Scotland', which contrasts the rare beauty of a summer day with a Scotswoman's Calvinist prediction that nature will exact its payment.

Alan Riach (1957–)

Born in Airdrie, Lanarkshire, and educated at the universities of Cambridge and Glasgow, Alan Riach went to the University of Waikato, New Zealand, in 1986. He returned to Scotland in 2001 as Reader in the Department of Scottish Literature at the University of Glasgow, where he is now Professor. He is the author of works of criticism on the poetry of Hugh MacDiarmid, editor of MacDiarmid's collected works, and has published several collections of poetry, including *This Folding Map, An Open Return, First & Last Songs, Clearances,* and *Homecoming: new poems 2001–2009* for which he drew upon his own experiences as an ex-pat. He is interested in comparative studies in Scottish poetry and painting, and has made a translation into English of Alasdair Mac Mhaighstir Alasdair's epic Gaelic poem *The Birlinn of Clanranald.*

Sir Walter Scott (1771–1832)

Sir Walter Scott studied law at the University of Edinburgh, becoming an advocate in 1792. In 1799 he was appointed Sheriff Depute of Selkirkshire and in 1806 he was made a Clerk of the Court of Session. His first major publication was his three-volume collection of ballads which he had gathered and edited, *The Minstrelsy of the Scottish Border*. This was followed by his long romantic poems, *The Lay of the Last Minstrel*, *Marmion* and *The Lady of the Lake*. His historical novels, such as *Waverley*, *The Antiquary*, *Old Mortality*, *Rob Roy*, *The Heart of Midlothian*, *Ivanhoe*, *Redgauntlet* and many others became world famous. In 1826 the printing company in which he was involved collapsed, and in order to clear his enormous debts he undertook a punishing writing programme. He paid back what he owed but ensuing ill-health led to his death at the age of sixty-one.

Adam Skirving (1719–1803)

Adam Skirving became a farmer at Garleton Castle, near Haddington. His eldest son, Archibald Skirving, painted portraits whilst his second son, Robert, inherited his mother's musical talents but went into the army. All three wrote verses but it is Adam who is best remembered as a song writer. His reputation rests on two Jacobite ballads on the Battle of Prestonpans, one of which, 'Johnnie Cope', whilst very far from an accurate narrative, is popular enough to be found in many collections of Scottish songs. In this case Skirving wrote the words to a well-known tune. After his death, he was buried at Athelstaneford in East Lothian.

William Soutar (1898–1943)

Born in Perth, William Soutar served in the British Navy during the First World War. He began to study medicine at the University of Edinburgh in 1919, but soon switched to the study of English literature. Despite crippling ankylosing spondylitis, which caused him to be bed-ridden by 1930, he became a leading figure in the Scottish literary Renaissance. Collections of his work include *Seeds in the Wind*, a volume of bairn rhymes in Scots; *The Collected Poems of William Soutar*; *The Diary of a Dying Man*; and *At the Year's Fa: Selected Poems in Scots and English*. His poetry is lyrical, reflective and often humorous and his use of Scots in his bairn rhymes is inventive and assured.

Alan Spence (1947–)

Alan Spence is a poet, playwright and novelist. He is based in Edinburgh, although he was born in Glasgow and attended the University of Glasgow. Known as a novelist and playwright as well as a poet (his first publication was the collection of short stories *Its Colours They Are Fine*), he became writer-in-residence at the University of Aberdeen in 1996, and has held a personal Chair in Creative Writing since 2001. He writes in a variety of poetic forms borrowed from Eastern tradition, including haiku and tanka, often blending Glasgow dialect with Zen phrases. His first book of poetry was *Glasgow Zen*. In 1996 he was named Scottish writer of the year. In his collection *Clear Light*, each three-line poem sits on a page of its own, promoting a meditative pace of reading, often revealing a new world in the mundane.

Robert Louis Stevenson (1850–1894)

Born in Edinburgh, Robert Louis Stevenson entered the University of Edinburgh in 1867 to study engineering with the intention of following the family profession of lighthouse design. He changed course to study law, qualifying as an advocate in 1875, but he chose not to practise. Originally known for travel-writing and essays, in the 1880s he wrote *Treasure Island*, *Kidnapped*, *The Strange Case of Dr Jekyll and Mr Hyde* and *The Master of Ballantrae*. His poetry collections include *A Child's Garden of Verse* and *Underwoods*. His novellas, *The Beach of Falesá* and *The Ebb Tide*, and his novels, *The Wrecker* and *Catriona* were written in Samoa. He died of a stroke while working on his novel *The Weir of Hermiston*. His novels have become classics of world literature.

Ruaraidh MacThòmais/Derick Thomson (1921–2012)

Born in the same village that produced Iain Crichton Smith and known as Ruaraidh MacThòmais in his native Gaelic, Derick Thomson was educated at the universities of Aberdeen, Cambridge and Bangor, and went on to lecture in Edinburgh, Glasgow and Aberdeen before becoming Professor of Celtic at Glasgow in 1963, a post he held until his retirement in 1991. He published widely on Gaelic poetry, including his own collection *Creachadh na Clàrsaich* (*Plundering of the Clarsach*), and took Gaelic poetry from its traditional heartlands in the Highlands and Islands to Scotland's Lowland cities, Glasgow in particular. Thomson's early poetry draws heavily upon his upbringing in Lewis. One of his most famous poems, 'Clann-Nighean an Sgadain' ('The Herring Girls') describes the women from the island who used to travel to the mainland to make a living in the fishing industry. He was the first poet to develop free verse as a serious medium for poetry in the language.

Valerie Thornton (1954–)

Valerie Thornton's poems and short stories have appeared in literary magazines and anthologies in the UK, Ireland, Europe, Canada, and America. She has received a Scottish Arts Council bursary, been shortlisted for the Macallan/*Scotland on Sunday* short story prize and has been a winner of the biennial Asham short story prize. She also teaches creative writing. Her creative writing textbooks are *The Young Writer's Craft* and *The Writer's Craft* (both Hodder Gibson). She has had two poetry collections published with Mariscat Press: *Catacoustics*, and *If Only Coll Were Two Floors Down*.

Margaret Tollick (n.d.)

Margaret Tollick was born in Glasgow, brought up and married in Edinburgh, moved with her husband to Airdie, Port Glasgow, and finally to Fife where she was a primary teacher, and subsequently a head teacher. She is a member of the Scottish Storytelling Network, working with schools, adult groups and libraries, offering stories to children and adults in a variety of venues. Her collection of poems, entitled *Tapsalteerie,* are all in Scots and include her own versions in Scots

of well-known nursery rhymes, as well as many original poems. She also worked on a project called 'Dreamcatcher' for a performance at the Byre Theatre in St Andrews.

Rab Wilson (1960–)

Rab Wilson was born in the Ayrshire village of New Cumnock. After an engineering apprenticeship with the National Coal Board he left the pits following the miner's strike of 1984–1985 to become a psychiatric nurse. His first main published work was his version in Scots of the famous medieval Persian work *The Ruba'iyat of Omar Khayyam*; this was followed by three collections of his own poetry 'chiefly in the Scots language'. He has collaborated with the artist Hugh Bryden in adaptations of Horace's satires in Scots, and with Calum Colvin in a book of responses to Robert Burns. He has also edited an anthology of contemporary poetry by Dumfries and Galloway writers. In 2008 he won the McCash Scots poetry competition. In 2013 he was selected as the first James Hogg Creative Resident, living and writing in Ettrick Valley, home of the poet and writer James Hogg.

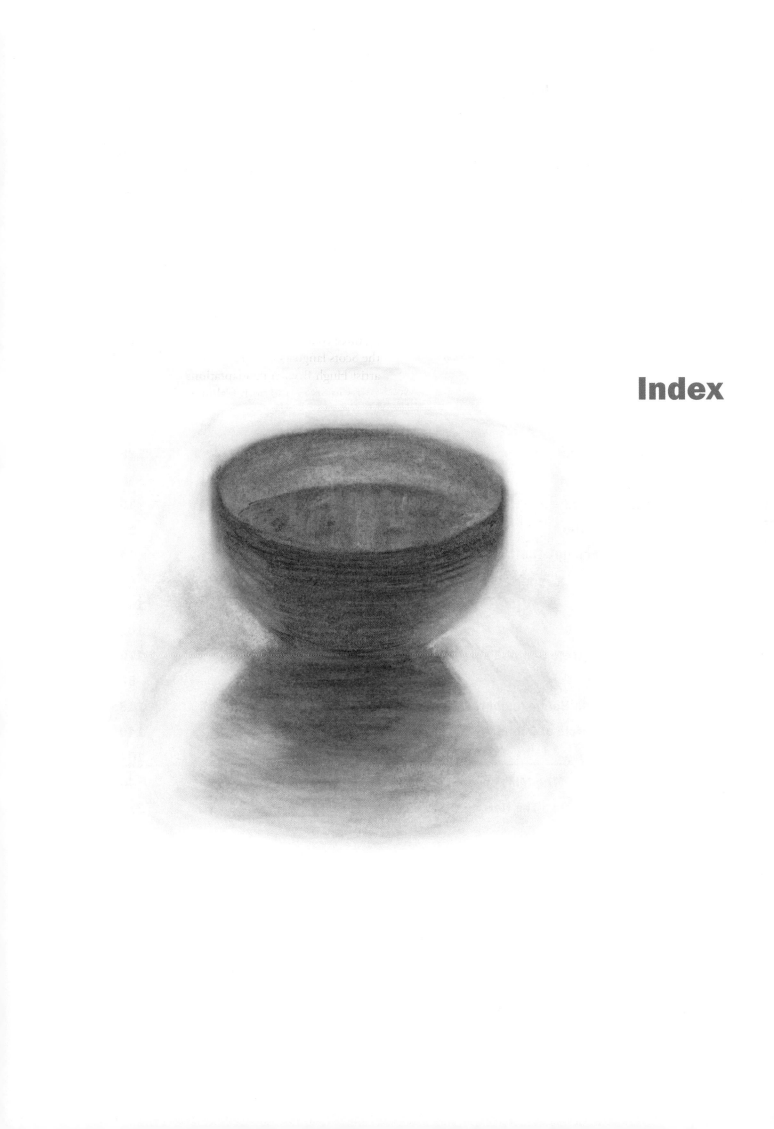

Index

Index of Titles

Key Words Index

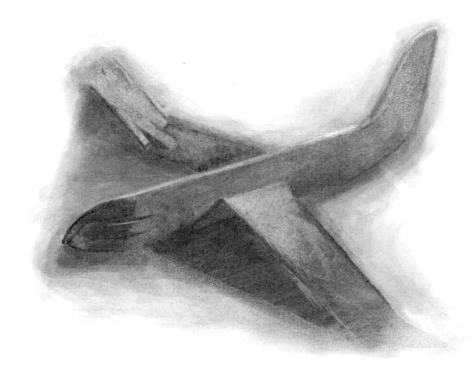

Bibliography

ACKNOWLEDGEMENTS

The Association for Scottish Literary Studies gratefully acknowledges the help provided and the permissions granted by the following people and publishers. Apologies are offered to those copyright holders who could not be traced, and they are encouraged to get in touch with us.

Sheena Blackhall: "The Eruption of Vesuvius", *Dead Men's Whispers (17 Scots Poems and Owersetts)*, Lochlands 2008

John M. Caie: "The Puddock", *The Kist/A'Chiste*, Thomas Nelson and Sons 1996

W. D. Cocker: "The Sniper", *From the Line: Scottish War Poetry 1914–1945*, Association for Scottish Literary Studies 2014

Stewart Conn: "Heirloom", *Ghosts at Cockcrow* Bloodaxe 2005; "Springtime" *The Best of Scottish Poetry: An Anthology of Contemporary Scottish Verse*, W & R Chambers 1989

James Copeland: "Black Friday" *The Kist/A'Chiste*, Thomas Nelson and Sons 1996

Joe Corrie: "Image o God", *The Penguin Book of Scottish Verse*, Penguin 1970

Robert Crawford: "Alba Einstein", *Dream State: The New Scottish Poets*, Polygon 1994

Iain Crichton Smith/Iain Mac A' Ghobhainn: "Rhythm", "When We Were Young/Nuair a bha sinn òg", *Iain Crichton Smith: Collected Poems*, Carcanet 1992

Christine De Luca: "Russian Doll", *North End of Eden*, Luath Press 2010

Jim Douglas: "The New Teacher", *Dugs, Doos and Dancing*, Windfall Books 2003

Carol Ann Duffy: "Nippy Maclachlan, "The Loch Ness Monster's Husband", *New and Collected Poems for Children*, Faber & Faber 2009; "The Scottish Prince" *The Good Child's Guide to Rock 'n' Roll*, Faber & Faber 2003

Alec Finlay: "New Model Glider", *Question Your Teaspoons*, Calder Wood Press 2012

Ian Hamilton Finlay: "Fox" from "Glasgow Beasts", *The Dancers Inherit the Party; Early Stories, Plays and Poems*, Polygon 2004

Matthew Fitt: "Captain Puggle", *The Thing That Mattered Most: Scottish poems for children*, Scottish Poetry Library 2006

Robert Garioch: "I'm Neutral", *Collected Poems*, Polygon 2004

Alexander Gray: "On a Cat Ageing", *Selected Poems*, William Maclellan 1948

Margaret Green: "The Ballad of Janitor MacKay", *The Kist/A'Chiste*, Thomas Nelson and Sons 1996

William Hershaw: "Dysart Tide Sonnet", *The Cowdenbeath Man*, Scottish Cultural Press 1997

Kathleen Jamie: "Arraheids", *The Queen of Sheba*, Bloodaxe Books 1994

Jackie Kay: "Brendon Gallacher", "Darling", "Grandpa's Soup", "In My Country", "Maw Broon Visits a Therapist", *Darling*, Bloodaxe Books 2007

Tom Leonard: "The Dropout", "The Good Thief", *outside the narrative*, etruscan books/Word Power Books 2009

Liz Lochhead: "For My Grandmother Knitting", *A Choosing: Selected Poems*, Polygon 2011; "The Metal Raw", *The Colour of Black and White: Poems 1984 – 2003*, Birlinn 2011

Brian McCabe: "Seagull", *100 Favourite Scottish Poems*, Luath Press 2006

Norman MacCaig: "Aunt Julia", "Praise of a Collie", "Toad", *The Poems of Norman MacCaig*, Polygon 2005

Hugh MacDiarmid: "The Bonnie Broukit Bairn", *The Kist/A'Chiste*, Thomas Nelson & Sons Ltd 1996

Calum MacDonald/Calum MacDhòmhnaill: "Circle of Ocean/Cearcall A'Chuain", *The Kist/A'Chiste*, Thomas Nelson & Sons 1996

John McEvoy: "The Wee Magic Stane", *One Singer One Song*, Glasgow City Libraries 1990

Matt McGinn: "The Ballad of the Q4", *One Singer One Song*, Glasgow City Libraries 1990

Ewart Alan Macintosh: "In Memoriam", *From The Line: Scottish War Poetry 1914–1945*, Association for Scottish Literary Studies 2014; "On Vimy Ridge", *In Flanders Field*, Mainstream 1990

George Mackay Brown: "The Hawk", *The Collected Poems of George Mackay Brown*, John Murray 2006

Jim McLean: "Farewell to Glasgow", *One Singer One Song*, Glasgow City Libraries 1990

Sorley MacLean/Somhairle MacGill-Eain: "Death Valley/Glac a'Bhàis", *From the Line: Scottish War Poetry 1914–1945*, Association for Scottish Literary Studies 2014

Kenneth MacLeod/Coinneach MacLeòid: "The Old Lady's Holiday/Holiday na Caillich", *The Songs of The Red/Orain Red*, Acair 1998

Adam McNaughtan: "Yellow on the Broom", *The Best of Scottish Poetry: An Anthology of Contemporary Scottish Verse*, W & R Chambers 1989

Angela McSeveney: "Changing a Downie Cover", *Dream State: The New Scottish Poets*, Polygon 1994

Ewan McVicar: "Shift and Spin", *One Singer One Song*, Glasgow City Libraries 1990

Edwin Morgan: "Canedolia", "The First Men on Mercury", "The Loch Ness Monster's Song", *Edwin Morgan: Poems of Thirty Years*, Carcanet 1982

Edwin Muir: "The Late Wasp", *The Complete Poems of Edwin Muir*, Association for Scottish Literary Studies 1991

William Neill: "Despatches Home", *Despatches Home*, Reprographia 1972

Nancy Nicolson: "Listen to the Teacher", *They Sent a Wumman: The Collected Songs of Nancy Nicolson*, Grace Note Publications 2016

Liz Niven: "Feart", *The Thing that Mattered Most: Scottish poems for children*, Scottish Poetry Library 2006

Catriona McIvor Parsons/Catriona Nic Iomair Parsons: "Memory/Cuimhne", *Brigh Na Gaelic/The Strength of Gaelic*, The Gaelic Society of America/An Comunn Gaidhealach Aimeireaga 2001

Alastair Reid: "My Father, Dying", *The Best of Scottish Poetry: An Anthology of Contemporary Scottish Verse*, W & R Chambers 1989

Alan Riach: "A short introduction to my Uncle Glen", *Dream State: The New Scottish Poets*, Polygon 1994

William Soutar: "Ae Night at Amulree", *Poems of William Soutar: A New Selection*, Scottish Academic Press 1988

Derick Thomson/Ruaraidh MacThòmais: "The Herring Girls/Clann-Nighean an Sgadain", *The Penguin Book of Scottish Verse*, Penguin 2006; "The Norsemen coming ashore at Ness/Na Lochlannaich A'Tighinn Air Tir An Nis", *The Kist/A'Chiste*, Thomas Nelson & Sons Ltd 1996

Valerie Thornton: "Prospecting in Partick", *If Only Coll Were Two Floors Down*, Mariscat Press 2010

Margaret Tollick: "Mairi's Sang", *My Mum's a Punk*, Scottish Children's Press 2002

Rab Wilson: "The Big Man", *Accent o the Mind*, Luath Press 2006

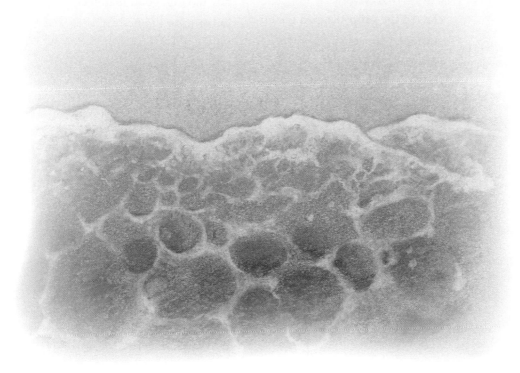

Glossary

A

adversar: enemy

almaser: almoner

amendis: revenge

anarmyt: armed

ane futt yeid ay onrycht: one foot kept going wrong

anidder: another

at bait: in confusion

austre: hostile

aver: worthless

B

bab: baby

baiginets: bayonets

bandster: person who binds sheaves

barne: offspring

barres: lists (in jousting)

barrowtrammis: pole shafts

baurent: baronet

bawd: hare

bedirtin: foul with excrement

begowthe: began

bigsy: conceited

birk: birch

bisselye: actively

blaw: boast

bleit: bleat

blydeness: gladness

bogle: ghost

boist: menace

boss: hollow, concave

bouk: body

bour: bower

braunis: muscles

braxie: disease of sheep

brose: dish of oats or pease-meal

broukit: neglected

bruke: brook

brunt: burned

but gilt thus de: to die without cause

byde ane unsuspect assyis: await an impartial jury

C

cadgeris: packmen

campionis: champions

cared na doit nor docken: cared very little

carline wife: old woman, witch

carlingis: old women

channerin: grumbling

cheris: spare

chestitie: chastity

chiel: young man, fellow

clanjamfrie: crowd

clawed the caup: scraped the bowl

compeer: appear

contenance: manner

continuance: steadfastness

contrarie: contradict

convoy: bearing

crak: boast

crammasy: crimson

cratur: creature

creillis: panniers, creels

crukit: crippled

cubularis: bedroom attendants

D

da: the

Dame Dounteboir: disparaging name for a court lady

dang: hit

dat: that

daunce: dance

deir: harm

demyng: suspicion

deray: trouble, disturbance

dirrye dantoun: lively dance

dirt partis: excrement

dispone: prepare for

doit: a small coin of little value

dreid: timidity

dryfe: drove

dukkie: doll

dule: grief

dyt: compose

E

ee: one

endytit: created by

erd: earth

ergo: (Latin) therefore

esperance: hope

F

fa: foe

fail dyke: turf wall

failyeis: departs

fair having: good manners

fairm toon: homestead

fald: bend

falt: fault, defect

familiaries: confidential servants

fassoun: appearance

fecht: fight

feirsnes: fear

feit: feet

fin: when

flure: floor

fock: folk

frackar: active

frawart: brash

futt'ratt: weasel or stoat

fyle: defile

fynyearis: fingers

G

ganyie: arrow

gar mak hir body till: have made for her body

garneist: ornamented

gentill: well-born

gif ressoun: hear my reason

girnand: bared (teeth)

glar: mud

glaumed: snatched

gluifis of plait: gauntlets

govirnance: conduct

gree: agree

grieve: overseer on a farm

gudlines: goodness

H

haill: whole, all of

hairst: harvest

halflin: half-grown boy

hals: neck

harnes: harness

hause-bane: collar-bone

hedit: beheaded

heill: health

heillis: heels, feet

helme: helmet

hing: hang

hint him be the hals: seized him by the neck

hit: it

hobchackellt: hobbled

hoddous: hideous

hoidin: hiding

hois: honesty

hommiltye jommeltye: confused, disorganised

houms: low-lying land beside a river

hud: hood

hunkered: crouched

hurdies: haunches

hussyfskap: housework

I

instant wyis: current procedure

J

juffler: stumbler

K

kirtill: bodice and skirt under gown

knokkis: blows

kynthis: knights

L

lachter: laughter

laeffe: rest

lasit: laced

lauchful: lawful

lave: the rest

leid: lied

leif: permission

leill: justice

lernit: taught

lesum: lawful

lickit: punished

lift: sky

lof: palm

lufe: love

lustie: beautiful

lyart: of hair streaked with white

M

magryme: migraine, severe headache

maid a bred: made a sudden movement

mailyeis: eyelets

mak ascence: run up, ascend

makar: poet

makin mane: lamenting

man off the self discend: must of itself descend

mantill: outer garment

marrow: comrade

mastevlyk: mastiff-like

medicinar: physician

melle: combat

menstrallie: minstrelsy

menyie: disable

mintiest: tiniest

mirrear: merrier

mis: misdeed

moderis: mothers

mone: moon

morgeownis: contortions

N

nae fat they eesed tae be: not what they used to be

neeps: turnips

nouther: neither

O

oblis: vow

of his band: from his leash

off kynd: by nature

on pace: apace

onything that he do mycht: despite anything that he could do

P

pais: consequences

pane: pain

panton: slipper

peerier: smaller

perfyt: perfect

perseing: piercing

pietie: a shame

pillie: amorous person

piscence: power

pleid: argument, claim in law

pleyis: quibble

ploo: plough

plycht: blame

potestatis: potentates

poynt: argument

preif: prove

prelotis: priests

property: sovereignty

propone: plead

puddock: frog

purfillit: trimmed

Q

queets: ankles or fetlocks

quhill: until

quhou: how

quhyt: white

quinies: girls

quod: said

R

raicis: courses

raips: ropes

raucht: dealt

rax: stretch

ream: cream

red the men: separate the men

reif: villainy

renowne: reputation

reply: rebut

resave: receive

ressoun: reason

reveir: river

rewth: pity

rink: contest

rodden tree: rowan tree

rokkis: distaffs (used in spinning)

rotche: cliff

rout: heavy blow

runkled: creased, rumpled

S

saikles: innocent

sancts: saints

sark: undergarment

sary: sorry

saulls: souls

schame: modesty

schone: shoes

seggs: sedge

seill: happiness, prosperity

selie: innocent

sheugh: ditch

sicker: sure

sickerness: confidence

son: soon

sough the catechis: recite the catechism

sowkand: suckling

speche: speech

spilt: killed

spows: spouse (referring to the Church)

spreit: spirit

stackarand: blundering

stakkeret: staggered

steipill-heid: steeple top

stirk: young bullock

stour: dust

strae: straw

straik: strike

straikis: strokes

strummall: horse, nag

swa upon cace: so it happened

swankies: strapping young men

swarf: faint, swoon

sweird: sword

syne: then

T

termin time: time when contract of employment on farms could be terminated or renewed

teuchat: lapwing

theek: thatch

thochts: thoughts

thrapple: throat

till: to

ting: little one

tink: think

tint: lost

togidder: together

tour: tower

travise: partition, screen

triggit: dressed up

tyke: cur

U

uncan: unfamiliar

W

waels: selects

waes me: woe is me

waiffit: waved, flung out

walkin: waken

wame: belly

war: worse

wheen o blethers: pack of nonsense

wir: was

wirk: work

wissit: wished

wot: know

wpryse: uprise

wraithit: angered

wrokin: wreaked

wynd: wind

Y

yak: ache

yeid: moved around, went

youkie: itchy